Battleground 1

Le Cateau
26 August 1914

Battleground series:

With the continued expansion of the Battleground Series a **Battleground Series Club** has been formed to benefit the reader. The purpose of the Club is to keep members informed of new titles and to offer many other reader-benefits. Membership is free and by registering an interest you can help us predict print runs and thus assist us in maintaining the quality and prices at their present levels.

Please call the office on 01226 734555, or send your name and address along with a request for more information to:

Battleground Series Club Pen & Sword Books Ltd,
47 Church Street, Barnsley, South Yorkshire S70 2AS

Battleground Europe

Le Cateau
26 August 1914

Nigel Cave and Jack Sheldon

Series editor
Nigel Cave

Pen & Sword
MILITARY

This book is dedicated to two individuals: Colonel Pat Love MBE of the Worcestershire Regimental HQ, who stands for all those who work in regimental headquarters and museums throughout the country; their assistance and knowledge is invaluable for authors such as us. The second person is Tony Spagnoly. Tony was the inspiration to Nigel Cave to study the battlefields in a way which is the characteristic of the Battleground Europe series. For Tony the battlefields have always been first and foremost places that have involved individuals; he never let the sheer immensity and depersonalising of war overcome the need to remember them and salute them. To him I am immensely grateful.

First published in Great Britain in 2008 by
PEN & SWORD MILITARY
an imprint of
Pen & Sword Books Limited
47 Church Street
Barnsley
South Yorkshire
S70 2AS

ISBN 978 08 505 28428

A CIP catalogue record for this book is
available from the British Library

Printed and bound in Great Britain by
CPI UK

Pen & Sword Books Ltd incorporates the imprints of
Pen & Sword Aviation, Pen & Sword Naval, Pen & Sword Military,
Pen & Sword Select, Pen & Sword Military Classics
Leo Cooper and Wharncliffe Books

For a complete list of Pen & Sword titles please contact:
PEN & SWORD BOOKS LIMITED
47 Church Street, Barnsley, South Yorkshire, S70 2AS, England.
E-mail: enquiries@pen-and-sword.co.uk
Website: www.pen-and-sword.co.uk

CONTENTS

French women dole water out to German troops in the streets of Amiens.

LIST OF MAPS

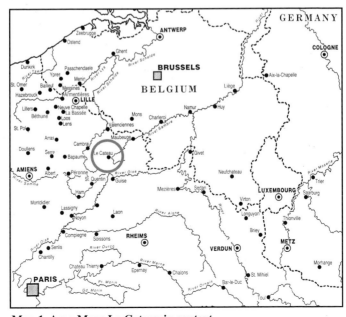

Map 1. Area Map: Le Cateau in context.

ACKNOWLEDGEMENTS

As for all the Battleground books, we owe most of our information to the authors of the regimental histories of both sides. Although by definition, almost, these are likely to be partisan works, they provide a wealth of information and personal accounts of the events on the battlefield. The Battle of Le Cateau is blessed by very full accounts in many of these works, particularly on the British side. We are extremely grateful to them. Ironically, the official records tend to be very patchy and never very full – an inevitable consequence of the conditions under which these early battles of the Great War were fought. Some of the battalion War Diaries, for example, consist of only a couple of lines. We would particularly like to express our thanks to Colonel Pat Love, MBE, of the Worcestershire Regiment's RHQ, who has always been the source of a wealth of information and who can also stand for the many other volunteers who carry out this function for the regiments of the British army of the time.

As usual we are indebted to Roni Wilkinson (and the other members of the Wilkinson dynasty, Paul and Jonathan) at Pen and Sword; the working relationship now spans twenty years and the same patience – and enthusiasm – has been displayed to at least one of the authors throughout those years.

Thanks are due to Arlene King, Directrice of the Beaumont Hamel Newfoundland Memorial, for her generous hospitality during the period in which the field work for this book was undertaken. Nigel Cave particularly thanks Brother Shinto Kumminiyil IC for sacrificing a couple of days of his very limited time in France to touring this battlefield in search of photographs. We also acknowledge the help provided by the Le Cateau tourist office and to various enthusiasts in the area who have made available some of their collection of illustrations: Gérard Lemoine of St Benin, Gérard Delmotte of Caudry, Philippe Gorcyzinski of Cambrai and Dominique Lechef.

The Commonwealth War Graves Commission continues to impress with the never ending hard work that makes even the most remote and unvisited cemeteries gardens suitable for the resting place of those who gave their lives during the war; whilst its excellent web site has ensured that it is much easier to direct people to the place of commemoration of so many who died as a result of the fighting on 26 August 1914.

Crowds in front of
the Houses of
Parliament
waiting for news
of the declaration
of war.

British infantry in
northern France.

British artillery
passing through a
French village.

Le Cateau: British Introduction

Despite the fact that Le Cateau was a short battle and, in the great scheme of things in 1914, not perhaps as significant as British historians tend to make it, it has long remained one of the most controversial of the Great War. It is a sobering thought that the battles of 1918 in the same area (as is clearly shown in the CWGC cemeteries) cost far more lives than did the battle on 26 August 1914.

However, it was the most costly of the engagements fought by the BEF in the first months of the war. Evidence on the ground suggests that the official casualty list for the battle – some 7,800 casualties – is overstated. One only has to look at the confusion in the days between the beginning of major fighting at Mons and the retreat to the Marne, with units hopelessly jumbled and some of them ending up miles away, to doubt the validity of roll calls. The actual fatalities for the British can be calculated reasonably accurately – and this comes in at rather under 500. Even allowing for a tendency to record some of those killed at Le Cateau by date of reporting the fact (thus some come under 5 September), this total is not likely to be much higher than 600. One can then make an allowance for wounded – say four times the figure; a significant number of those would have been amongst the prisoners, which are not likely to have been above 2,500. Thus the total for the battle *per se* is more likely to be in the region of 5,000, and even that is likely to be on the high side. In turn, what that means is that the total is somewhere around the ten percent mark of British troops engaged on the day; in Great War terms a small ratio for such an engagement. At least fifty percent of the casualties were prisoners. Far more research could be done on this, but it is evident that the established figure must include casualties in II Corps from at least 25 August and then a number of subsequent days. This does not stop it being a battle with very large casualties (by British standards), but perhaps not quite as people have tended to see it. I am very grateful to Jack Horsfall for the laborious research he has done in this regard.

Similarly, German casualties on the day were not large – or not as large as the British would have liked them to be. The vast majority of the casualties would have been wounded or killed – the number of prisoners insignificant. German casualties are not likely to have been any more than 2,000.

Why begin this introduction with the problematic one of casualties? I thought it best to get the issue out of the way, because it is one on which, perhaps, an undue emphasis is placed. Of course, for the people concerned and for their battalion these losses were very much to the point; but they are only a factor in determining the significance of the battle and the relative success of it. Another issue is the matter of the various eyewitness accounts and their reliability. It seems from the evidence here that men from both sides tended to overstate – sometimes wildly so – the number of casualties inflicted by those around them. Men falling were assumed by all too many to have been casualties, whereas in fact they were just going to ground. In the heat of the battle this was understandable; and it is only natural that men would want to put the best possible gloss on their unit's part in an action.

It will be recalled that II Corps' commander, Smith-Dorrien, had been rushed out to France to replace Grierson, who had died in his railway compartment, a victim of his enjoyment of life as a *bon viveur*. Almost as soon as he arrived he had to fight his Corps through Mons and then conduct a retreat whilst in contact with the enemy, a most difficult military manoeuvre. His men were exhausted and conducting a fighting retreat. Because of the retreat route (and this was no one's fault), he had lost contact with I Corps on his right and hardly anyone was where they were supposed to be by the evening of 25 August. GHQ (ie French and his staff) must take its share of responsibility for the scale of the losses of the 4th Division. Signals, engineers, divisional cavalry, some elements of the artillery and the train as well as most of its medical support were kept back at St Quentin: thus the Division's communications were hampered, it had no 'eyes' to send out to keep track of the enemy and it was extremely difficult to evacuate the wounded.

Lieutenant General Sir Horace Smith-Dorrien

The British Official Historian, JE Edmonds, wrote in a foreword to the English edition of Walter Bloem's fascinating *Advance from Mons*, *About 1pm during the battle of Le Cateau, he* [Smith-Dorrien] *asked that a senior General Staff officer of the 4th Division should be sent to his headquarters to report the situation and receive orders. Major-General Snow sent me. On my arrival I saw that General Smith-Dorrien was obviously perturbed. He said to me at once, "Jimmy Grierson having died, I am sent out here without time to collect even a kit, still less to make myself fully acquainted with the situation, and I have had to make two great decisions. When I arrived before Mons the C-in-C [French] told me to give battle on the line of the Condé Canal and, when I asked whether this meant the offensive or the defensive, he told me to obey orders. That fellow said to me this morning, "If you stand and fight there will be another Sedan." ' I could only reply, "Please don't let that worry you; we all feel you have done the only possible thing." Indeed, had he not decided to stand with his 3rd and 5th Divisions, the fate at least of the 4th Division, sent up by GHQ without signal company, cavalry, cyclists or engineers, would have been sealed.*

Looking at the situation on the ground, whatever French wrote about it after the war, it is very difficult to see what alternative he had but to fight at Le Cateau, on ground not of his choosing and with units widely scattered and with only the haziest idea of what was going on. If he had continued the retreat it is likely that the resulting situation would have been far more dire.

What has struck me whilst writing this book is the sheer professionalism of the members of II Corps. The chain of command, from battalion level up, had become severely dislocated – a number of battalions had companies fighting a considerable distance from their main body, in some cases a matter of miles away. Decisions had to be made by junior officers for which they had certainly not been trained. One can only marvel at what they managed to achieve – they and their exhausted, tired, soaked, hungry and battle weary men.

Without a doubt the Germans could claim a victory – they were in control of the battlefield late in the day. But the advance had been dislocated and their commanders left in confusion as to what exactly was going on. Even when most of II Corps had left the battlefield, those who had not received orders in time managed to make the German advance difficult by maintaining a vigorous defence of their area, a defence perhaps not significant in terms of casualties inflicted but certainly formidable enough to leave the Germans wondering what was going on and forcing their own tired infantry and cavalry to deploy again and again to remove isolated pockets of resistance. This is an exhausting process and the German troops were themselves in no condition to chase after the (generally) utterly confused units that formed the bulk of II Corps on the evening of 26 August. Although the retreat continued to make huge demands on the men of II Corps over the next days, the Germans never came close to maintaining the level of pressure that they had imposed on the BEF on 25 August, for

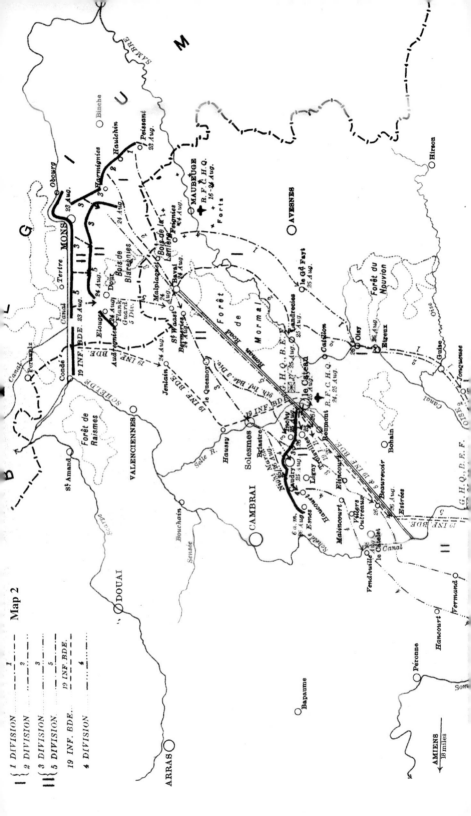

Map 2

example; and the consequence was that the BEF was able to restore order and be in a suitable condition (whatever French says in his memoirs) to be able to take its significant part in the Battle of the Marne. Le Cateau and the events over the following couple of days was a major lost German opportunity. For the British it probably saved much of II Corps at the cost of some guns and the loss of large numbers of soldiers and officers who were trained to a high standard and whose professionalism would not be seen again in the BEF until the fag end days of the Somme in 1916.

Le Cateau, therefore, at a large cost, achieved what Smith-Dorrien hoped that it would do. The decision to stand says much about the man; the men who obeyed his orders and their subsequent actions say much about the soldiers of the BEF in August 1914.

Nigel Cave,
Lushoto, December 2006

Enthusiastic crowds greet British troops in their requisitioned vehicle.

Le Cateau: German Introduction

In any examination of the battle of Le Cateau, the question always arises as to why it was not possible for the considerable forces of *First Army* at von Kluck's disposal to deal the BEF a mortal blow during the retreat from Mons. The short answer and the most important reason is that the commander was let down by his intelligence organisation. There were inherent systemic deficiencies in the way information was collected, communicated, collated and processed by the German army at the time and these problems, coupled with failures on the ground, meant that for much of the campaign von Kluck was forced to take decisions based on incomplete and misleading intelligence appreciations.

Despite the arrival on the scene of aircraft, in 1914 the cavalry was still the primary means of gaining intelligence about the enemy. The enclosure of the countryside and increasing urbanisation both complicated the work of the cavalry and forced it to divert around major towns and cities, which in turn increased the distances it had to cover and reduced its flexibility. These difficulties were compounded by numerous other problems. The German cavalry lacked firepower and had to rely on infantry *jäger* battalions to make up the deficiency. In fast moving operations only the *jäger* cycle companies could maintain contact with the advancing squadrons, which in turn tended to tie the cavalry to roads and to force on it a policy of advancing on narrow fronts; the very antithesis of the requirement for reconnaissance units and formations to operate on as broad a front as possible.

A commemorative medallion of Generaloberst Alexander von Kluck.

As a result, the slightest check meant that time was lost whilst the units deployed into line of battle or waited for their infantry to close up. The hard surfaces of the pavé roads and the habit of German cavalry of riding at all times, rather than marching to spare their horses as the British did, meant that shoes were often cast or worn out more swiftly, leading to lameness, an intolerable workload for the farriers and, even worse, the horses quickly

Von Kluck and members of his staff.

became exhausted and thus incapable of hard work. Despite the apparently generous allocation of cavalry, on the ground there was such a shortage that throughout the campaign von Kluck operated in a partial intelligence vacuum. He was, for example, unaware of the BEF's actual deployment at Mons and the same was true at Le Cateau.

Command and control, already glossed over in pre-war training, which never succeeded in thoroughly exercising the cavalry chain of command required to support mobile operations efficiently, suffered further from poor communications. The field telegraph had many limitations. The telephone network of the day was embryonic and it was extremely difficult for signallers to maintain field telephone networks during mobile operations. Radio was in its infancy and although attempts were made to harness all these means of modern technology and there had been some limited pre-war trials, the problem was that if procedures were used which exploited the potential of the latest technological means and then the system failed, the outcome was worse than reliance on messengers mounted on horseback or motor cycle, or making use of staff cars – despite the fact that the totally inadequate road network was completely overloaded. Consequently reporting was a woefully slow process.

It is possible that better use of the few reconnaissance aircraft available could have compensated for some of these deficiencies, but here again, instead of these valuable assets being centralised and their product made available to all senior commanders who required it, a few aircraft were allocated to each army and active corps. Reserve corps, however, had no access to aerial reconnaissance. This was particularly unfortunate for von Kluck. He had *IV Reserve Corps* as flank guard on the right of his advance and so never received any information from this vital source as far as a large part of his command was concerned.

One consequence of this lack of accurate intelligence was that von Kluck believed that he had only been facing a British advance guard at Mons and that the main body was located between Valenciennes and Maubeuge. His intention, therefore, on 25 August was to attack the

A brief halt for a German headquarters during the advance through northern France.

BEF in the flank and rear with the *II Cavalry Corps* and *II Army Corps*. Orders to this effect were issued during the evening of 24 August, but it then became clear that the BEF had been deployed in far larger numbers at Mons and that it was now in retreat in the direction of Landrecies. Initially there was no need to change the orders, because the direction of movement ordered had been generally southwest, but then an unfortunate report from an air reconnaissance pilot arrived and muddied the waters: Overall impression: General retreat in the direction of Maubeuge.

As a result, during the morning of 25 August, the corps were ordered to march in a south easterly direction on Maubeuge, right flank on Le Cateau. Within hours it had been established that the report was false and fresh orders shifted the direction of advance more to the west; *II Corps*, on the right, being directed to thrust south to the west of the Valencienes-Solesmes road. All this order and counter-order and switching of direction made a confused situation even more so. There is little doubt that had *First Army* been ordered to advance in the first instance towards the southwest, with one flank heading for Cambrai and the other for Le Cateau, it would have been far better placed to react to whatever course of action the BEF chose to follow. Despite that failure by the operational planning staff at First Army, it was clearly a cavalry responsibility to locate the direction of withdrawal of the British left flank, but it failed to do so. By the evening of 25 August, *II Cavalry Corps*, having been involved in skirmishes with French territorial forces and one British brigade, was located only about halfway between Cambrai and Solesmes, whilst the remainder of *First Army* was not well deployed to conduct effective pursuit operations and even less so to affect the freedom of manoeuvre of the BEF decisively.

The leading elements were spread out in a huge arc from Denain, via Solesmes, Landrecies to Aulnoye, south west of Maubeuge. *IV Reserve Corps*, following up in rear of *II Corps*, was well placed, but the same could not be said of *IX Corps* on the left flank, whose ability to manoeuvre was constrained by the geography around Maubeuge. Nevertheless, air reconnaissance on 25 August showed conclusively that the BEF was in full retreat along the main roads from Bavay to Le Cateau, Landrecies, Avesnes and either side of Solesmes. It should have been clear to the *First Army* Staff that the BEF had no intention of mounting a serious defence north of the Somme and, even if resistance had been forthcoming, *First Army* should have been able to deploy overwhelming strength against it – despite the need to counter the potential risk of a threat developing against its right flank as it advanced.

Throughout its history the German army has always paid great attention to the war-winning potential of wide outflanking manoeuvres and encirclement. To this day the Bundeswehr Command and Staff College in Hamburg displays as a mural a stylised representation of the Battle of Cannae yet, faced with a superb opportunity to achieve such a triumph during the retreat from Mons, it failed to do so. With hindsight it is clear that the German Army High Command should have concentrated its entire cavalry forces – *I* and *II Cavalry Corps* – in a wide sweeping movement designed to hinder or cut off the BEF's retreat and to drive forward as far as the Bapaume area, at least, as quickly as possible. The positioning of *I Cavalry Corps* to the south of Mons during the night of 25/26 August meant that this would have been quite feasible. In the event, nothing of the kind occurred.

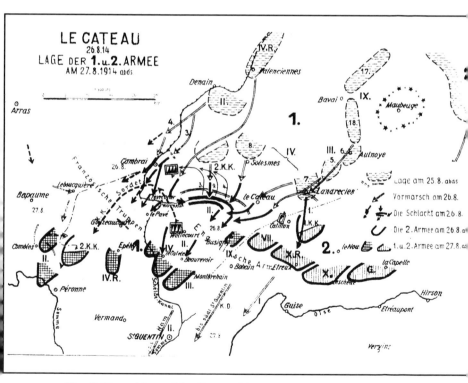

Map 3. Dispositions of the German First and Second Armies 25–27 August 1914.

Extraordinarily, on 25 August, *II Cavalry Corps* requested and was granted permission by First Army to advance towards Bohain, ie to the area forward of the army's left flank. This was a timid decision; one which was to have serious consequences for the future course of the campaign.

By the very early morning of 26 August, *II Cavalry Corps* was already in the saddle and, supported by its *jäger* battalions, was advancing south to the west of Solesmes in three great columns. Within a very short time battle was joined and the cavalry, instead of spending the day ranging out wide to the west and threatening to cut off the British retreat, became bogged down in minor battles for the possession of unimportant villages. It could be argued that, in so doing, it engaged the attention of the British defenders for long enough to enable the leading infantry regiments to close up. Be that as it may, the end result was that the German cavalry was drawn progressively into a dismounted battle in unfavourable circumstances, was fixed in position by the British II Corps and effectively prevented from acting decisively and cohesively.

Fortune favours the brave, but General Smith-Dorrien was, nevertheless, lucky to be able to be able to fight a delaying battle at Le Cateau and then to extricate II Corps the way he did, especially when the result of the fighting at Landrecies was to widen further the gap between the British I and II Corps. It was just as well for him that faulty German intelligence and poor handling of the cavalry at the operational level meant that von Kluck's *First Army* was off-balance and ill-placed to carry out the great encircling movement which might have seen at least the whole of II Corps defeated and captured. In the event *II Cavalry Corps* was unable even fully to probe the western extent of the British line and then, after the battle, did not, or could not, pursue the British vigorously to the south.

Once more lacking soundly based intelligence, persisting in the belief that the general line of the British retreat from Le Cateau was to the southwest, over the next forty eight hours the gap between von Kluck's army and the BEF simply widened. Faulty dispositions at the start of a battle can rarely be corrected; never is this more so than in an encounter battle such as Le Cateau. German errors had let their chance of dealing a truly crushing blow slip through their fingers. The opportunity never arose again.

Jack Sheldon
Vercors
September 2007

Visiting the Le Cateau Battlefield

General

The Le Cateau area is relatively quiet and peaceful, yet is easily accessible by road from popular battlefield areas such as the Somme and Arras. It is much easier to get around it than Mons, which has become a tourer's nightmare, requiring enormous patience on the part of the driver and lightning map reading qualities from the navigator. Here, if an error is made, it is never too difficult to turn around and get back on the correct route. There is nothing of the war left to see – even the British gun preserved in the library in Le Cateau is a replacement; apparently the original fell victim to the needs for metal in the Second World War. Le Cateau also offers some cultural opportunities, with the impressive Matisse Museum, in the old palace, which had been used by the Germans during the war. In fact the town had figured prominently earlier in English history, for the Treaty of Cateau Cambrésis in 1559, soon after Elizabeth I came to the throne, ended English occupation of Calais and thus terminated a part of its history that had its origins in the Norman Conquest. There were, from that date, no more English possessions in France. The treaty also resolved Franco-Spanish rivalries, at least for the next thirty years or so.

Insurance and Medical

Travel and breakdown insurance is very cheap in comparison to the potential cost of an emergency, so although you are embarking on a simple visit to a nearby EU country, rather than an expedition to the North Pole, the peace of mind obtained is probably well worth the modest outlay involved. In any event do not venture out of the UK without a European Health Insurance Card, the successor to the old E111 form. You can apply online for the card at www.ehic.org.uk" or by calling 0845 606 2030. Cards take about three weeks to be delivered, but it is possible to obtain a temporary number at short notice. For those living in France it is normal to have top-up medical insurance to complement state provision, so this is another argument for taking out some form of travel insurance, in order to ensure that you are entitled to the highest standards of treatment, should it be necessary. You will be visiting an agricultural area where there is a risk of tetanus. Make sure that your vaccination is up to date.

Independent Travellers

Most visitors from the United Kingdom tend to travel independently by car. This method probably provides the best combination of value for money and flexibility and, if you prepare carefully and bear a few straightforward rules in mind, you should have a trouble-free trip. The first point to remember is to drive on the right. This may seem obvious, but visitors from the UK are involved in accidents every year because they forget this simple fact. Danger times are first thing in the morning, or setting off after a stop for refreshments or to visit a point of interest, especially if you are on a minor, quiet country road. Put an arrow on your windscreen or have a drill to help you to remember. Carry your driving licence, log book and proof of insurance and passport at all times, *but do not leave them unattended in the car.* You also need a red warning triangle (indeed, it is better to have two of them) in case of breakdown and spare light bulbs. If you are stopped by a policeman and informed that a light is not working, production of a spare bulb from the glove compartment means that no offence has been committed. It would also be as well to have one of the slip on reflective vests that are becoming mandatory in many parts of the EU – and there should be one for everyone on board in some countries, so if the French law has not changed by the time you get this, it doubtless will!

A small first aid kit and fire extinguisher are also sensible items to carry. Make sure that you familiarise yourself with the speed limits in France (motorways 130 kph in dry weather, 110 kph in the rain; dual carriageways 110 kph; normal roads 90 kph; urban areas 50 kph, or less) and about the need to give way to traffic approaching from the right, unless you are on a priority road. Do not even think about drinking and driving. The legal limit is lower than in the United Kingdom and easily breached.

Accommodation
There are a couple of hotels in Le Cateau and in some of the larger places on the battlefield, such as Caudry. Honnechy boasts a rather smart bed and breakfast as well as a gite and there is an upmarket hotel and restaurant in Ligny. Cambrai would make a good centre, as would St Quentin. However, Le Cateau is quite manageable from popular stamping grounds such as Arras and the Albert area.

Useful Books
Le Cateau has never merited a book to itself thus far. However, the Mons campaign is well covered by John Terraine's first book, *Mons*, and David Ascoli's *Mons Star* is equally readable and authoritative. The battle also plays a prominent part in a number of other books, such as those by Lyn MacDonald and several others on the theme of the Old

"'French's contemptible little army', who have already made the Kaiser eat his words. Panoramic view of a British camp in France." News photograph with the above caption was released to the British press in late August 1914. It shows the Welch Regiment somewhere in France.

Contemptibles. Usually I have taken great chunks out of the numerous regimental histories, nearly all of which had been reprinted in recent years by the Naval and Military Press at affordable prices. The battle gets good coverage in the Official History – 1914 Volume 1 – and the appendix volume I has an excellent map of the battle; full use of this has been made in this book.

Maps
See the Tours section for fuller details on this, but I would strongly recommend that you have the IGN Green Series Map 4 (Laon Arras) with you. It is very good for navigation. We would hope that the maps in the book will enable you to place yourself on the ground once you are in the area of the battlefield; please note that Tour 4, from Le Cateau to Cambrai on the German side of the line, comes without a tour map, though we consider that the written instructions should be adequate.

Clothing and Personal Equipment
Clearly this will depend on what time of year you intend to visit. Good boots are essential for all but the simplest walks and, regardless of the season, we always take Wellingtons to wear when squelching up to

distant cemeteries and points of interest. This minimises the amount of mud transferred into the car each time you get in and out. As a general rule always carry a waterproof jacket and wrap up warmly against the wind and rain in the winter. In the summer the sun can be fierce. Wear a hat and use sun screen. None of these walks is really off the beaten track, but you need to carry drinks and snacks so as to be self-sufficient. Do not forget your camera and notebook and a day sack with which to carry everything.

Refreshments
There are plenty of places in which to eat at Caudry and Le Cateau itself and we have never found parking a particularly difficult problem. One or two recommendations are made in the touring section of this book.

Dogs
Now that the quarantine laws have been changed, it is much easier to transport domestic animals to and from the United Kingdom and it is quite common to see dogs accompanying their owners around the battlefields. For the latest rules which govern the import and export of pets you are advised to check on the website: www.defra.gov.uk/animal/quarantine/index.htm. The critical point, which travellers often get wrong and which makes the vets in Calais wealthy, is the fact that dogs arrive at the terminals not having been treated for internal and external parasites in the correct manner. They should arrive at the port in France having been treated by a vet more than 24 hours and less than 48 hours previously. Make sure when you have this done that the vet signs and dates the paperwork, adding in the time the treatment was administered. If not, the dog does not travel and it is another job for a vet in Calais, not to mention a twenty four hour delay.

Dogs are welcomed, or at least tolerated, in a wide range of hotels and gîtes in France, but it is as well to check in advance, unless you intend to use a chain such as Formule 1 www.hotelformule1.com www.hotelformule1.com, or Campanile Première Classe www.envergure.fr, where pets are automatically welcome. Currently there are no hotels of this type in Albert or Bapaume, but there are in places as close as Arras, Péronne, Cambrai or Douai, all of which are convenient for the area covered by this book.

Make sure that you keep control of your animal at all times. There are very few places on the battlefield where they can easily be allowed to run free, but if they walk well on a lead and you can cope with the amount of mud that they will transfer into your vehicle, they will enjoy the walks as much as you do. Be especially careful during the hunting season in the autumn. Local hunters will let fly at anything, including your dog if it is free. It is not a good idea to take them into cemeteries; use your judgement and all members of the party, including four-legged ones, will enjoy the visit.

Battlefield Debris

There will be very little material left over on the battlefields from the Le Cateau 1914 battle, but it must be remembered that much of the area was heavily fought over in October 1918. Modern ploughing depths and the natural action of the soil means that rusting battlefield debris, including small arms ammunition, grenades, mortar bombs and shells (both conventional and chemical) appear in small quantities every year. Such material is dumped by farmers at the sides of fields awaiting collection by the *démineurs* who are responsible for disposing of these items safely. Leave all such items strictly alone. Do not touch or kick them; above all do not tamper with them. Even after all these years they are still lethal. Possession of live or defused items is a criminal offence in France, as is the use of metal detectors on the battlefield; so be warned.

A British gun crew dug in during the open stages of the Great War. Although practically no dangerous munitions are likely to remain from the Battle of Le Cateau, 1914, there was plenty of lethal fighting over the same ground later. Leave all suspicious items alone.

Chapter One

THE RIGHT OF THE LINE:
THE FIFTH DIVISION

The right of the Fifth Division: part of 14 Brigade

Amongst the first to be involved in the fighting at Le Cateau were the two elements of the 5th Division that happened to be to the east of, and almost in, Le Cateau itself – that is the 1st Duke of Cornwall's Light Infantry (1/DCLI) and the 1st East Surrey's (1/E Surrey). This part of Fifth Division was to maintain contact with I Corps, further to the east (or, at least, that was the idea). The DCLI's excellent regimental history (The History of the DCLI 1914 – 1919, Everard Wyrall) provides most of the material for what follows. At the outbreak of the war it required no less than 650 reservists (ie about 60% of a mobilised battalion's establishment) to bring it up to strength, These men had to be assembled at Bodmin, the Regimental Depot, kitted out and shipped to the Curragh, near Dublin: and this was achieved within two days of mobilisation being ordered. Almost every man called up appeared at the depot – the exceptions (two) were at sea. If nothing else, this is a tribute both to the telegram system of the day and the quality of the contemporary public transport.

See Map
p. 201

1st Battalion Duke of Cornwall's Light Infantry (1/DCLI)

*Note that letters in **bold** and in parenthesis are to be found on the map extracted from the DCLI history.*

1/DCLI had suffered relatively few casualties during its time on the extreme left of the line (for much of the time) at Mons. Similarly, although being the rearguard of 14 Brigade and of the 5th Division from early morning until about 2pm on 25 August, it suffered few casualties from the enemy. However, from that time onwards, men began to fall out, utterly exhausted. It was very hot indeed, a heat that was relieved somewhat by a torrential downpour that commenced at about 5pm. The bivouac positions for 1/DCLI and half of 1/E Surrey were to the east of Le Cateau; they arrived at about 6pm after a march of over twenty three miles and were utterly worn out and completely soaked. Not only was it a march of twenty three miles – one has to include the heat, the extremely crowded

25

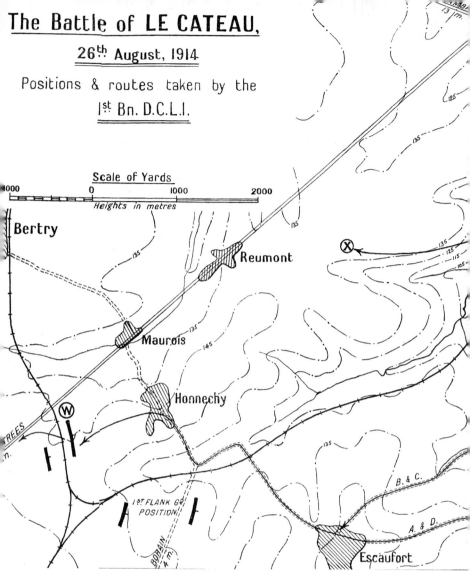

The Battle of LE CATEAU,

26ᵗʰ August, 1914.

Positions & routes taken by the
1ˢᵗ Bn. D.C.L.I.

Scale of Yards

1000   0   1000   2000

Heights in metres

Bertry

Reumont

Maurois

Honnechy

1ˢᵗ FLANK GD
POSITION

Escaufort

B. & C.

A. & D.

BOHAIN

TREES

Map 4. The east of the battlefield, particularly that of 1st Duke of Cornwall Light Infantry.

and confused road traffic conditions and the great clouds of dust through which they would have had to march, never mind the rumble of firing and the threat of a probing enemy.

We bivouacked, in a drenched condition, in a field at the fork road [ie the Pommereuil road] on the south eastern outskirts of the town just as it became dark. The men were served out with rations, the first since 8pm the previous night. It may safely be

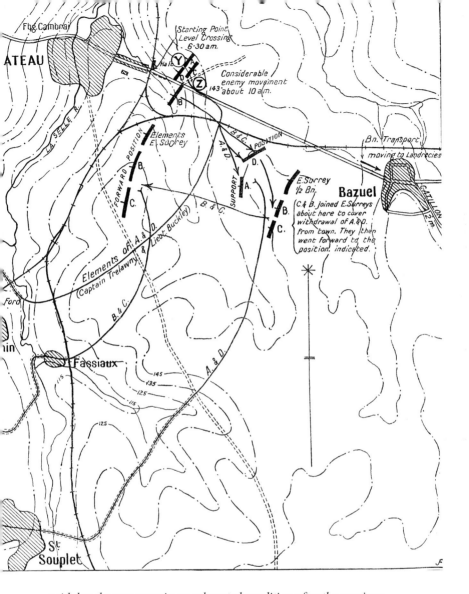

said that the men were in an exhausted condition after the previous four days' continuous strain and a rest was much hoped for.

'Early on that memorable day the Cornwalls, after a wretched night, 'stood to arms'. It was still dark and their clothes were sodden with rain: many had not slept at all, even exhausted as they were on the previous night. 'Stand To' was the worst hour of the day: chilled through and drowsy, the bitter change from oblivion to consciousness amidst all the gloomy surroundings of war was a thing men experienced not only in those early days of 1914 but throughout the long years in France and Flanders that followed. Sleep was the only sedative, an anodyne which took away all remembrance: the thing which allayed pain, blotted out for an all too short period the ghastly horrors and surroundings of the battlefield.'

The Battalion was due to continue its retirement at 6.30am in line with French's original orders – and no official order arrived to change that intention. It was all set up, in column of route **(Y)**, with its head near the level crossing, to proceed from the eastern end of town through it and then off in a south westerly direction when, at the very moment set for departure, it came under small arms fire. Although some shelling had taken place to the west of the town shortly before this time, the DCLI were the first to be fired upon by infantry in what the British subsequently called the Battle of Le Cateau. The shots came from houses on the town side of the railway, about a hundred yards to the west of the assembled Battalion; although the Commanding Officer's horse was hit, most of the damage was done to the Brigade Signals Section, which was already on the west side of the bridge Situated with them was part of 14 Brigade HQ, and Lieutenant J Dennis of the DCLI, the Brigade Machine-Gun Officer, was killed. (He has no known grave.) Immediately the men retired, through fields of allotments, to some high ground to the rear and occupied positions across the road **(Z)**. The two and half companies of the East Surreys took up a position south of the road and to the rear of 1/DCLI.

The situation was uncomfortable, as there was a gap of some miles between these easternmost troops of II Corps and Haig's already retreating I Corps; the only possible elements of support were some horse artillery, part of 1 Cavalry Brigade and Gough's 3 Cavalry Brigade which were covering the gap between the two corps. The British were now under fire not only from the houses but also the railway embankment, which continued in a south easterly direction. There was no question of trying to force their way through the town. The solution was to take positions to the south, in more open ground. The situation became gradually more confused. Two companies (B and C) were sent forward to take up a position on the east side of the railway line that ran south from Le Cateau, towards St Souplet. A and D companies, with the East Surreys on their right, came up in support.

In the process, some men from A and D companies became separated and, hearing considerable fire from the west, moved towards it and eventually ended up on the high ground to the east of Reumont **(X)**. They attached themselves to the 2nd Manchesters and then to the

Argylls; eventually returning to the Battalion late at night.

By 10am the position had become serious. The Germans were keeping up an effective fire from positions on the railway embankments and cuttings, whilst at about that time considerable German activity could be observed north of the Le Cateau-Bazuel road. It was time to move on, and the Commanding Officer, Lieutenant Colonel MN Turner, decided to head south west in an attempt to rejoin the rest of the 5th Division. It was fortunate that the cavalry was available to provide some cover for the manoeuvre, which otherwise would have been all but impossible. It was not an easy move, as the Battalion (and the East Surreys who were with them) had to move separately; but they combined, by some miracle, as accounts make clear, at Escaufort and reorganised there, making contact with higher headquarters at about 1.30pm. The Battalion was moved to a position just south of Honnechy **(W)** as a right flank guard for the 5th Division; at 4pm it carried out a similar function nearby, on the Roman Road; and, finally, at 5pm set off southwards along the road.

However, in the confusion, some troops went east from Le Cateau; indeed the Battalion transport, under Lieutenant Benn – who was the Battalion Machine Gun Officer and whose account follows – was not to be heard of again until the early hours of 1st September, having earlier arrived miles south of here at Crépy-en-Valois.

Being a minute or two early [for the start of the retreat, at 6.30am] *we sat down in fours on the right of the road where there were but few houses and had scarcely done this when fire was opened on us from houses at the bottom of the street, and at once the Battalion took to the open ground on the right* [north] *side of the road. This operation naturally led to companies getting mixed up as it appeared that there was no time to be lost, and in the absence of superior orders each officer did immediately what seemed good to himself. In a very short time the Battalion had opened up, but the general intention was not clear, though the East Surreys, who had not been fired on, and at least two companies of the DCLI, took the ground on the left of the road and began an advance. Gradually more and more men were transferred across the road and across the railway cutting from the high ground near which little groups of men could be seen advancing towards the more obvious Germans who, however, seemed to be firing at us from several directions.*

I found that it was impossible to get vehicles across country so kept the Machine-Gun Section on the road on the right of our line [ie the Bazuel road] *to prevent the Germans turning our flank, and all the first line transport of the Battalion together with that of the East Surreys was on the road, only further back behind, out of the way of stray bullets.*

About 9am, or perhaps later, I discovered that I had lost touch with the Battalion and could not find them, although stragglers indicated that they had retired in a south westerly direction. Eventually I decided to take charge of the vehicles and try to work round and rejoin from behind.

On coming to the first branch road [presumably the road from Bazuel heading south west] *I was met issuing from it by two officers of the East Surreys with about fifty men and a few belonging to the DCLI and a number of wounded, including* [Second Lieutenant] *Savile in a cart. They were also lost, so I judged that it was no good to attempt that road. I had now some seventy men of my Battalion and with them proceeded towards Catillon where I met a party of Scots Greys guarding a canal bridge* [to the east of Catillon].

Having contacted 5 Cavalry Brigade HQ and got no information, he proceeded with his group until he came into I Corps area. This account is typical of the experience of many men at Le Cateau, who got mixed up in the inevitable disorganisation of a retreat conducted under fire. In his case he eventually made his way back to the Battalion by train, but had to leave thirty men behind *whose feet were too bad to march anymore.* Major Cornish-Bowden, the second in command, was in a base hospital some days after the end of the Retreat. Some of the cases there were suffering simply from complete exhaustion.

But the most tragic thing about them was the state of their poor feet. I was told that, in certain instances, it was impossible to remove the socks as they had become practically a part of the feet, the raw flesh and the sock just welded together to form one substance. When one considers the pain caused by walking with a mere blistered heel, the sheer agony that these poor fellows must have endured becomes dimly apparent.

And bear in mind that the majority of the Battalion consisted of called up reservists, who would have been issued with brand new boots, with no time to break them in.

1/DCLI lost surprisingly few men, given the conditions under which they fought on 26 August. Two officers were wounded and made prisoner – Major Petavel (repatriated in January 1918) and Lieutenant Richardson (interned in Holland in January 1918 and sent home the following October); another was wounded and 185 other ranks were reported as dead, wounded and missing. Ninety of these, however, rejoined later. Again, the experience of 1/DCLI in this respect was not unusual.

In passing, it would seem appropriate to note the ending of an era. During the confusion of the day and the separation of the Battalion into a number of parts, some elements of the Battalion tried to use buglers and the Regimental Call. For example, the second in command, Major Cornish-Bowden, was amongst those who fell back first after the initial assault by the Germans.

Arrived at what seemed to be the crest of a hill we were astonished to find ourselves again under fire. Somebody expressed the opinion that the whistle of the bullets denoted that they were British and that therefore we were under the fire of our own side. I replied that my ear for music was not sufficiently well developed to enable me to distinguish between the note of British and German bullets; but, as I thought it would do no harm to attract the attention of the firers and as we could not locate them, I ordered the bugler to sound the regimental call. Of course I was quite unaware at the time that the Colonel had used the same expedient to attract my attention; but I had better luck than he, though not in the way that I had intended. The fire continued just the same as ever, but the bugle call produced Captain Oliver, who presently appeared on the scene with a considerable number of his company, and also the OC East Surrey Regiment and some of the men of that regiment. The result was that I had the better part of Captain Romilly's and Captain Oliver's companies [ie B and C companies].

Was this the last time that bugle calls were used for such a purpose in the Great War? Probably not, but there cannot have been very many other occasions.

1/East Surrey was a Battalion split in half, with two of its companies to be found on the east side of the Roman road, in rear of 2/Suffolks. The remainder, including the CO, the Battalion cyclists and transport, were with 1/DCLI to the east of Le Cateau. When the shooting started, at 6.30am, the CO moved his men astride the Catillon road and then gradually moved them south and across the railway line. The Surreys was unable to move west by proceeding directly south of the town, coming under fire from Germans

31

in a wood. The two companies (plus one of the DCLI) launched a spirited counter attack which helped to reduce the volume and accuracy of the fire coming from it. Like the DCLI, the East Surreys made their way south westwards, not without considerable difficulty, and with the support of 3 Cavalry Brigade, and rejoined the Division at Maurois at about 2.30pm. However, it too lost its transport, which eventually joined up with the 1st Division and only returned to the Battalion two weeks later, during the Battle of the Marne.

1/East Surrey, which required over 400 reservists to bring it up to full strength at the outbreak of the war, suffered rather less – in the two battles at Mons and Le Cateau and in the Retreat it suffered some 230 casualties, of whom twenty-nine were killed and 117 missing, of whom about fifty were wounded.

The centre right of the Fifth Division: part of 13 and of 14 Brigades, supported by 19 Brigade.

The 2nd Battalion Suffolk Regiment

Le Cateau will always be associated by the battlefield visitor with 2/Suffolk; the memorial on Suffolk Hill, commanding such excellent views as it does and unique in its kind, has been the one 'permanent' memorial on the battlefield since soon after the war was ended. The Battalion was also honoured, uniquely so far as I know, with an introduction in the Regimental history (published in 1928) to the chapter on the fighting at Le Cateau by Smith-Dorrien himself. In part, he wrote:

> Under instructions from the commander-in-chief I had issued orders for the retirement to continue and the 14th Brigade, to which the 2nd Battalion of the Suffolks belonged, had been detailed as rearguard to the 5th Division.
>
> Thus, when in the small hours of the 26th I was able to gauge the situation from the accumulating reports of the scattered positions of the troops in my area, I learned that many of them were still on the march, that more than one whole division would not have reached the line we had taken up until daylight and, further, that all were exhausted and foot-sore, and therefore issued orders to stand and fight. The 14th Brigade automatically became the first troops who would have to meet the first attack

of the enemy. There was no time to choose, much less to adequately entrench, a position; so they had to fight where they were, practically in a salient, fully exposed to the enemy's fire, and their right flank en l'air, owing to the failure of I Corps to come into their place in the line on the previous evening.

Some one, certainly not I, ordered that on no account were the Suffolks to retire. Such an order was enough for the Suffolks. For nine hours they fought with desperate losses, their CO, Lieutenant Colonel Brett, being killed comparatively early in the day; but no thought of retirement entered their heads, for had they not been told to fight to the last? I was not surprised when I heard of their grand behaviour, for I had had previous experience of

Lieutenant Colonel Brett DSO.

this magnificent regiment, especially in the Boer War, but it was never my intention that any troops should have been called upon to fight to the last. My intention was to fight a serious rear-guard action and, when the pressure became too great, to order a general retirement by divisions, and this I actually did about 2pm. It may be some satisfaction to the regiment that their gallant adherence to the letter of the order they got materially helped the remainder of their comrades in the 5th Division to fall back practically unopposed; in fact, had not the Suffolks and other intrepid troops refused to budge, there would have been nothing to prevent the enemy sweeping on the scattered units of the Division before they had had time to get on the road allotted for their retirement. Had this happened, the safety of the whole force fighting at Le Cateau, and indeed of the whole BEF, would have been jeopardised…it was the blow to the Germans delivered on the field of Le Cateau which upset their plans and prevented their descent on Paris.

The Suffolks were one of the units that made that blow possible. I thank them, and the whole nation should be grateful to them.'

Sufolk Hill Memorial. Inscription memoralizing those killed resisting the German advance in August 1914.

33

.303 ammunition being distributed under fire.

On the evening of 25th August, 1/Suffolk were to form part of the force guarding the north front of Le Cateau, but this was changed and they finally arrived, at about 10pm, at Pont des Quatre Vaux, the crossroads with the Cambrai – Le Cateau road and the Montay – Reumont road, the latter better known as the Roman Road. The Battalion was exhausted, not helped by the fact that the scene in Le Cateau was one of utter confusion, as French (and some British) cavalry tried to move – in some cases east, in some cases west – through it, whilst hordes of British troops were coming down from the north and heading in a generally southern direction. Physical exhaustion was accompanied by worries about the proximity of the Germans, about whom rumours were flying. At 4am the CO, Lieutenant Colonel Brett, was told that the retirement would be continued and that 14 Brigade would form the rearguard for the division. The Battalion then moved off in artillery formation, keeping to the east of the road, but the leading companies had only got to the crossroads about 800 yards away when Major Peebles was told by an ADC to the Divisional commander, 'You are going to fight it out here'.

Once the decision became widely known, the adjutant (Captain Cutbill) rode after the Battalion transport (which, naturally, had gone on ahead) to rescue the regimental tools. A and B Companies took possession of these and 'took up a line in some stubble on which the corn stooks were still standing'. The position the Battalion held was far from promising, as the *Official History* pointed out:

> *The Suffolks, in particular, who lay immediately to the west of Le Cateau, were badly placed for a general action: there was much dead ground on every side; the field of fire was, for the most part, limited and could nowhere be called good; and small valleys and sunken roads at sundry points gave hostile infantry every opportunity of concealing their approach.*

At about 6am a Uhlan patrol was fired upon, whose officer was killed. More patrols and scouts were observed. Brigadier-General Rolt came up and explained the situation as he understood it, adding, 'You understand, there is to be no thought of retirement'. The story is taken up by the Regimental History [*The History of the Suffolk Regiment 1914 – 1927* by Lieutenant Colonel CCR Murphy, 1928].

> *The stooks had scarcely been flattened down, and the shallowest*

Patrolling Hussars – the British did not much distinguish between them and Uhlans.

British infantry enjoying a rare respite during the retreat.

of trenches dug, when one of the enemy's guns opened fire. The second shell landed in the middle of No 15 Platoon, killing Second Lieutenant Myddleton [no known grave] *and Sergeant Molineaux. Major Peebles, finding his company enfiladed, withdrew them to the main position. About this time Lieutenant Colonel Brett fell mortally wounded* [no known grave].

The enemy's infantry did not show up much at first, but it became immediately evident that their artillery was in vastly superior force to that of the British. Some German skirmishers, who had crept up to the knoll of the Montay spur, now opened fire on the British gunners. Upon these and also upon a concealed German machine gun on the Cambrai road the left company of the Suffolks opened fire; but there was some doubt as to the situation, for it never occurred to any of the officers that the high ground immediately to the east and west of Le Cateau would be left open to free occupation by the enemy.

'It was not, however, until about ten o'clock that the German infantry began to offer a target. In spite of the losses they sustained from rapid individual and machine gun fire they continued to advance steadily for some time, but were eventually checked. ...

By this time the hostile artillery had increased to a pitch of tremendous severity. The deafening storm of high explosive shells, with the roar of the British guns, which on the right were less than a hundred yards behind the Battalion, rendered communications between units well nigh impossible. German aeroplanes, circling overhead, dropped smoke bombs of various colours to direct their artillery. The enemy were already seeking to turn our right flank and two battalions of 19 Brigade [1st Middlesex and 2nd Argyll and Sutherland Highlanders] *were therefore sent to reinforce that flank.*

Early in the day the enemy had succeeded in getting a number of machine guns into the cutting on the Le Cateau – Cambrai road, immediately in front of 2/Suffolk. By 11am the fire from these guns had increased to such an extent that the position of the Battalion became critical. Before noon two heroic attempts were made by the 2nd Manchesters and 2/A&SH to reinforce them, but only a few of these splendid men managed to reach the trenches.

A German officer samples food from a field kitchen.

Ammunition for the machine guns was running out by this stage; the acting CO, Major Douglas, and a sergeant brought up some bandoliers, but the former was soon afterwards severely wounded, as was the adjutant. The two front line battalions of 13 and 14 Brigade, 2nd King's Own Yorkshire Light Infantry and the Suffolks, continued to be assaulted by very heavy shrapnel and high explosive shell fire as was their supporting artillery, much of which was positioned practically in the front line; but for almost six hours the right of the line held firm.

At 4.30 am German time the regiments of **HKK 2** [Higher Cavalry Commander 2] had started to advance from north of Solesmes in a southerly direction, aiming to skirt Cambrai to the east. The infantry of *7th* and *8th Divisions* of *General der Infanterie* Sixt von Armin's *IV Army Corps* were also on the move early. All the men were tired, having marched thirty eight kilometres the previous day. Shortly before 6.00am the companies of *Infantry Regiment 72 (16 Brigade, 8th Infantry Division)* were picking their way forward through or around the town of Le Cateau. During the next sixty to ninety minutes they were involved in constant small-scale actions with British rearguards or delaying parties scattered in the buildings but, having already taken numerous prisoners in the town, their forward elements were already probing the southern exits of Le Cateau by 7.00am. A short time later they became engaged in a heavy fire fight with the British who had taken up positions up on Suffolk Hill. Until the arrival of regiments from *7th Division* about 9.00 am *Infantry Regiment 72* was carrying the entire weight of the battle in this area unaided. The problem faced by its commander, *Oberst* von Zehman, was that he could not expect reinforcement from other regiments of *8th Division,* because they were increasingly being drawn towards the battle for Caudry. The only hope was assistance from *13 Brigade* of *7th Division*, which was advancing along the axis Le Cateau-Reumont. For a critical two hour period, therefore, there was considerable concern on the German side.

Already by 6.00am Reserve *Leutnant* Halbrock of *Kürassier Regiment 7*, who was scouting forward, was reporting the exits to the

General der Infanterie Sixt von Armin, commanding IV Corps.

town all blocked off or covered by fire. Half of a platoon (about thirty five men) were despatched forward in support and told to keep advancing to contact. This was closely followed by additional sub units, until about half a battalion was on the move. Coming under brisk fire from houses and buildings off to a flank and also from a railway embankment, *12th Company Infantry Regiment 72*, with fire support from *9th Company* mounted a quick attack, captured the railway embankment and occupied it.

Leutnant Edelmann, 6th Company, following up, described the situation later:

> *'Emerging out of the built up area, I deployed my first platoon and, in accordance with the good old tradition, I followed up at fifty paces interval. At my side, as he always was, was my very brave drummer Österitz. We soon reached the railway line,* [This is the line which runs north towards Solesmes] *which passed through a deep cutting and which was under fire from somewhere. Initially I led my company in single file along the railway, then, at a suitable spot, I dropped down, crossed the tracks and climbed up the other side. We passed a sunken road, entered a field of sugar beet and came under heavy enemy fire.'*

By 7.30 Edelmann, who lost his right arm on 1st April 1915 whilst serving with *Reserve Infantry Regiment 264*, had been badly wounded in the neck, the bullet just missing his carotid artery. More companies and machine guns were fed into the battle as a result of this resistance, including *5th* and *6th*, who were reinforced by elements of *2nd Company*.

Progress was somewhat easier on the other flank, where *4th Company*, supported by two guns of the *Machine Gun Company*, rushed forward, just failing to be able to bring fire down on a train which was pulling out from the station. *Infantry Regiment 72* was informed later by prisoners that the train had been carrying a high level staff and probably Sir John French himself. Doubtless, had the rumour been true and had not Sir John French established his headquarters the previous day at St Quentin, the men of *Infantry Regiment 72* might have pulled off one of the great coups of the war. As it was they continued to work their way forward as best they could.

On the extreme eastern flank, *Infantry Regiment 72* was dealing only with isolated British outposts. 5th Company had by now taken the lead on this line of advance, with *Reserve Leutnant* Kühlhorn's platoon in the lead.

Just to my front was a brickworks [might have been making

tiles], *the buildings of which were strongly defended by the British. Initially their shooting was poor and I had no desire to present them with easy targets. We were perhaps 300 metres from the buildings. I gave my platoon the order 'On your feet! Forwards! Go!' and we advanced in short rushes. When I looked around, during a pause, I found that I only had about eight men and some NCOs with me. The remainder had stayed where they were. Luckily the British seemed to be perturbed by the attack of my little band and about forty of them pulled back swiftly to Bazuel. I had also forgotten to order the fixing of bayonets, but everything turned out well again and the fleeing enemy was brought under heavy fire by my few men. We searched the buildings but found nothing. A bed sheet was hanging on a pole from the north window of a house, so I had it withdrawn because I had no idea what it was supposed to signify. Now what? I was located on the extreme flank of our position, alone with my men. To advance was impossible. In addition, the British who had been driven off had established themselves about 1,400 metres away in a little copse near Banuel, whence they sent us their greetings from time to time. We saw them located diagonally across a road, but could do nothing about them. We had little time to deliberate, because we were suddenly brought under a hail of shells. They exploded on all sides. We had the British to our front and shells to our rear. We sought much-needed shelter*

in a clay pit. I then remembered the 'white flag' and it was swiftly re-erected. The fire eased almost instantly. The British batteries must have believed that their fellow countrymen were hard on our heels. Finally I pulled back to my right, towards Le Cateau, where luckily I made contact with my company once more.'

Hauptmann Emil Frucht, IR72, buried at Le Cateau Cemetery.

Infantry Regiment 72 was extremely pleased with itself for what it thought it had achieved. It seemed not to appreciate the fact that the town of Le Cateau was essentially undefended and occupied only by a few stragglers and delaying parties.

Utterly alone (they later recorded) the regiment had marched along the front of the enemy army and broken in amongst them in Le Cateau! Not only that! Its energetic advance and the surprise entry into Le Cateau had pushed back the front,

40

apparently forcing small parties of enemy to pull back in an easterly and southerly direction, before presenting a defensive line to the regiment. The main enemy defensive line, however, was located along the line of the road Le Cateau-Cambrai, where the 8th Division appeared to be fighting. It was now important to establish contact with our own troops. Because the enemy artillery fire falling on Huber's half-battalion was coming from the direction of Pommereuil, contact had to be sought there first. Leutnant *Rauch*, the regimental adjutant, displaying his usual skill and daring, managed to make contact successively with the 7th, then the 8th Divisions and later with HQ IV Corps, making use of British car which Hauptmann Rogge had captured. Apart from a few bullet holes in the

Generalleutnant Hildebrandt, Commanding 8th Division.

Map 5. Operations of IR72 around Le Cateau.

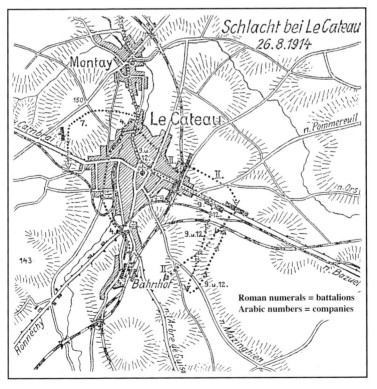

car, the journey passed off smoothly. In the meantime 9th Company, out to the east, had launched an advance which was completed by 12.00 pm. The enemy withdrew to its front, was brought under heavy fire and so energetically pursued that after an advance of about one kilometre, it found itself completely outside the regimental area. It was ordered to pull back to conform to the general line and it achieved this about 1.00 pm, just as the 2nd Battalion advanced in a southerly direction. This advance was accompanied by Huber's half battalion, echeloned to the left. The troops reached the heights to the south of the town, where Leutnant *Kühlhorn's platoon was in a blocking position, then moved forward to the area of the station.'*

Hauptmann Huber later provided his impressions of the scene which he observed from the heights to the east of St Benin:

As I orientated myself, I was greatly amazed to realise that we were situated well in rear of the enemy battle line. An unforgettable scene unfurled before me. To the west of Le Cateau, some of the British batteries and their teams of horses were destroyed, initially by infantry and later by artillery fire. Further to the north, German infantry could be seen winning ground in the area of the road from Cambrai.

Meanwhile, for the Suffolks, as morning turned to afternoon, 'the Germans had worked so far round our flank that Second Lieutenants George and Burnand had to turn their men about to face their original rear'. The *Official History* recorded the last minutes:

Between 2.30 and 2.45pm the end came. The Germans had by this time accumulated an overwhelming force in the shelter of the Cambrai road, and they now fell upon the Suffolks from the front, right flank and right rear. The turning movement, however, did not at once make itself felt and the Suffolks and Argylls opened rapid fire to their front with terrific effect... The Germans kept sounding the British 'Cease Fire', and gesticulating to persuade the men to surrender, but in vain. At length a rush of the enemy from the rear bore down all resistance and the Suffolks and their Highland comrades were overwhelmed. They had for nine hours been under an incessant bombardment which had pitted the whole of the ground with craters, and they had fought to the very last, covering themselves with undying glory.'

2/Suffolks suffered some 720 casualties in the battle, with four officers being killed, only one of whom, Second Lieutenant GH Payne, has a

A tranquil pre-war scene in Le Cateau. Looking up the high street is the town hall (centre left) and parish church (centre).

known grave, in Le Cateau Military Cemetery. Many of the wounded officers were made prisoner, as it was impossible to get them off the field. The Battalion was only able to have a muster at dawn on 27 August, when there were found to be 111 men, then commanded by Lieutenant Oakes; by the evening of the 28th this had grown to 229 men, organised into a company and attached to 1/E Surrey. Mixed in with the Suffolks was a small party of men from the 1st Dorsetshire Regiment, about thirty strong and under the command of Captain Williams. They had got separated from their battalion during the retreat from Mons; when the fighting commenced at Le Cateau they

came under the Suffolks and took up a position in the forward positions, on the north eastern front. Most of them managed to make their way back during the retirement. Williams, who commanded the battalion for a while in the fighting in the Ploegsteert Wood area in mid November 1914, died of pneumonia in March 1915 and is buried in Boulogne Eastern Cemetery.

2/Manchesters suffered 353 casualties, including fourteen officers. Of the officers killed or died off wounds, only Captains Brodribb and Trueman have a known grave, in Le Cateau Military Cemetery. At roll call that night only eight officers and 339 other ranks were present – but the numbers grew as the Retreat continued. A number of these, including the Medical Officer and the grooms with the led horses, had taken a wrong turn at Bavai during the retreat from Mons, and did not eventually rejoin the battalion until six weeks later after they found themselves in I Corps area. Some of the Battalion was moved forward at about 10am to support 2/Suffolk, and it was amongst the men of these companies that the Manchesters' casualties were highest. Other men were sent to extend the right flank and to form a flank guard, with the machine gun section covering the approaches from the north east from the Selle Valley. It was their presence here that helped the artillery to remove what guns they could.

It is now necessary to look at the contribution to this right flank part of the battle of **19 Brigade**. It was formed on 22 August from four battalions originally allocated as lines of communications defence troops, under the command (unusually) of a major general, LG Drummond.

During the initial retreat from Mons (where the Brigade had been on the extreme left flank) it suffered few casualties and on the evening of the 25th was moved into the town of Le Cateau itself. When dawn broke on 26 August there was a thick mist hanging over the hills and valleys. The men of 19 Brigade had got what rest they good either in the main square or in the goods yard of the station; the town itself was a scene of complete confusion, with ambulance and GS [General Service] wagons fighting it out for road room with civilian carts and battalion transports. 1st Middlesex (appointed rearguard) was scheduled to be clear of the town by 5.30am, but because of the congestion was unable to think of actually setting off until 6.30am – at

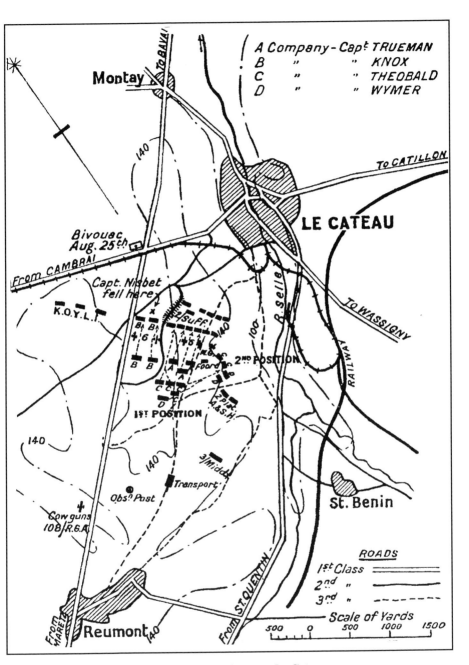

Map 6. 2nd Battalion Manchester Regiment at Le Cateau.

which time the Battalion came into action. German artillery came into action at 6am, firing from the area of Rambourlieux Farm, a few miles to the north east and north of the Cambrai road. These guns were ideally placed to hit the positions south of Le Cateau in enfilade.

'Under cover of their artillery the German infantry advanced, and by 6.30am had penetrated the outskirts of the town even as the British troops were withdrawing. A little street fighting took place in Le Cateau and, as the Middlesex acted as rear guard, it is possible that the Battalion exchanged shots with the enemy, but there are no records to that effect. The War diary states:

> Germans had entered town before we got away; leaving town, came into action, keeping enemy back till all clear; leaving town, going SW, passed through hastily thrown up trenches of 5th Division and took up position in support of 5th Division by wood [Bois des Dix-Sept, ie Seventeen Wood] north of Reumont.'

[Most of the material for this section comes from *The Die-Hards in the Great War*, Vol 1, Everard Wyrall, n.d.]

About 9am 1/Middx and 2/A&SH were ordered to take up positions on the right flank of 14 Brigade; the other two battalions were also made available, but in fact were never heavily engaged, going first to hold a covering position in Montigny, well south of Caudry, and then acting as a rear guard defence in front of Maurois, astride the Roman Road, at which place they arrived at about 4.30pm.

The two former battalions (along with two companies of 1st Royal Scots Fusiliers, 9 Brigade, which had become temporarily attached to 19 Brigade the night before) deployed about 10am, with 1/Middx on the right of 2/Manchester and occupying the high ground above the Roman road, lying across the track that now runs south east from Le Cateau to Reumont. From here the Battalion could offer support to the battalions in front and also cover possible

German advances from the north east and east. 'Both battalions were now under heavy shell fire, for which there was no shelter as their hastily dug entrenchments were but scrapings in the ground, for entrenching tools [ie the picks and shovels] had been lost or thrown away during the first phase of the retreat from Mons. The time was now between noon and 1pm.'

By about that time it had become quite clear that the position of the right flank was fast becoming untenable – Fergusson 'could see that the right of his Division was shaken and might shortly give way.' It was also clear that Germans were moving far over to his right, and might envelop the position. II Corps told him that he should hold on 'a little longer', but could then withdraw as he saw fit.

Also at about this time – around 2pm - the Middlesex, along with 59 Field Company Royal Engineers, two half companies of 2/A&SH and two companies of 1/RSF, moved down the western slope of the valley of the river Selle to meet any threat from the right flank.

> Soon (towards 3pm) the Germans were seen advancing from the east across the spur on the opposite side of the valley. At once the Highlanders and the machine gun section of the Middlesex engaged them at 1,200 yards range, whereupon the enemy hesitated and finally beat a retreat. Half an hour later the Germans again ventured to show themselves, advancing in extended order, and although it was not so easy for the machine guns to beat them back, the guns of two Horse Artillery batteries

A firing line such as this would soon become a rare sight on the Western Front.

[presumably including L Battery] *compelled them again to seek shelter. Thus the further advance of the Germans was, for the time being, held up and the retirement began.*

1/Middx, on the right of part of 2/A&SH, now withdrew up the valley of the Selle towards Reumont. The War Diary takes up the story:

About 4pm, on all remainder of force retiring, retirement was ordered by Lieutenant Colonel Ward, commanding Battalion. [Colonel Ward was mortally wounded near Fromelles on 21 October 1914 and is buried at Boulogne Eastern Cemetery.] *Retirement was successfully carried out in good order via Reumont, where hospital was established in Church, which was shelled. Battalion, after Reumont, now became somewhat broken up owing to congestion of road. Retirement proceeded S. of Estrées, where Battalion went into bivouac about 10pm.*

The WD casualty lists gives two officers wounded, two other ranks killed, thirty six wounded and seventy four missing but *many more probably*. The Royal Scots Fusiliers, on the other hand, for both its parts – divided as they were on the day – only suffered three wounded in casualties.

13 Brigade
2nd Battalion King's Own Yorkshire Light Infantry (2/KOYLI).

This Battalion was on the right of 14 Brigade; the bulk of the men were to the west of the Roman Road, but its front did extend over and just to the east of it. The CO received a written order in the early morning: *There will be no retirement for the fighting troops – fill up your trenches, as far as possible, with water, food and ammunition.* This order was repeated by a staff officer, verbally. The 5th Division's history tells the Battalion's story succinctly.

Surrounded on three sides, swept by a concentrated rifle and machine gun fire from front and flanks, battered by shells and with their ammunition exhausted, the Battalion stayed to its death, faithful to the order. Lieutenant Denison, though mortally wounded in the head and blind, continued to encourage his men until he became insensible. [He is buried in Le Cateau Communal Cemetery. Strangely enough, the Regimental history says that he died of his wounds in a hospital in Mons; presumably this is an error.] *As the final German rush came, Major Yate gave an order to meet it with a charge, refusing the call to surrender.*

Lieutenant Colonel Bond

48

A highly dramatized version of the 2/KOYLI action at Le Cateau.

Sixteen officers and 320 other ranks of this gallant regiment were captured, and there were many killed and wounded.

Amongst the captured was the CO, Lieutenant Colonel Bond, the author of the Great War volume of the regimental history from which much of the following account is taken. Of the captured officers, most were moved to internment camps in Holland in January 1918, but two were repatriated, one in 1917 and the other, the highly respected post war commentator on the German army, Lieutenant GC Wynne, on 18 February 1918.

Major Yate, awarded the VC for his actions at Le Cateau.

The reader will have already noted that there were a substantial number of officers who went into internment in Holland (sic) in January 1918. This was the result of a long drawn out negotiation whereby an equal number of British and German officers were sent there by their respective captors to see out the war in rather more comfortable circumstances.

2/KOYLI had been involved in the fighting at Mons, though their casualties had been relatively light (one officer killed and twenty seven other ranks missing – killed, wounded or prisoner). They had put up a strong performance (as had 1/RWK). It may be interesting for the reader to see an account of this action by Walter Bloem, a military classic entitled *The Advance from Mons*, who was a company commander in the Brandenburg Grenadiers, the troops who came up against them.

The Battalion arrived in the Le Cateau area in mid afternoon; and settled down for a disturbed rest. The Battalion was allocated the role of divisional rearguard for the continued retreat on 26 August and, during the very early hours of that morning (indeed it was still dark), the men were moved into position. It was anticipated that they would have to hold their line until about 11am, which would give time for the Divisional transport to get well clear. Positions were taken either side of the Roman road; C Company held the ridge that was later to be held by the Suffolks and other units, whilst D Company covered the other side of the road. Like other battalions, the only tools available for entrenching the new line were the small, multi-purpose entrenching tools or 'grubbers', the others having been abandoned. At daylight new

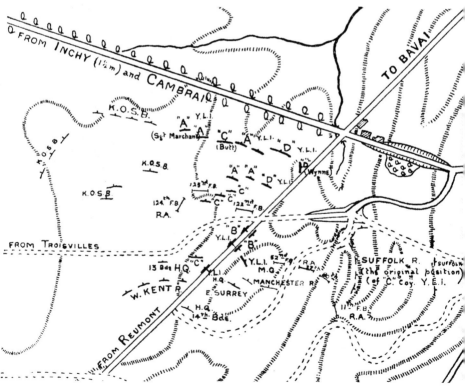

Map 7. **The battlefield to west of Le Cateau from KOYLI regimental history.**

dispositions were made, and C Company was withdrawn from a position that could certainly not be held for any length of time by only a company; part of it was used to extend the left of the Battalion line whilst the rest provided some depth to the position. A Company, which had been pushed forward to hold an outpost line, was also brought back to the new line and further extended it towards the KOSB on the left. D Company, meanwhile, had dug a series of trenches, unconnected, a few hundred yards south of the Cambrai road. B Company was instructed to take up positions astride the Roman road, facing south east, to provide enfilade fire for the front of the Manchesters. By placing them carefully, the effect was to create two tiers of fire; whilst a culvert under the road made communication relatively easy. The Battalion's position was complicated by the placing of guns within the line of the infantry supports; the limbers and teams of 28 Brigade Royal Field Artillery (RFA) were packed into the Troisvilles road, which severely disrupted communications between the various parts of the Battalion.

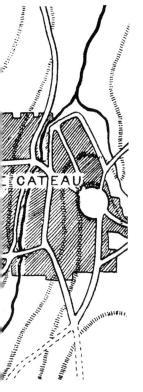

Brigadier-General Cuthbert, whose headquarters were in the sunken Troisvilles road, issued the order, quoted above, to hold the line at about 6am. The Battalion ammunition reserve was brought up shortly before the German bombardment really got under way; and the buglers (who performed the function later taken on by runners) distributed it as best they could amongst the nearby companies. Once the action commenced and daylight was complete, 'the weak spots of a position taken up in a half light, and only half prepared, were soon only too apparent'.

To the right of the Battalion's position, in the first phase of the battle, the men were mainly observers of the events taking place on and around Suffolk Hill. Immediately to their front they were able to view the attempt by 2/Manchesters to clear some of the Germans from the low ground to their (the Manchesters') front and towards Le Cateau. Eventually, at about 11am, Major Yate had the target he wanted and B Company opened fire; up to then it had refrained from firing so as not to disclose

51

its position. 'From that time forward the company was constantly engaged.' The Battalion machine guns were placed to the south and right of B Company and were in action constantly from 8.30am until about 2.30pm, by which time one gun had been knocked out, several men were wounded; the second gun was got back into B Company's trenches and there broken up and made useless.

D Company was engaged in dealing with frontal attacks across the Cambrai road, whilst at the same time trying to bring effective fire against the several German machine guns situated above the cutting of the road as it descended into Le Cateau. Elsewhere the other companies were fairly heavily engaged. By about 11am some Germans had established themselves on the rise in the ground on the south side of the Cambrai road and were able to fire in enfilade on some of 2/KOYLI's trenches. Meanwhile the artillery positioned within the lines came under increasingly effective German fire, even more so when 14 Brigade's positions were gradually overrun.

German Infantry Regiment 26

The German regiment involved was *Infantry Regiment 26* from the Magdeburg area. As part of *13 Brigade* of *7th Division*, it was advancing in a southerly direction astride the Solesmes – Le Cateau road. *Leutnant* Schacht of the Machine Gun Coy describes what happened next:

> *Completely shielded by a deep gully we approached Le Cateau. We could see no trace of any trenches. The British had a brilliant understanding of the art of digging in. The eerie emptiness of the battlefield, which we had often discussed on quiet winter evenings in the mess, was very evident here. All we could make out, because of the muzzle flashes, were the enemy artillery positions. To our half right we could see a battery which, according to our doctrine, was located far too far forward, in amongst the line of infantrymen, to which we had already approached very closely. To our front, by the village, we could see several batteries preparing to move off. Right! Sights at 1,400 metres! Rapid fire. Slightly short. Higher! Soon we could observe the effect of the fire. There could not be greater activity around an upturned ant heap. Everywhere men and horses were milling around, falling down and, in amongst all this brouhaha, was a constant Tack! Tack! Tack! ... Soon many had disappeared. There now followed a rare spectacle. Half right among the flashes appeared a dark mass. It was the teams approaching at a*

mad gallop. We could not help but think, 'Are they mad?' No, with extraordinary bravery they were attempting to pull out their batteries at the last minute; to save what was left to save. 'Half right! 1,000 metres! Double-tap! Rapid fire!' and in a hectic rhythm, twelve machine guns poured bullets at the sacrificial victims. What a dreadful tangle there was up there. One vehicle was ready and drove off, with three horses in front and one man on top and managed to get away...a second dashed up; six riderless horses, tripping and stumbling, emerged over the hill...a third could not get away. Men lashed out at the poor creatures, but soon could do no more as they were hit and fell. One [horse] remained standing in amongst this wild hail of fire from batteries and machine guns, started to graze, whinnied for water and shook its head tiredly. What a cruel ironic fate...the other three guns and teams were one dark, confused mass.

Everywhere new scenes unfolded! On the extreme right up on the hill, sharply defined silhouettes appeared against the sky. One, two, three, ever more of them, running downhill from right to left. Are they ours? They have no weapons; they must be British, although their green drab colour can still not be distinguished. But what's that? Yes, now they are running back. The same scene is being played out elsewhere. From our right comes a hail of pursuing fire. My runner Bloch and I ignore our cover; we want to be able to see better. Thuddd...Now then what's happened to you? Don't look at me so stupidly! My hands are

British position overwhelmed.

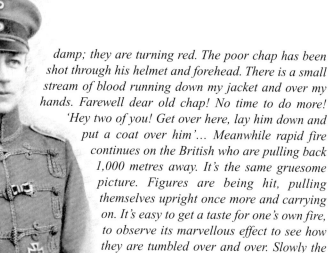

damp; they are turning red. The poor chap has been shot through his helmet and forehead. There is a small stream of blood running down my jacket and over my hands. Farewell dear old chap! No time to do more! 'Hey two of you! Get over here, lay him down and put a coat over him'... Meanwhile rapid fire continues on the British who are pulling back 1,000 metres away. It's the same gruesome picture. Figures are being hit, pulling themselves upright once more and carrying on. It's easy to get a taste for one's own fire, to observe its marvellous effect to see how they are tumbled over and over. Slowly the beast in each man takes over. Now our own infantry are advancing.

Rittmeister von Etzdorff, OC 1 Sqn Hussar Regt 10.

At 12.45 orders were given to withdraw as many of the guns as possible from the central part of the 5th Division's front; very few of those in the KOYLI lines were in fact extracted. There was a lull in the German gun fire after the British guns had been either silenced or withdrawn; but about a half hour later it started again, this time being exclusively directed against the infantry, who were now effectively without any artillery support. An advance by two German battalions over the ridge which had been held by the Suffolks, some 600 yards distance from B Company's position, was met with rapid fire from the two tiers that the men held once the German infantry had come well down its forward slope. This halted the advance, at least for a while. A and D Companies continued to hold their positions, but at a great cost in casualties. Some attempt was made to push forward, but reinforcements were severely mauled whilst trying to get to the new positions.

At about 3pm the brigade reserve battalion was seen to be retiring to take up a new covering position. But, as the regimental history points out:

There was no question of retirement for the companies in the firing line. Even if it had been possible to communicate an order to retire, had such an order been intended, very few men could have got away owing to the proximity of the enemy and the nature of the ground. Some of the occupants of the line of supports, however, did receive the order to retire directly from Brigade, and thus a portion of the Battalion was saved.

Some of the trenches were without ammunition and, in the last stage of the fight, when a determined advance by the enemy must at any moment have settled the business, some officers told their men they could take their chance of getting back to the column. Many men who made the attempt must have lost their lives, but a few managed to win through, for there were men who later in the week were able to give evidence of what had taken place within the trenches in the last phases of the action. Such evidence was impressionistic, as evidence gathered under the conditions was bound to be. [This is a very important point; often too much weight is put on eyewitness accounts when the witness could only have had a very limited understanding of what is always the confusion of battle.]

For the last hour of the fight, so far as they could see, the KOYLI were alone in the line to stem the German advance; it was conceived that their duty [remember, the author of the history commanded the Battalion at Le Cateau, so this was the CO's reading of his duty] lay in blocking the great high [Roman] road and in denying it until the last possible minute to the advancing enemy. Though their troops surrounded 2/KOYLI on three sides, completely dominating their flanks, and were supported by field guns brought up within 900 yards of the trenches, the Germans still hesitated to rush in. Time after time their bugles sounded the British cease fire, and attempts were made to send forward a flag of truce. Each overture was met with a burst of fire and the remnants of the companies made it evident to the enemy that resistance was being maintained.

B Company made one final attempt to deal with the advance of a mass of Germans, by launching themselves into a charge led by the extraordinary Major Yate. The position did not actually surrender so much as it was completely swamped. A few of the men were bayoneted but, to the credit of the German soldiers, be it mentioned, most of the unwounded were made prisoners and the wounded in the trench were respected.

The cost had been terrific. A British officer PoW walked past B Company's trenches the following day whilst under escort and counted sixty two dead in the trenches by the side of the road [B Company] alone, with the wounded already cleared from the battlefield. The action was over at about 4.30pm.

These lone, desperate actions by a number of battalions had been costly – very costly – in men; but they had served a purpose. A German commented:

**Lance Corporal
FW Holmes VC.**

In front of us there still swarmed a number of scattered English troops, who…again and again forced us to waste time in deployment, as we could not tell what their strength might be.

The total losses of the Battalion at Le Cateau were returned as: officers 18; sergeants 21; corporals 22; buglers 7; privates 532, making a total of 600. Out of this number a total of 310 were later reported to be prisoners in Germany, 170 of whom were wounded. 2/KOYLI won two VCs at Le Cateau: Major CAL Yate and Lance Corporal FW Holmes. Yate died as a prisoner of war under somewhat confusing circumstances; some accounts say that his skull was smashed whilst trying to escape. He is buried in the suburbs of Berlin, in one of the few Great War CWGC cemeteries in Germany – casualties were concentrated here after the war. Holmes won his VC for rescuing a wounded soldier and then returning and helping to remove one of the guns; he survived the war (and was commissioned) and died in Australia in 1969.

Denison is ranked as a captain on his headstone.

The only known grave for an officer fatality of the Battalion is that of Lieutenant Denison; the others are commemorated at La Ferté sous Jouarre.

German casualties.

Following up onto the position the men of *Infantry Regiment 26* were confronted by chaotic scenes of death and destruction.

We call our vehicles forward and follow up across the battlefield. Shocking...indescribable. We confront the entire effect of our own fire. We had been able to enfilade almost all the trenches, because they had expected us to approach from a different direction. There lay the first, then another and another and so on. For a change there was an ammunition box, machine guns, a young Second Lieutenant; tough –looking, with typically British features. The ground is torn up, better ploughed by German shells than French ploughs. All is deathly quiet in the battery position. There are piles of wrecked equipment, ammunition is strewn everywhere and there in the midst of it all is a horse, tiredly shaking its head.'

1st Battalion Royal West Kents (The Queen's Own) (1/RWK)

This Battalion had had a relatively hot time at Mons, but the retreat See Map p. 63 towards Le Cateau was generally uneventful. The two biggest problems were the heat and rations: between dinner on the 23rd and the evening of the 25th, when emergency rations were authorised to be used – but only one between four men – no rations were issued. As they passed through France on their way south 'the poor inhabitants did all they could to mitigate the men's sufferings with substantial offerings of bread, fruit and water; this in spite of the fact that the army was retiring and abandoning the district to the Germans.' The Battalion had a bivouac on the Roman road, some two miles south west of Le Cateau.

The Battalion occupied its position soon after daybreak on the 26th, behind 2/KOYLI. 'The Battalion entrenched itself in two lines in the cornfields, where the corn had nearly all been cut and stood in stooks, about six hundred yards behind the first line positions.

As the German attack developed, the battalions holding the first line suffered heavily both from shell and rifle fire. By about 3pm the enemy had succeeded in working round the right flank to a position from which he could enfilade the forward battalions of 13 Brigade. A retirement was then ordered. The Queen's Own, remaining until the other battalions of the Brigade had moved to the rear, retired in extended lines of half battalions. Taking up a succession of fire positions, they held up the German infantry until the rest of the Brigade was well clear. The last two companies then formed a rear party to cover the troops moving on St Quentin.

This bald account is amply filled out with the diary entries of Major P Hastings, who commanded C Company during the battle.

Wednesday 26th August: First of all we were told that the retirement was to be continued. C and D Companies were sent off to dig fire trenches to cover the battalions who were forming outposts. After we had started this all the plans were changed and we were told that the big fight was to take place there and that we were to hold a long line of trenches prepared by civilian labour. [These had been constructed by the local people in the day before the retreat reached Le Cateau. They were not particularly good, as they were straight, too wide and too shallow – but at least they existed!] ... *In local reserve, we were behind the KOYLI and the Dukes were rather behind us on the left. We started working very hard making shelter trenches with entrenching implements (all our tools had been lost at St Ghislain* [Mons battlefield]*).*

The soil, fortunately, was very favourable, and we obtained some big picks but no shovels. The men used the entrenching implements, mess tins and their hands, with the result that we had a very fair lot of trenches before the guns began.

C Company's trenches were behind a crest, and A Company's could be seen about fifty or seventy yards ahead of us. D Company was on our right. We could see nothing to our left, but had an excellent view to the right and right front. At first the guns began searching the slopes behind us, and we watched the limbers of the batteries being quietly moved about to avoid the shells. They suffered a little. Most of our guns appeared to be in front of us, but I could only see one battery, which was on a spur to our right front. A 60-pounder battery appeared to be in rear of us and also, I think, a Howitzer battery. The main line of infantry trenches appeared to have been about five hundred yards in front of A Company, but I never saw them. I heard they were very badly made by civilian labour, too wide and shallow. All the enemy guns were firing as hard as they could, and the noise was terrific. Sometimes they searched the ground we occupied, but they did not hit a man, as we kept well down at the bottom of the trenches. Sometimes we got a spell of machine gun fire, but it was no doubt aimed at something in front. The noise was like a whip being swished backwards and forwards. Fortunately we appeared to escape most of the Howitzer fire, which burst beyond us while trying to get the 60-pounders. The ordinary shrapnel from guns did not get into our trenches, but splinters and bullets fell all around us. During the lulls I was able to observe what was happening on our right. Across the main road I saw a number of wounded men, probably gunners, running or crawling back. Of these many were wounded again during the journey. The gun wagons and limbers were very quiet and frequently changed their position, sometimes coming close behind us.

... Sometimes during a lull I walked round the trenches to see our men...In any part of the line one could stand up and not be seen from the front. Part of the time I read the Daily Mail and, being very tired, also went to sleep. ... After what seemed hours to me, we saw the limbers galloping forward to try and get the guns back. One battery galloped past our trench within a few yards. The captain was leading and shouting 'Come on boys!' at

Saving the guns.

the top of his voice. *Another lot went forward to the battery to our right and another past the left of our trenches, but I did not see the others. After a bit they came back, but it was a sad sight. Very few returned and these had the greatest difficulty in moving the horses. I saw one gun from our right front coming back at a slow walk, dragged by four horses. The two drivers were flogging for their lives, and shells were bursting all over them. A few gunners were hanging on to the limbers and others were straggling back wounded. I think that was the only gun that came back from that battery, but there may have been two. ... There was a good deal of fire, but I could not keep down as it was so exciting. It was impossible to see what happened to the battery which passed on the left of our position. To our right front I could see a dismal wreck of guns and limbers where the battery on the spur had been* [This was almost certainly 52nd Battery of XV Brigade RFA]. *Several wounded gunners came into C Company's trenches, one having three wounds in one leg. We could do very little but give them water, as I could not find our doctor, who had been in a trench behind us. I then saw large bodies of German infantry appearing on our right front, but they were invisible except with field glasses. Many of the infantry on our right across the road kept retiring, and it looked as if the spur would shortly be occupied by the enemy, and that we would be outflanked. Then the KOYLI came back through our lines, they*

Stacks of hay or straw or the roofs of farm buildings were frequently used as observations points.

had suffered terrible losses in their trenches and had lost most of their officers. Some of their men joined my company. A Company then passed through our lines and shortly afterwards the CO ordered me to retire. We made short retirements and were most fortunate in escaping shells. ...'

Retirement followed, with occasional halts to hold a firing line. Behind Reumont the Battalion began its retreat march. *'There was a hopeless block of transport, guns and infantry extending for miles. It rained lightly the whole evening and everyone was nearly dead with fatigue, lack of sleep and want of food. ... Every wagon was full of wounded or men who could not march. We got a bivouac about 10pm and then both men and officers had some tea and bread, and lay down anywhere (mostly in the mud) and slept.'*

Major Hastings was killed in the fighting at Crépy on 1 September. He is buried at Perreuse Chateau Franco-British National Cemetery.

2nd Battalion Duke of Wellington's (2/DW)

This battalion had had a hard time of it at Mons, suffering over 350 casualties on the 23rd and, the great majority of them, 24 August. It took up positions on the morning of the 26th to the rear of 2/RWK, in trenches on the northern slope of the high ground west of Le Cateau. They had spent the night making best use of the corn stooks, spreading them on the ground: as Lieutenant Ince commented, *we had been able to sleep out in the open in real comfort.* From here the Battalion was able to get an excellent view of the opening of the battle; whilst it did not get involved in any great way with the fighting during the day and began retiring around 4pm. Captain Kelly gave an account of his 26 August.

We had a good night's rest before Le Cateau, were wakened about half an hour before dawn and started to dig trenches where we had been sleeping. We had a splendid field of fire and could see a low level plateau for about 1200 yards. At Le Cateau we did not see any infantry

Lieutenant Ince.

Captain Kelly.

advancing at all except at a great distance. Just as we were dug in, shells began to burst over our heads. Personally, I had made quite a good trench for myself. I was at the time in command of half a company. We stayed there all day under very awful shell fire, with our guns firing right beside us. I saw that day the gunners doing most extraordinary feats of bravery. I saw one officer with his arm blown off, still riding his horse giving instructions. Of course he soon fainted from loss of blood, but just imagine doing your duty with your arm blown off, in awful agony, knowing that you had only a few minutes more to live. I also saw batteries blown to pieces, one gun being left intact in one battery; immediately a team of gunners galloped out with their horses and hooked in and galloped back with their gun safe. I saw an artillery major blown high in the air and falling down in pieces...

About 4 o'clock we were told to retire on to the main road. I happened to be the last to leave the front trenches. When the major and myself got on the road we found huge columns of transport, guns, wagons, ammunition columns, etc., etc., all struggling to get on, and infantry crowded up in hundreds.

In the ensuing confusion, Captain Kelly got split up from his Battalion and even from his small group of men; eventually he was picked up off the road three days later by an ambulance wagon of the 4th Division.

It had been a harrowing day for the Dukes, but the Battalion itself suffered very few casualties.

The centre left and left of the Fifth Division: Part of 13 Brigade and 15 Brigade front.

2nd Battalion King's Own Scottish Borderers (2/KOSB)

2/KOSB only heard of the decision to stand and fight after they had made preparations, on the basis of their previous orders, to form the rearguard of the Division with 2/KOYLI. C Company took up a position in trenches close to the

Map 8. Fighting south of Inchy, 5th and 3rd Divisions (OH extract).

Cambrai road – about three hundred yards south of it; to its right was A Company, extending the flat salient of the line towards the Roman road, but still out of sight of 2/KOYLI. D Company was in support, arranged in two half companies in dead ground and without a view. B Company was on the left, holding a position that, at that time, had no trenches and formed a link with 15 Infantry Brigade's right, held by the Bedfords. The Regimental history takes up the story:

Fortunately few men had been guilty of the unpardonable crime of throwing away their 'grubbers' [light entrenching tools] *and quite fair shelters were made as a result of feverish digging with these. This sector was not so heavily shelled as others, but the reserve company* [D] *saw a battery of our artillery literally blown to pieces and the one surviving officer most gallantly brought in by Colonel Stephenson* [the CO] *and an orderly in full view of the enemy. About 11.30 am a tendency to retire was observed on our right, but before the cause was ascertained to be due to orders failing to reach the particular body, the GOC* [General Fergusson] *himself was seen to gallop forward and turn the troops back to the original positions. They were joined by D's reserve under Major Haig, who found a fair field of fire and a view to the right as well. But beyond the Cambrai road there were folds by which the enemy could be dribbled up out of sight. It was soon evident that the brunt of the attack was nearer Le Cateau and against the KOYLI and 14 Brigade, and also on the right* [sic] *against 15 Brigade covering Troisvilles. But about 2.30pm artillery from a new position opened on the KOSB. Some of the trenches were conspicuous on account of newly turned earth, and casualties began to occur so that the trenches had to be evacuated and open ground right and left occupied.*

For the first time masses of German infantry were observed about two miles off on the other side of the Selle [ie, to the east, well beyond the Suffolks' lines], *apparently past the British position. Major Haig was then wounded in the shoulder but managed to report the situation to the CO before painfully walking to Reumont dressing station. As bad luck would have it, this was overrun by the Germans, and Major Haig awoke from the opiate the next morning to find himself a prisoner* [which he remained until October 1918, having been interned in Holland the previous January].

The order to retire reached the CO soon after 3pm and was passed on. But one off the difficulties of war is to get orders through to everybody. On this occasion C were the sufferers. One platoon under Lieutenant Harvey, nearest D, did retire in sympathy, but the remaining three platoons were out of sight, and having orders to hold out until the last, did so till completely surrounded and outnumbered. Thus ceased the participation of nearly three-fourths of what had been a practically intact company.

Meanwhile A had occasionally had long range targets of infantry and had wonderfully few casualties considering the way that shells fell all around. Soon after 3.30pm they also retired in a south westerly direction, dictated by the German thrust on the right, until the Tree, where a stand was made for nearly an hour, while the men fired at and checked the enemy at about 900 yards range. Then came a further retreat on Maurois. Intense shelling caused casualties, among them the CO, Colonel Stephenson. A horseless (because the horses had been taken by civilians) ambulance was found [in the sunken road] *and the CO and six other wounded were hauled by hand as far as the Bois de Gatigny* [now Bois de Dix-Sept]*, where it was left by order, as its retention would have merely led to the capture of the team. Thus by the hard fate of war 2/KOSB was deprived of its two senior officers* [Haig and the CO]*...As it was, pursuit was so close that Lieutenant Jonson, while trying to rescue a wounded man of another regiment, was charged by cavalry, hit on the head and made prisoner. Another prisoner was Lieutenant Sherwin of B, made delirious and unconscious by the close passage of a shell. On coming round, a confused idea that a medical armlet might help him to escape, induced him to put one on. This might have earned him a bullet, but the Germans took the sensible view that he was not in his sound senses.*

Those officers killed in the battle (remarkably few) have no known grave; many of these (as also the missing) have erroneous dates because the casualty returns, understandably, given the circumstances, were not made until about 10 September. Most of the officers taken prisoner were interned in January 1918 in Holland – in this way the Germans avoided having to feed their prisoners, the British refunded the Dutch and the men had more freedom; unfortunately this happy arrangement, by and large, only applied to officers, with the exception of severely wounded soldiers who would only be a burden on the hard pressed Germans, suffering as they were from years of blockade. The CO, Colonel Stephenson, was interned in Switzerland in the Christmas of 1916, returning home in March 1918. The Regimental history gives no casualty figures for the Battle of Le Cateau, but they could not have been insignificant and were probably at least 250 of all ranks.

15 Brigade:
1st Battalion Bedfordshire Regiment (1/Beds).

The Regimental History of the Bedfordshire and Hertfordshire Regiment (the two were amalgamated in 1919) did not come out until the late 1980s. Unusually, some of the narrative of actions is left entirely to eyewitness accounts, without editorial comment. This can lead to confusion, especially when the account is from a relatively junior rank, who may have had only slight knowledge of what was going on beyond his immediate area. This is certainly true of Le Cateau 1914; of the two accounts, that of the adjutant (Captain J Macready) is the more accurate, though that of Lieutenant JS Davenport is certainly of interest and is clearly indicated.

We passed Le Cateau, turned off the main (Roman) road towards Troisvilles and about two kilometres further on came to a road junction where one tree was standing [the famous Tree]*; strange, this one tree was marked on the map, it struck me as being dangerous as an aiming mark, but I never thought there was going to be a great battle on this ground the next day. We left the road and turned off on our right, ie northwards, roughly one a half kilometres east of the northern end of the village of Troisvilles, where we bivouacked. Joy of joys, there was RQMS Bartlett with our second line transport and a MEAL. We must have reached our bivouacs at about 3.30pm.* [Davenport] *Here we managed to brew a little tea and get some rest. Six* [sic: in fact there were three] *divisions of French cavalry then appeared from the right and cantered past, going out to the left flank...they looked very fine indeed in all their full rig out and their Horse Artillery. Going as fast as they did, they took about three hours to go past us. After our meal we reconnoitred some trenches to our front, ie on the enemy side. They were only half dug, having been prepared by civilians.*

[Davenport] *They had sited the trenches rather badly and had dug them worse. Some of them were about eight feet broad and only two feet deep. Most of them were facing in the wrong direction. We put out outposts and evening fell.*

[Davenport] *at 9pm we – D Company – were sent off to relieve B Company and to find the outposts. I was in the centre trench and Wagstaff on the right...the main road to Cambrai ran across our front and parallel to it about 600 yards away and we posted our sentries along it.*

We arose early on the 26th having received orders to march again at 9am, but before we had gone two hundred yards a staff officer rode up and told us to get into the trenches; that there was to be no retirement. As he was dashing off I heard him say to another officer, whom I did not know, that II Corps was to be sacrificed to save the other. This sounded unpleasant. However, I do not think that anyone else heard it. So we marched back, past our bivouacs of the night before and got into the trenches, the Colonel and I in a trench in the centre of the line. There was one platoon of A Company in battalion reserve. C Company was on our left and D Company on our extreme left, A and B being on our right. The men started to deepen the trench. [Davenport, D Company, left flank.] *In my trench I had one and a half sections (about fifteen men) and we started straight away to make the trenches serviceable. We dug down and also undercut the parapet to make a shelter (terrible folly in view of after events) as we did not want to be caught by shell fire similar to that experienced before, without any shelter. We had just got the trench almost perfect and beautiful little funk holes made and were on the top assimilating the turned up earth to the surroundings, when the extra weight thrown on the parapet gave in and our shelters collapsed. One or two men were partially buried in the collapse. The case was desperate and we stood and swore, we were now absolutely exposed to view and the Germans were beginning to attack. However, we spotted down near the road some old plough-shares and other implements by a rick, so I raced down with a party and collected all we could and brought them up and propped up the trench and set it up a best we could. This was the best defence position I have ever taken up in my life. It was sited on a gentle reverse slope, and well down the reverse slope, therefore anyone coming over the crest had a long way to come to reach the trenches. Behind us ran a sunken road, which towards D Company (where also was posted the machine gun section) on our left was no longer sunken.*

A battery, much to our disgust, had unlimbered about 200 – 300 metres behind the trench where I was and another took up position behind D Company. The battery behind me fired hard all the morning and the Boches retaliated, luckily over our heads, at the guns. Rifle fire came over, but nothing to worry about. MG fire and gunfire became intense, especially on our right and got even heavier as the day proceeded.

About 4pm order came that we were to retire by bounds, if we could, but it was to be a very gradual withdrawal. We saw the KOSB retiring on our right. Bit by bit men were got out of the trenches, A, B and C retiring by driblets. I went over to D Company to give them the message; enemy MG fire was very heavy and the grass at the crest of the sunken road was being cut up just as if by a mowing machine. Finally I got a message to them. I returned to our trench and informed the CO, who then retired with a few men; shortly after I retired with the remainder. I could hear the swish of the bullets coming nearer, then it traversed away, back it came again quite close and, Heaven be praised, it traversed back again. I passed the battery position, a heap of dead lay around the guns.

I arrived at La Satiere [sic: La Sotière] *crossroads* [ie with the sunken road] *and halted there. The crossroads were sunken and we faced about. Troops of many units passed through and I found Major Allason and the CO a little further down the road shortly afterwards. We waited there until we saw that no others were coming back. Davenport and I went forward to look for Wagstaff* [D Company], *who had been wounded, but we could not find him.'*

Davenport, who had by this time retired with his men to the same area, gives his version of the story:

In front of us the ground was covered with mangold [a type of beet] *and some gunner horses were galloping madly about in pairs, some dragging a dead pair with them. Suddenly in the mangolds in front we saw something move and a khaki figure just exposed itself. We shouted at it to come in and soon it go up and ran like a hare for us and fell at my knees!! It was Corporal Holloway, who belonged to Wagstaff's platoon and who had got left behind. He gurgled out that Wagstaff was lying wounded in the thigh in his trench and could not move but who sent to say that he was all right and quite comfortable...So we went off and scrambled about in front, in and out of trenches and in the open to about where we thought he was but we could not find him near his trench and anywhere about although we howled out for him as loud as we could.* [Wagstaff was taken prisoner and interned in Holland in January 1918].

Macready continues:

The Boches began to shell the crossroads heavily with shrapnel and we crouched under the bank as bouquet after bouquet arrived. Finally, about 6pm, we split into artillery formation and moved in a south westerly direction – other direction we had none as there were no maps.

I finally reached the [Roman] road. It was a dismal sight as the exhausted men of the 5th Division marched by; no sign of a rearguard, everyone tired to death. On we trudged and it must have been nearly to Maretz before I saw one battalion stretched across the road on either side, in one line, a battalion of the Cameronians (Scottish Rifles).

Night came and the CO and I had A and B Companies, or what remained of them, with us; where C and D were we had not a notion. Darkness closed down upon us. We would walk a few yards, halt, walk half a mile, ten yards, halt, three yards, halt, 200 yards, halt and so it went on. One dare not sit down. To do so would have meant sleep and capture. One's knees were simply breaking. Weariness quite outmatched hunger and thirst.

1st Battalion Norfolk Regiment (1/Norfolk).

The Norfolks had been in a hard fight during the retreat from the Mons position. On 24 August the Battalion fought an action at Elouges (see Battleground Europe, Mons), which cost them some 250 casualties; about a hundred of their wounded had to be left behind. At Le Cateau their bivouac position for the night of the 25th was near Troisvilles; and in the early hours of the 26th they took up a position in the sunken road between Troisvilles and the Roman road. The regimental history notes:

During the earlier part of the battle even the front line in this part was not seriously attacked, and the Norfolk battalion, dug in on the sunken road, was not disturbed at all. What a contrast to what was going on only a mile or so away!

At 1.15pm the Battalion was sent back to Reumont, acting as a cover for any withdrawal from the positions in front of

69

the village. Some of the men – about one and a half companies – were sent to a quarry south west of the village and was able to bring down fire on Germans advancing from the north east. By 4.30pm the whole Battalion had taken up a position on the eastern edge of Honnechy, where it was able to open effective fire on German troops advancing along the eastern side of the Selle from the general direction of Le Cateau. The furthest the Germans got to the Norfolk's position was about 1500 yards; and in due course the Battalion fell back in successive companies and joined the retreat. Casualties had been negligible.

1st Battalion Cheshire Regiment (1/Cheshire).

Along with the Norfolks, the Cheshires had also fought at Elouges and suffered extremely heavy casualties there, losing about 800 men. It took little active part in the fighting at Le Cateau. It occupied a well protected position south of La Sotière and just east of Troisvilles, forming a second line of defence behind the right and left flanks, respectively, of 1/Dorsets and I/Bedford.

1st Battalion Dorsetshire Regiment (1/Dorset).

The Battalion had been engaged at Mons, but had suffered relatively few casualties – a dozen killed, some fifty wounded and seventy missing. The decision to fight at Le Cateau reached the brigade commander by about 5am, but he had previously been warned that if the 3rd Division were to be attacked his Brigade would not move at the appointed time of 7am. Thus some preparations had been made the previous day to establish a reasonable defensive position: To the troops on the spot, at the time, there seemed nothing surprising in the order to occupy the trenches along the ridge between Le Cateau and Troisvilles, which had been reconnoitred the previous day, This was done at 5am.

Half of C Company was placed so as to be in touch with the Bedfords on the right; the remainder dug themselves in on the northern edge of La Sotière. The Battalion's machine guns were also sited near here, so that they could sweep the approaches to the village. B Company was positioned at the northern end of Troisvilles, overlooking the valley which ran down to Inchy, on the Cambrai road. D Company dug in behind La Sotière, in the open ground on the reverse slope whilst A Company occupied some orchards between Troisvilles and La Sotière. As battle commenced, despite the mayhem going on around them, most especially towards Inchy, which was in flames, nothing much at all happened on the Dorsets' front. As the Battalion was not being hard pressed, the CO (Lieutenant Colonel Bols) decided to hold his position, although he did order the first line transport to withdraw at about 3pm. The machine guns seemed to be doing a fine job in preventing any significant advance; but at about 4pm the Germans began shelling the Battalion's front. Seeing that the Battalion was isolated, Colonel Bols ordered a general retirement, which commenced at 4.20pm, the men moving back through Bertry, Maretz and then Estrées. The Dorsets were the last battalion of the 5th Division to retire from the battlefield. During the withdrawal, Colonel Bols decided that, because of the chaotic road traffic and the condition of his men, who were exhausted, that he would call a halt at the hamlet of Ponchaux, some four kilometres short of Estrées; the whole Battalion fitted into a sugar refinery. It was 11pm and they had four hours of blessed rest.

The regimental history makes no mention of casualties; they were probably very modest.

Brigadier General Count von Gleichen's story (commander 15 Brigade).

Gleichen wrote a short volume of memoirs, *The Doings of the 15th Infantry Brigade, August 1914 to March 1915*, published in 1917. He then went on to command the *37th Division*, whose fine memorial (sculpted by his sister) may be seen at Monchy le Preux.

15 Brigade was the front brigade when the *5th Division* moved off on the 25th; hence it arrived quite early onto what was to become the Le Cateau battlefield. By 3pm the Brigade was either in the trenches (these constructed by the French – on this front he considered they were quite well sited, but only three feet deep) on outpost duty or bivouacked half a mile behind. Gleichen managed to procure some food for the men; not only army rations of bully beef and biscuits but also a cart load of 'very smelly cheeses' as well as ham, vegetables and bread. When instructions came in the early hours to hold the position, the trenches were deepened, Troisvilles was put in a state of defence and telephone wires were laid. Brigade HQ was established to the left of the Norfolks in the sunken road:

The morning was distinctly cool after the rain [of the previous night], *and I remember that I wore my woolly until about 11am.*

Our horses were stowed away a few hundred yards to the left in a hollow; and the extraordinary thing was that neither they nor ourselves got shelled as long as we were there, though some shrapnel burst occasionally only a hundred yards off or so in different directions.

By and large the morning was for him rather uneventful: *during the first hours it was really more a spectacular piece for us than a battle.* Apart from getting on his horse soon after midday to halt a company of Bedfords from retiring (in fact they had been ordered to a new position, but he put them back whence they had come), much interest seems to have been caused by a working party from 1/Norfolk.

On our immediate right the Norfolks were occupied for several hours in trying to cut down a very big tree, which was about the most conspicuous feature in the whole of our position, and formed an excellent object on which the enemy could range. It was all very well; but as soon as they had cut it half through, so as to fall to the south, the south wind, which was blowing pretty strongly, not only kept it upright but threatened to throw it over to the north. This would have been a real disaster, as it would have blocked completely the sunken road along which the ammunition carts, to say nothing of artillery and other wagons, would have had to come. So it had to be guyed up with ropes, and even then when teams hung on and hauled on the ropes, they could make little impression, the wind was so strong. Eventually they did manage to get it down, but even so it formed a conspicuous mark. (It was so big that it was marked on the map.)

The battle progressed, with the right of the 3rd Division being hard pressed but managing to hold their own. The wounded started coming through Gleichen's headquarters' position and his veterinary officer was turned to working on human suffering.

...some of the shrapnel wounds were appalling. One man I remember lying across a pony; I literally took him for a Frenchman, for his trousers were drenched red with blood, and not a patch of khaki showing. Another man had the whole of the back of his thigh torn away; yet after being bandaged he hobbled gaily off, smoking a pipe. What struck me as curious was the large number of men hit in the face or below the knee – there seemed very few body wounds in comparison; but that may have been because those badly hit in the body were killed or unmovable. But one would see men apparently at their last gasp,

with gruesome wounds on them and no more stretchers available, and yet five minutes afterwards they had disappeared.

The time came to withdraw, as formations on either side were either giving way under the pressure or had begun to pull back. Gleichen gave a general instruction to withdraw to Estrées in the direction of Bertry and then set off across country.

By this time units had become a bit mixed [a certain amount of British understatement there!], *and lines of troops belonging to different battalions and even different brigades were retiring slowly over the open ground and under a heavy fire of shrapnel – which by the same token seemed to do extraordinarily little damage…*

It was hard work making our way mounted across country because of the numerous wire fences we came across, not to mention ditches and hedges…(German shrapnel) then very nearly got us just when we had got to a hopeless-looking place – the railway, with thick fence and ditch on each side of the track and a barbed wire fence as well, with signal wires knee high just where you expected to be able to jump down [on horseback, of course] *on to the track. Luckily Catley, my groom, had some wire nippers; but just as he was cutting at the wire, and we of the Brigade staff were all standing around close by, trying to get over or through, whack came four shrapnel* [shells]*, one close after the other, bursting just short of us and above us – a very good shot if intentional, but I don't think they could possibly have seen us. Horses, of course, flew all over the place; Cadell and his horse came down and I thought he was hit, but he only lost his cap and his horse got a nasty flesh wound from a bit of shrapnel in his hindquarters. Again, why none of this shrapnel hit us was most extraordinary: there we were, seven or eight of us mounted and close together and the shells bursting beautifully with terrific and damnable cracks – yet not one of the Brigade staff was touched.'*

Gleichen and his staff continued on. By this stage they were on the Roman road:

As we proceeded along the [Roman] *road we did our best to get the troops collected into their units, getting single men collected into bunches and the bunches into groups and platoons and so on. But many of them were wounded and dog-tired, and it was hard work. Ballard and his Norfolks joined us in bits* [a minor miracle in itself, considering how detached they had been from the Brigade] *and we heard that they had had a hard time falling back through Reumont and had done very well as rear guard. There were stories at first of their having suffered terribly and lost a lot of men; but it was not in the least true – they had comparatively few casualties.*

Gleichen comments on the general chaos, as units and formations of the 3rd and 5th Divisions were hopelessly jumbled and the road was choked with transport of various types and conditions. As it got blacker there were ever more unintentional halts; eventually Estrées was reached, but there was no-one there to give any orders.

Weatherby [the Brigade Major] *and I moved aside into a field full of corn stooks, unsaddled our horses, gave them a feed and went fast asleep in the wet corn. We had meant to sleep only half an hour, but were so dead tired that it must have been more than an hour and a half.'* They were awoken by the arrival of a battalion in the field *'...and so we guiltily saddled up again, thinking that the whole Brigade must have passed us in the dark. But, as a matter of fact, it had not.*

Infantry Regiment 66, also from the Magdeburg area and commanded by *Oberst* Freiherr von Quadt-Wykradt-Hüchtenbruck [who, fortunately, was usually known only as von Quadt], was the regiment which fought against the left flank of *5th Division*. It acted initially as the advance guard of *7th Infantry Division* and was already advancing to the west of and parallel to the modern D932 towards the west of the town by 5.30 am. In a day of heavy fighting, it suffered severe losses at the hands of the units of the British 15 Brigade, losing a total of five officers, including three company commanders, and seventy five OR killed. Eighteen officers and 398 OR were also wounded. The regimental history of *Infantry Regiment 66* is one of the better German ones, containing as it does a great many eyewitness accounts, a selection of which now follow. The regiment deployed for battle between 8.00 am and 9.00 am, but found itself in the very difficult position of being observed and brought under fire by the British units, manning the heights about 500 metres south of the Le Cateau – Cambrai road from positions described as 'superbly hidden and offering excellent fields of fire and superb observation'. The advancing battalions of *Infantry Regiment 66* on the other hand had no covered approaches and were too far away to begin a fire fight. There was nothing for it but to attempt to advance southwards towards the road and close the range.

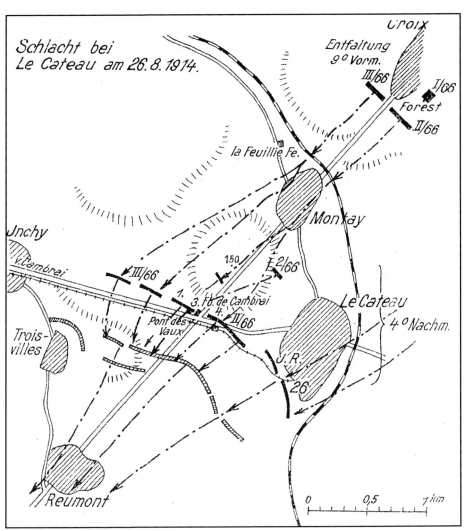

Map 9. The advance of Infantry Regiment 66 astride the Montay – Reumont road.

Leutnant Siegener of *9th Company* later recalled:

We were able to find cover behind a rise, reorganise, then advance in a skirmishing line. Now bullets began to whistle past us, despite the fact that we were in full cover. We moved along a hedge line, then there was a another small hollow. We had found our way to the right place. Left forward of us, the 10th Company was already engaged in a fire fight. We had to cover a one hundred metre bound, then we had linked up once more and the line was complete again. We crawled forward to the crest. We could see nothing of the enemy, but their bullets continued to whistle past our ears. We had no choice but to go forward. In one bound we reached our fire positions and now we could see, on the far side of a line of great poplar trees (the Le Cateau – Cambrai road), the British in their trenches. With sights set on 900 metres, we opened fire. It was about 11.00 am. We were now lying in our positions and there we would spend several hours, because there could have been no question of advancing. A real hot fight now unfolded and it was interesting to be able to follow the course of a real battle in this way for the very first time. There were constant crashes, clattering, whizzing and whistling! It was a noise which is impossible to describe and yet one which left an unforgettable impression. Our men were soon using their knapsacks as shooting rests or had dug themselves shell scrapes. Our losses in the front line were slight.

Reserve *Leutnant* Roebbling of *6th Company* had a similar experience.

We were lying in a field of clover, where haystacks were still standing. We were waiting for fire orders, but none came. Instead of just waiting I looked through my prismatic telescope and searched and searched, but there was nothing to be seen. At the same time things were whistling past, or crashing into the ground. Then, all of a sudden, the man two to my right called out, "Adieu Süßenbach (my Gefreiter, responsible for estimating ranges), I've had it!" "Don't say that Busse, it won't be that bad!" – "Keep your chin up!" – then a little later comes a groan, "Oh, I've only got it in the shoulder and ear! Hey, you! Take my pack off it's pressing on me." Despite the hail of fire, the good lad crawled over and helped him, by laying him down on a bed of hay! "Süßenbach", I shouted, "bring me his rifle and a few rounds over!" He brings them over. In the meantime I keep searching for something to shoot at, but I still cannot see anything. From the right comes a report that they are located in the roadside ditch. The right hand half platoon opens fire. I search the line of the ditch, but I still cannot locate a target. Then all hell breaks loose! Shrapnel rounds burst over us. First there is an approaching howl, then a crack, followed a little later by the rattle of the balls landing around us. It makes a decisive impression on us and, almost as a duty, we greet each round by ducking our heads, until our noses are buried in the earth. We can already count them: one, two, three, four; up to four three more times, then there is a pause. At long last I have discovered something with my telescope. "Halfway along the line of poplar trees, trench in a stubble field! Sights at 800 metres!" With all the racket, it is impossible to think of a fire order being heard by everyone. I am pleased when I see that my neighbours are obeying the order. With that my duties are almost over for the time being. I keep observing and I fire now and then, which helps me master my nerves. I maintain all round observation whenever the shrapnel rounds permit it. There is still no sign of fresh troops to our left or right. We are still the sole object of all this concentrated fire! To our left I can see our company commander on top of a pile of bricks. He has an excellent, but extremely dangerous, position there. The pile of bricks seems to be attracting the shrapnel balls. A haystack in front has already caught fire. Suddenly, a different type of shrapnel round bursts. The earlier sort had white smoke, this is reddish brown and it smells clearly of sealing wax. They burst with a far louder report and the shower of bullets released is far denser. "Can't we get forward?" demands the impatient Busse. "No, not yet, but there are some reinforcements arriving to our right!"

If only there was not such a dense hail of small arms fire every time we try to raise our heads during pauses in the artillery fire. But we do not have to endure the shrapnel as much as before; the gaps in the firing become longer. At long last we are able to consider working our way forward. I shout the order down the ranks to my left, but then comes the report, "We're out of ammunition!" What a situation! A rifle bullet hits the forward sling swivel of my rifle and fizzes away vertically as a ricochet. It feels as though I have been whipped on the hand. There is a groove down the back of my hand. The artery behind my middle finger is damaged and the skin is torn open behind my three centre fingers. I am bleeding freely. For an instant my nerve almost fails me and I consider crawling back to the aid post. But what would happen here if the men were to see the sole officer present yielding! Out of the question! One good lad tears open a first field dressing and expertly binds up the wound. Splatt! Another round cracks past my ear and rips through my knapsack (it turns out later that my coat has eighteen holes in it); then down come more shrapnel balls – particularly densely now. One shrapnel pot impacts five paces to our front, spins up into the air above our heads and finally lands ten paces behind us. So many shrapnel balls land around us that we can harvest them. Constant reports of wounding arrive. "Unteroffizier Winnig has had a heel shot off." "Vizefeldwebel Eule is wounded in the chest and leg!' 'Hold fast!' I say to myself and, really, I have hardly thought the thought than it does become easier. We have the feeling that the shrapnel fire is not being directed so much against us; evidently the enemy artillery is having to cover a much greater length of line. Then we see our own rounds begin to land amongst the enemy trenches. It becomes easier to lift our heads. I look behind me and see a long line of infantry behind the railway embankment at Forest. Our artillery has to bring down the fire perfectly. We watch and clearly see it doing just that. The enemy artillery fire becomes weaker and less certain. If we only had ammunition, we should certainly be able to advance. A greater weight of fire begins to whistle around us and we see why. Some men of the 10th Company have rushed up to our line and packages of ammunition start flying along the line. The longed-for resupply of ammunition has arrived. I wait until everyone has the opportunity to load up, then we move forward. We are just in time, because things start to get hot once more. A gun moves into position close behind our line.

I envy the artillery men their gun shield, which protects them completely from small arms fire. The periscope sight enables the officer to observe over the gun shield, whilst remaining within its protection. There was barely five centimetres available beneath the shield that would permit the passage of a round. They had only fired two rounds when artillery shells began to burst around us. Hill 150 was all too easy to aim at and the map provided the enemy with the exact range.

By 11.00 am *Infantry Regiment 66* was still trying to launch a coordinated attack.

Leutenant Fricke tried to get 7th Company moving. Waving his sword high in the air, he moved off in front of his men, but everyone who attempted to follow him was shot down by the British. Leutnant Fricke fell and with him, Fahnenjunker [Officer Cadet] *Roegglen. Despite the fire, Hauptmann Bonsac tried to get his company up on its feet. Leutnant Seldte's weapons* [presumably machine guns] *hammered away at the enemy. All was in vain. Hauptman Bonsac was killed. The sword, which his*

Hauptmann Bonsac, Commanding Officer 7th Company IR66.

78

father had dropped when he lay mortally wounded at the head of the same 7th Company before Beaumont in 1870, fell to the ground for ever.

The situation was much the same in *5th Company*. Reserve *Leutnant* Thierkopf reported:

The major had already given the order to attack twice. One section which threw itself forward out of its cover was shot down as soon as it had gone ten paces. Only one unteroffizier returned. Our guns then opened flanking fire and infantry began to advance on the left [east] towards the British. 'Leutnant', one of the Musketiers suddenly shouted, 'They're waving handkerchiefs over there; they want to surrender.' Sure enough they had tied white cloths to their rifles, which they were constantly waving to and fro.'Up and at 'em lads! Get up, move, move!' At that all who were left around me got up and stormed forward. Then suddenly there were cracks and we came under fire from the flank at close range. One of my rangefinders lay groaning, shot through the stomach...We hit the ground, pressing down into the stubble field. Taking cover behind a corn stack, I observed through my telescope...in vain...there was nothing to be seen. As though laid out on a display counter we lay there, whilst rounds whizzed and cracked past us. Suddenly I received a blow on the back, which bowled me over. What was that? Had I been hit? Cursing, I rolled back on to my stomach and started to check my limbs. I drew them towards me slowly and stretched them out again, one after the other, just like a spider in a web. Thank heavens! Everything seemed to be all right! My eyes stared again through the telescope. A shrapnel ball tore through my sword knot and fell on my knee. Then I received another blow on the back. Then something hot was flowing along one of my arms. It was blood. I needed to check that out undisturbed, so I pulled myself carefully upright and, ignoring all the British bullets, I returned unscathed to the sunken road, where a stretcher bearer bandaged up my upper arm, which had been shot through.

Hauptmann Bonsac's temporary grave.

As the morning wore on the German artillery support in this area increased. The guns of *Field Artillery Regiment 40* were reinforced by heavy guns of *Foot Artillery Battalion 4*, then the 6th and elements of 10th and 3rd Companies under *Oberleutnant* Holscher, *Leutnant* Hesse and Reserve *Leutnant* Roebbling made a further attempt to close with the British positions.

Reserve Leutnant Roebbling of 6th Company later wrote:

'So now came the order: "On your feet. Move, Move!" With two short pauses to catch our breath, we advanced seventy five metres to the edge of a sugar beet field. But we could not see a thing! The enemy knew exactly where we were and brought down very accurate fire on us. We infantrymen had the feeling that we were clear of the worst of the danger and we tried to expose ourselves as little as possible. Here at least our heads were not sharply silhouetted against the sky, whilst our field grey uniforms disappeared against the green field. We could immediately feel that our situation had improved. Only the occasional round cracked against our line; the majority passed well overhead. The field of beet was a good 150 metres long and it fell away in front. I gave the order, "Crawl forward!" It was just an attempt and it succeeded! Everyone was very relieved that we were able to advance without being on the receiving end of unpleasantly heavy enemy fire. Admittedly my left hand hurt badly. I could not carry a weapon in it, and could not use it to crawl, but I was still well out in front of the rest. I suddenly realised that bullets from below were no longer whistling around us; that they were all passing much too high. I stood upright and sure enough, we could see nothing of the enemy trenches. We were in dead ground to them. I called out the happy news to the advancing line. Cautiously at first, but then with increasing daring, they stood up. Now there was no obstacle to our forward movement and we could calmly cut our way through the fences. The way forward led to the road and on over the railway. Artillery shells howled overhead.'

All this took a great deal of time, but during the afternoon they closed up on the British trenches, with the greatest progress being made on their right [western] flank, where elements of *10th* and *11th Companies* were first led onto the British position by *Reserve Leutnant* Mende. Then it was the turn of the *9th Company*. Of course, by then 5th Division was in the midst of its withdrawal. *Leutnant* Siegener *9th Company* described how the attackers were able to take advantage of this change in the tactical situation:

Just before 4.00 pm, we saw signs of life in the British lines and we established that they were withdrawing slowly. Finally whole sections at a time leapt up and made off, whilst our lines brought down an enormous weight of fire We could see how the enemy were taking casualties from the moment they began to move.

Entire sections went down under our fire. We now began to advance, at first in tactical bounds, then we continued steadily, despite enemy artillery and small arms fire. Our losses had been, and continued to be, great, but we wanted to get on and we had to. We arrived at the main road, doubled across it and went into fire positions the other side. 200 metres to our front was a trench that was still occupied. We intended to bring it under fire and then to charge it. But already white flags were being displayed over there. The men had their hands up and they surrendered. An officer came up to me and handed over his sword, but there was still fire coming down on us from further up. I pointed this out to the officer and threatened to shoot him immediately. The Briton waved towards the rear and the shooting stopped.'

At this point the regimental history of *Infantry Regiment 66* includes a section of purple prose to describe the subsequent events:

It works like an electric shock. "Fix bayonets!" comes the order. Cheeks are shining everywhere and eyes are flashing. It is now 4.00 pm. Suddenly the battlefield is full of advancing lines of

A highly stylised sketch of German infantry in the attack – though colours were still being carried into action in 1914.

infantry. Colours flutter in the wind, trumpets blare. Swords flash. Battle cries of 'Hurra' drown out the sound of the guns. The men of both regiments of the Brigade [Infantry Regiments 26 and 66 of 13 Brigade] *launch themselves forward in lines, flags flying and are followed up by support waves...It is a magnificent unforgettable sight. Enemy countermeasures were still fairly effective, so a daring battery came galloping up to send showers of shrapnel flying at the retreating British lines. Leutnant Siegener and Reserve Leutnant Kreidner were severely wounded, but there was no more stopping. Soon the enemy was in general retreat...*

Reserve *Leutnant* Roebbling of *6th Company* took part in the final moments of the battle:

Now the artillery fire fell silent too. We were in a fold in the ground. I could now see the left of our line charging forward.

2nd Company IR72 marches out of its depot at Torgau, August 1914.

Hauptmann Bergansky had his sword raised. Further to the left I thought I could see Hesse, with Westphal beyond him. To our front a row of soldiers clad in brown stood up, waving white flags. Hands raised, the British left their trenches. Some were supported by their comrades, but others moved towards us, hands high and continuing to wave white flags. Victory was ours! God be praised! Tears of joy rolled down! How great, how wonderful! We have won. It's a victory! God be thanked! It really was Hesse and Westphal over to the left. I waved at them and they approached. To our left was Hauptmann Bergansky, who has halted in front of six ammunition wagons. They kept shouting "Hurra! Hurra!", whilst ever more British streamed towards us.

Infantry Regiment 66 later claimed to have captured thirteen guns [type unspecified] and 600 prisoners. Whilst picking his way through the town of Le Cateau that evening, *Leutnant* Kühlhorn of *Infantry Regiment 72* saw a sight which made him smile:

We saw a pretty sight at the station: six bath tubs were peacefully lined up alongside one another. It transpired that the British, who had only arrived in Le Cateau that morning, had brought the bath tubs with them. We were not so fussy. The generality of British soldiers presented a very clean appearance. Every one of them carried a razor in his knapsack. Above all they were superbly equipped and from what we discovered in their knapsacks, their rations must have been really excellent. From the station, we marched back into the town, which in places had been badly shot up by the British [Not the Germans, of course!!]. *One complete row of houses was in flames. Luckily we found our field kitchen untouched.*

Some elements of *Infantry Regiment 26* found themselves in Reumont during the night following the battle. The situation was still very fluid and there were numerous clashes. *Oberstleutnant* Faelligen wrote:

The enemy was pursued to the east of Reumont. In the village the regiment gathered in and divisional orders were issued [presumably 7th Division, commanded by Generalleutnant Riedel]. *Whilst this was going on there was a diverting little incident. The officers were listening intently to the words of the divisional commander at the crossroads in the centre of Reumont when the sound of shots was heard to the left* [presumably west] *of the main road, followed by the sound of horses galloping by. Everyone believed that the British were on their way and prepared to give battle, but the situation was clarified rapidly. The Machine Gun Company of Infantry Regiment 26 had sent off men to requisition bread. In Bertry this group had bumped into a thirty man British cavalry patrol which had unsuspectingly entered the village. The* [German] *party had engaged them, hitting most of them and capturing eighteen horses.*

In fact there was not much for *IR 26* to smile at. The fighting had cost them four officers and fifty seven OR killed, twelve officers and 247 OR wounded and no fewer than 347 missing, although the majority of these turned up later as stragglers.

Chapter Two

THE CENTRE OF THE LINE: THE 3RD DIVISION

**The right of the 3rd Division (Major General Hubert Hamilton):
9 Brigade – before Inchy.**

The *Official History* account of the fighting on 9 Brigade front is
succinct – the account of events until about 4.30pm takes up less than
a page of text. It held a line south of Inchy, dominating that place;
battalions were positioned with 1st Northumberland Fusiliers (1/NF)
on the right and 1st Lincolns on the left, with the remains of 1st Royal
Scots Fusiliers (the other two companies, it will be recalled, had been
sent to the assistance of the right flank of the 5th Division) in between.
4th Royal Fusiliers formed a reserve. XXIII Brigade RFA had its three
batteries (107, 108 and 109) in close support, with a section (of four
guns) almost in the lines of the Northumberland Fusiliers. Essentially,
the German attack was held and the enemy was not able to make much

German cavalry in northern France.

progress from Inchy southwards; at about 3.30pm Brigadier General Shaw, the GOC, ordered a retirement in line with what was happening to his right, and his men were got away with very little interference from the Germans. The four guns of the advanced section of 108 Battery were disabled and abandoned. Elements of the Brigade formed a screen, roughly between Montigny and Bertry, for the other retiring troops of the Division before they continued on their way south.

Generalmajor von Reichenau, commanded 15 Infantry Brigade whic included Füs R36 and IR93.

Beaumont – Inchy was the particular objective of *8th Infantry Division*, commanded by *Generalleutnant* Hildebrandt. The division marched off via Solesmes at 5.30 am (German time), *Infantry Regiment 93* bringing up the rear, so that by the time the *93rd* was properly underway it was already 7.30 am. It eventually reached Viesly, via Biastre, about 9.30 am. By this time *Infantry Regiment 153* and *Fusilier Regiment 36* were already in action; *Infantry Regiment 153* attacking the British lines to the west and south of Beaumont and *Fusilier Regiment 36* the village itself and the positions to the east.

Shortly before 10.00am Infantry Regiment 153 was ordered to capture Béthencourt. Advancing 1st Battalion right and 3rd Battalion left astride the Viesly – Béthencourt road, the regiment came under heavy shrapnel fire the moment it appeared forward of Viesly. After a period of hard close-quarter fighting, the British were driven out of Béthencourt by about 11.00 am. Mopping up continued under heavy British artillery file, which damaged buildings, scattered roof tiles and almost toppled the church tower, which was hit by two shells.

Further to the east *Fusilier Regiment 36* was also having a difficult time of it. Deploying in mid morning just southwest of Neuvilly, it headed towards the Le Cateau-Cambrai road, with its 3rd Battalion east of the Neuvilly-Troisvilles road and its 2nd Battalion to the west of it. Under constant fire it closed up to the main road but could progress no further for the time being.

Oberst von Oertzen, commander FR36.

Despite coming under shrapnel fire in Viesly, *Infantry Regiment 93* up to this point had not taken any casualties. At 10.15 am it was ordered to leapfrog *Infantry Regiment 153* and to assault Beaumont, which was in dead ground to *Infantry Regiment 93*. Taking advantage of the fields of cereal and rape, much of which had already been harvested, the regiment shook out, with *1st Battalion right, 3rd Battalion left* to the east of the Viesly-Beaumont road and *2nd Battalion* in reserve.

As soon as the regiment emerged out of the dead ground it came under accurate shrapnel and small arms fire. At that the sub-units began to advance using fire and manoeuvre, but casualties began to mount, especially in *2nd Battalion*, whose commanding officer, *Major* von Puttkamer, was seriously wounded and unable to continue. The *1st Battalion* moved through the grounds of Clermont Chateau, about 1,500 metres north northwest of Beaumont, in an attempt to link up with *Infantry Regiment 153*, then continued. Shrapnel rained down on them, causing considerable casualties, including *Hauptmann* Ulrich von Scheven, commander of *11th Company,* who was killed. Von Scheven is buried in the German cemetery at Cambrai, Block 9 Grave 110.

Because the advance had tended to pull the regiment to the west, its

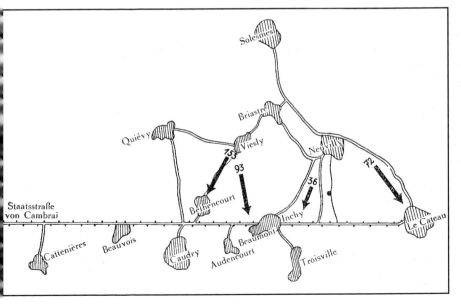

Map 10. The attack of the *8th Division*.

Original graves of *Oberst* Louis von Arnim and *Hauptmann* Alfred Theinert at Clary.

commander, Oberst Louis von Arnim, who by now had reached a good position of observation directed his *2nd Battalion* to close the gap which had developed with *Fusilier Regiment 36*. Soon this unit too was heavily engaged. The 1st Battalion, whose commander, *Major* von Huth, was also seriously wounded, linked up with elements of Infantry *Regiment 153* and together some progress was made against the British positions along the road. By about midday, *2nd* and *3rd Battalions* entered Beaumont itself and drove back a number of British outposts to the British main position. There was no opportunity to develop the attack to the south beyond the village; the German troops being pinned down by concentrated shrapnel and small arms fire along its edge.

See Map p. 63

9th and 12th Companies did make an attempt to launch an attack in conjunction with elements of *Fusilier Regiment 36*, but it was shot to a standstill by British marksmen and cost the lives of both company commanders: *Hauptmann* Alfred Theinert of *9th Company*, who is buried in the German cemetery at Selvigny, Block 1 Grave 191 and *Oberleutnant* von König from 12th Company. It is not possible to be certain where *Oberleutnant* von König lies. The regimental history does not mention his first name, but two graves exist which bear the name of *Hauptmann* von König, one in Caudry and one at Le Cateau. There was an even worse blow for the regiment about this time when *Oberst* von Arnim was also hit by shrapnel and killed, whilst calmly walking up and down smoking a cigar on his vantage point and directing the battle. He is believed to be the senior casualty on either side during the battle and is buried in the German cemetery at Selvigny, Block 1, Grave 192.

During the afternoon the regiment reorganised in and around Beaumont, but was unable to progress further until the British had withdrawn. In advancing to the point it had it had taken some of the worst German casualties of the day: six officers and 112 OR were

Officers of 10 Company, Fusilier Regiment 36, before march off to war.

killed, nine officers and 306 OR were wounded.

Dissatisfied with progress the divisional commander issued orders for a coordinated attack by all three regiments around 1.00 pm, but according to *Fusilier Regiment 36*,

> *there was insufficient artillery preparation and our attack came up against the British who were brilliantly entrenched along the line of the road. The losses of the lines of infantry as they attempted to use fire and manoeuvre were extremely high because of the heavy British rifle fire. Repeated attempts were made; the commander eventually deploying all his reserves. At long last at 4.00 pm Hirsch's battery of Field Artillery Regiment 75 came into action at Rambourlieux Farm, followed an hour and a half later by another, which did not need to fire, because by then the British began to withdraw.*

The story was much the same all along the divisional front, but there were unforeseen consequences for *2nd Battalion Field Artillery Regiment 75*. Its commander Major Hinsch, who had earlier played a leading role with his guns in neutralising several British batteries by means of a skilful flanking action, was keen to close up to a point from which he could support the infantry of *8th Division*. For the artillery, too, the British positions south of the road turned out to be so well

Oberst **Freiherr von Dassenbach, commander FAR75 at Le Cateau.**

camouflaged and sited that it was extremely difficult to bring them under accurate fire. Hinsch's adjutant takes up the story of what happened after the battalion approached Rambourlieux farm:

It seemed pointless to leave the observation point at Rambourlieux Farm and Leutnant Blomeyer received orders to remain there and to keep a look out, whilst I myself plus Sergeant Walter with the tripod mounted binoculars, continued forward. We could still not see the enemy, so we pressed on past some of our infantrymen, then we halted and, remaining standing, observed through our binoculars. With each step visibility improved. Because only a few stray bullets were winging their way past us, Major Hinsch decided to stay in contact with the enemy and call forward 6th Battery immediately then to move forward 4th and 5th Batteries under the covering fire of Hirsch's Battery. He therefore sent me back to pass on these orders. I had only gone a short distance, when I heard a shout from behind. Turning, I saw that the major had collapsed. Trumpeter Walther, who had been standing next to him, shouted 'The major has been hit!' Not knowing quite how serious the wound had been, I first galloped off to Hauptmann von Armin to inform him that the battalion commander had been wounded. At that Walther also rode up to say that the major had

Major **Eugen Hinsch. commander 2nd Bn FAR75, died of stomach wounds received at Le Cateau.**

a serious stomach wound. At the same time our line of infantry had come under heavy direct rifle and machine gun fire by the British and their movement stalled. Major Hinsch was lying about one hundred metres in front of this line. I grabbed the two nearest stretcher bearers and together we ran to the infantry position. We tried to crawl forward, towing the stretcher behind us, but it was out of the question. Enemy bullets were passing so close overhead that even with our noses pressed into the ground we could feel the wind from them on the napes of our necks. We lay there for ten minutes hoping that the wild firing would slacken, but it continued unabated, so we crawled back to the infantry line and took cover in a furrow in a field of sugar beet. A further attempt fifteen minutes later saw us further forward, but when one of the carrying handles of the stretcher was shot away, I ordered everyone to crawl back. It was not until a long time later, when the infantry had worked their way forward in a series of costly bounds, that Major Hinsch was within our lines and could be recovered. Supported by two men, who almost had to carry him, his face deathly pale, but his head upright, he made his way back and was then carried away. We were certain then that he would never return. He died in a field hospital two days [sic] *later. Everyone of us missed him; which is the highest degree of respect and devotion that can be granted to a soldier.*

The grave of *Major* Hinsch in Le Cateau Military Cemetery.

Major Eugen Hinsch, who was the only casualty that day from Field Artillery Regiment 75, is buried in the German cemetery at Le Cateau, Grave 664.

Major Herbert Stewart DSO of the Army Service Corps wrote a book published in 1916, *From Mons to Loos: Being the Diary of a Supply Officer*, in which some idea may be gained of the difficulties the Divisional Train and Supply Columns had during the Retreat. Stewart had particular responsibility for 9 Brigade.

At nightfall [of the 25th] *the Supply Column arrived, and I was ordered to take five of the lorries with supplies to my Brigade, which I should find at Troisvilles. I reached there in the pitchy darkness at 11pm, to find not a vestige of life in the place. Not a light was seen, every house was deserted, not even a dog barked. Leaving the vehicles near a church, I proceeded to reconnoitre on foot; my footsteps were the only sound that disturbed the stillness. Past the houses I came upon the fields, and leaving the road tramped across the ploughed land towards a light I saw in the distance. Suddenly a challenge rang out, followed by the crack of a rifle and the shrill crescendo of a bullet screaming into the darkness. "Friend!" I shouted, and looking around discerned the dark figure of a sentry standing in the shadow of a hedge. Being bidden to pass I remonstrated with the man in no measured terms. It appeared, however, that he had already challenged once and had received no reply. After this I remained on the road, taking no further chances across country, and came at last to the headquarters of 13 Brigade* [which were in the sunken road between Troisvilles and the Roman road, situated a

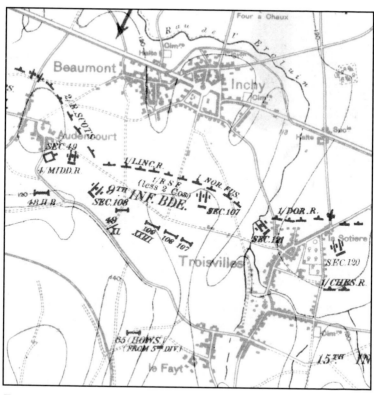

Extract from O.H Map 11: 9 Infantry Brigade's front.

few hundred yards from the junction with the latter]. *They,
however, could give me no news of my brigade* [13 Brigade was
in the 5th Division].

*There was nothing to be done but to return. I reached
Troisvilles again, but there lost myself in a maze of streets. I
seemed to find dozens of churches, but not the one where I had
left the vehicles. Suddenly, to my delight, I heard the rapid beats
of a motor-cycle engine, and a despatch rider appeared round a
corner. Taking me up on his carrier we quickly found the lorries,
the drivers of whom were by now considerably anxious over my
long absence. Returning to Bertry I reported at Divisional
Headquarters at 1am on the 26th. Round the sides of a long shed
at the back of a church officers and men were lying on straw,
worn out by their long exertions. In the middle of the room at a
table sat the General* [Hubert Hamilton] *dictating a despatch in*

a low voice to a staff officer. The light of a lamp fell on the General's fine, soldierly features; his face was drawn with fatigue and anxiety. The despatch finished, the General uttered a name in the same low voice; immediately one of the staff officers lying round the room rose to his feet, put on his cap, took up the despatch from the table, saluted and, passing out of the door, disappeared into the night.

Turning to me the General asked my business and, being informed, pointed out on the map the town of Inchy, where my brigade would be found. Again I started out into the night and this time with success. The troops were in Inchy, the wearied men lying on the pavements or in the road, too exhausted even to hear the approaching vehicles. Stopping the lorries, the drivers and I had to descend and make a path through the slumbering forms by literally dragging their bodies on to the pavements or sides of the road. At the junction of three streets by Brigade Headquarters we deposited the supplies in the midst of hundreds of sleeping soldiers and, at 4.30am, as the sun was appearing, we returned to the Train Headquarters (ie the divisional train, the main supply column) at Montigny, after twenty five and a half hours of continuous duty. I lay down to snatch a short rest.'

It was indeed a short rest – he was up by 6am for another very busy forty eight hours.

1st Battalion Northumberland Fusiliers (1/NF).

This account is largely extracted from *The Fifth in the Great War*, the regimental history; Naval and Military Press has reprinted this in recent years. It makes some interesting observations. For example, it notes that II Corps line had 'been partially prepared for defence by French Territorials'. Further, 'it was considered that the situation did not permit of II Corps standing on the defence and that the intention, therefore, was to resume the retreat after a brief halt. Orders were received by the 3rd Division shortly after 9pm that the defensive position would not be taken up.' '9 Brigade, accordingly, billeted in Inchy for the night, under cover of outposts.' The Battalion was fed and billeted by 10pm and with orders to turn out at 2am.

A statement after the war by the then second in command of the Battalion, Brigadier General Yatman, is, as the history notes, of great interest:

On the afternoon of 25 August Smith-Dorrien was at the side of the road, when I went over to speak to his ADC. Smith-Dorrien called out to me and said: 'Come here. I am going to tell you something which you may repeat to none but your CO. We are going to stand and fight tomorrow. What will your men think? Are they tired of retreating? I said that the men were certainly tired of retreating and would be delighted, It was some time before I could tell Ainslie [the CO], and he was then so harassed by other concerns that I have never been sure that he grasped the significance of what I told him...He said that he would fight at Le Cateau – and that is a fact.

The men duly turned out at 2am, only to be told, in the light of the decision to hold the position and make a stand, which by now had reached the Battalion, that they should return to rest until dawn. As the history notes:

One gathers that, where a Corps Commander should have been credited with an historic decision, a long-suffering adjutant was blamed for having issued the wrong orders in the first place. The pawns to the game know so little of the great issues that influence the small, though to them all important, moves on the chess board of war.'

This is a salutary warning about the value of first hand commentaries on battles when the speaker is referring to something well above his actual experience: of course such impressions are useful, but they are not blessed with first hand knowledge of the reasoning behind decisions that were made – though they are, of course, about the consequences at their level of such decisions.

The Battalion took up positions about 800 yards south of Inchy on a forward slope. The whole position had to be re-dug with a lack of sufficient heavy tools; so, as usual elsewhere that day, entrenching tools had to be used. B Company formed the Battalion reserve a few hundred yards to the rear, and both it and the 1st Line Transport suffered several casualties when the enemy opened fire, though the front line companies were unaffected. The German artillery was seen off by elements of the British artillery. Although heavy fighting could be heard from the flanks, the Battalion was little troubled, relatively speaking, through the morning and early afternoon. 'On the slightest indication of enemy movement in Inchy, the exits were smothered with by artillery and rifle fire, and the battalion undisturbed, except for an occasional hostile shell...' as far as the Battalion was concerned, all was going well until they could see that the troops on the right were withdrawing. This was the result of the unravelling of the 5th

Division's position.

At about 3.30pm orders reached the Battalion to withdraw.

Simultaneously a forward section of 107 Field Battery opened rapid fire on Inchy and shortly afterwards the Brigade Major, Captain [RWM] *Stevens, galloped up and personally conveyed orders to the forward companies of the Battalion to retire, being immediately afterwards mortally wounded* [he is buried in Troisvilles Communal Cemetery]. *The position, strong for defence, was most unfavourable for this operation. Retirement from the forward trenches entailed traversing an open slope for some four hundred yards.'*

However, withdrawal was carried out with quite light casualties. 'As it was, held in check by the fire of two guns of 107 Battery, which were sited close in rear of the trenches and maintained fire until the last moment before being perforce abandoned, the Germans did not advance to within 1,000 or 1,200 yards of B Company, which had taken up a position in rear to cover the retirement of the remaining companies.' The withdrawal had not cost a single casualty and the Battalion's losses for the day were three other ranks killed and two officers and fifteen OR wounded – most of whom came from the reserve company and the transport – suffered at the opening of the action.

1st Battalion Lincolnshire Regiment (1/Lincoln).

The Battalion reached Inchy at about 6pm, soaked through, the hungry, foot-sore troops entered the village ready to drop; there had been a violent thunderstorm between about 4 and 5pm.

Billets were small and overcrowded, but in some the men found washing and drinking water; that at least was a Godsend. No one, however, was permitted to undress, so that whatever rest was possible had to be taken in wet clothes. The village was bare of food.

The Battalion was allowed to get some rest, except for the men called on to provide guards and outposts; the anticipation was that the move the next day would start at 6am. However, it was not to be a quiet night, as sleep would be broken by frequent alarms; for example, at midnight the whole Battalion was stood to arms. News of the fighting between

British Infantry setting up machine gun positions.

the Division's rearguard (7 Brigade) and the cavalry against advancing Germans near Solesmes came through. It was difficult to get much rest in those circumstances, always half expecting to be called out for the next emergency. By 5am the whole Battalion was formed up in the main street enjoying their piece of bread and cup of tea as they stood in their ranks. Soon after they left Inchy and took up positions on rising, open ground about 300 metres from the large village (Inchy and Beaumont even then tended to run into each other in one, long, straggling settlement). Inchy lies in a dip in the ground and the position gave an excellent view over the long open slopes on the northern side of it and down which the Germans would have to advance. Shaw sent up the Brigade tool carts and so, unlike most other units on the day, the men had some reasonable equipment with which to dig themselves in. On their right were the two companies of the Royal Scots Fusiliers and on the left the 2nd Royal Scots of 8 Brigade. Behind the Lincolns were some guns (of 107 Battery and 108 Battery), at the top of the slope, well dug in and concealed. These were very effective throughout the attack and all survived the battle; but being in such an exposed position those of 108 Battery had to be spiked and abandoned when the time for the withdrawal came.

The German artillery began firing at about 6.30am, not very heavily at first. Their infantry came over the opposite sky line and down the open slope in extended lines. Our guns opened on them with some effect. By degrees the Germans got down to the village and into it, where they were out of sight, until they reappeared on the outskirts of the village nearest to us, when our companies at once opened a heavy fire on them... More and more lines of Germans came over the skyline and down the slope and established themselves in the village. They got their machine guns to work as well as sharpshooters, who had apparently spotted our piece of trench, as whenever a head was raised a bullet came past it. The trenches were fairly good, but it was impossible to keep a good lookout on the Germans, which was necessary lest they rushed us from the village [which was only

about three hundred yards away at the nearest point], *without exposing oneself. The Germans were thick on the edge of the village and our guns frequently turned on them and set some buildings on fire.*

At 3.30pm came the order to retire. The Official History takes up the story:

Pushing up the Royal Fusiliers [4th Battalion] *from the reserve to the north western edge of Troisvilles, he* [Brigadier General Shaw] *brought away nearly all his wounded, after which he withdrew in succession the Northumberland Fusiliers and the Lincolnshire with very trifling loss. The German skirmishers lining the southern edge of Inchy tried very hard to hinder the movement, but were silenced by the advanced section of the 107th and the 108th Batteries* [the latter were on the left of 1/Lincoln's line]. *As the last party of the Lincolnshire came abreast of the advanced section of the 108th Battery the officer in command, having fired off his last round of ammunition, disabled and abandoned his guns.*

The Regimental History describes the first stages of the withdrawal:

On the further side of the ridge and at the southern base there was a sunken road in which the seriously wounded were placed in safety. After crossing the sunken road and a railway line, the retirement was continued across a beetroot field which, owing to the rain of the previous night, was slippery, and clods of clayey earth clung to the men's feet, making progress slow. But fortunately the enemy failed to follow the retiring troops, and the latter, unmolested, plodded along, crossing ditches and fields until well out of range of rifle fire.

Eventually a road, crossing the line of retirement diagonally, was reached [It is not possible to identify this road with certainty; it might have been the Bertry-Caudry road or that running from south of Montigny to south of Bertry], *and here officers and NCOs formed the men into small parties and, directed by Colonel Smith (the CO), marched them to a rallying point at some crossroads near Clary, where the battalion was formed up without delay. Companies were, however, still somewhat scattered. The majority of A and B and about half of D were present, but the majority of C Company (which had held the right of the position at Inchy) had retired through Troisvilles and did not rejoin until the next day. Part of D, on the left of the line, caught up later on.*

...not a German followed, not even a cavalry patrol, not a shell was fired at the Brigade as it withdrew from Clary. The enemy was wholly occupied with the few remaining units which had not received orders to retire in time to get away...

The casualties suffered by the Battalion at Le Cateau were Major C Toogood wounded by a sniper and left in the trenches [repatriated to the UK in September 1918 after nine months in Holland and imprisonment in Germany]*, three other ranks killed, forty wounded and fifty missing, though most of the latter rejoined later.'*

The 4th Royal Fusiliers had suffered considerable casualties at Mons – some 150 (the Battalion also won the first two army VCs of the war there). It was withdrawn from the right hand of the Brigade line when the shelling commenced; they had been improving the previously dug and rather inadequate trenches prepared by the French. It moved back to a sunken line behind and parallel to the front line and acted as Brigade reserve. When the men were moving down to it the Battalion was caught by a burst of shrapnel that left one man killed and twenty or so wounded. After that, for the remainder of the battle the men had a comparatively good time. They were blessed with a hot meal, as the Battalion cookers were in Troisvilles. About 250 yards in the rear of the lane were two batteries of artillery and, as a result, shells from both sides continually crossed overhead, but without doing any damage.

The Battalion (plus the two companies of 1/RSF) withdrew in good order and acted as rearguard to the Division. Practically undamaged by the battle, the Battalion was able to cover the retreat as if on manoeuvres; so rested and in good shape was it that the Battalion was able to march 'through a village at attention, arms sloped and fours dressed'. Major General Hamilton, having watched a rag, tag and bobtail of men drifting past him, was suitably impressed and called out, 'Well done, Fusiliers!'

The Actions of the German Cavalry in the Battle for Caudry.

The fighting at Caudry involved various regiments from the *4th* and *9th Cavalry Divisions* of *HKK* [Senior Cavalry Commander] *2.* Moving south on all the available routes from their concentration area north of Solesmes, their advance guards were soon in action against the defenders of Caudry. Those involved were mainly from *13th*, *14th* and *18th Cavalry Brigades*. The German cavalry regiments notoriously lacked firepower, so they were quickly sucked into an unequal struggle with regiments of the British 3rd Division. *Rittmeister* [Captain] Freiherr [Baron] von der Horst of *Hussar Regiment 15* later recalled:

> *Battle was soon joined. The sounds of shooting were coming from all directions. We halted for just under an hour in a village then we were pushed forward. With my squadron I had the task of Brigade right flank protection, but when I detected heavy firing in the area of Husarenregiment 11* [14 Cav Bde 9th Cav Div] *just to my front, I ordered the squadron to dismount. Hardly had I pushed forward with my soldiers, when suddenly heavy artillery fire was coming down a bare ten paces to our front. I crawled with my men back to a road which offered some protection from the fire, but my men assumed that the command meant that they were to pull back to the led horses. I had to go back and fetch them, doubling them forward. Major von Madai* [Kürassier Regiment 4, 13 Cav Bde , 9th Cav Div] *waved at me to provide the Kürassiers with support, because they were pinned down by heavy British small arms fire. Bullets were whistling just past our ears. We took up position in a sunken road. I tried to keep the enemy position under observation so that I could give fire orders to my men. Reserve Leutnant Riemann was to my left. Suddenly there was a thud and Riemann was hit. Fortunately it was only a graze to the shoulder. Shortly after that a man on my left was shot through the head. Riemann's carbine was also hit, injuring Oberst Seiffert, who had taken up position next to us, in the hand. Doubtless the British had realised that there were officers around the tree, where we found ourselves, because they constantly shot at us. We lay in trenches until late evening, becoming so used to all the shooting that we were able to make ourselves really comfortable. We just had nothing to eat. The place was being hit by heavy artillery and it was interesting to view this from close range; it made a hellish row! Towards evening the British had withdrawn so skilfully from their positions that we had not noticed anything. We went forward and captured a large number of British coats. I took one for myself as well.*

The Regimental Commander wrote:

> *How grateful I am that the Regiment emerged so well out of yesterday. Despite being in a heavy fire fight with the British, we*

only lost seven men. Riemann was slightly wounded. The Kürassiers had heavy casualties. Before battle was joined, the Kürassier Weichs, the brother of ours, made me a cup of coffee in a village. It was pouring with rain. Weichs had lost his regimental coat and had replaced it with a civilian one. We had a real good laugh together, then an hour later he was dead. Westerholt was mortally wounded and Salis was shot through the arm. As a senior officer, it is certainly useful to show the men from time to time that you are not afraid; or better, that it is possible to overcome fear. There is, however, no need for a brigade commander to take part in the actual fire fight as Oberst Seiffert did with great courage. All command then ceased, because there was nothing for it but for the regimental commander to follow the good (or was it bad?) example!'

Much of what von der Horst recalled was borne out by members of Kürrassier Regiment 4, one of whose officers wrote:

The regiment as a complete entity was involved for the first time on 26th August with regular enemy troops. Unfortunately this was not the mounted action we had all hoped for; rather it was a battle conducted on foot. During the night 25th/26th, the regiment had bivouacked in St Vast [sic = St Vaast-en-Cambrésis, two kilometres north of Quiévy]. *By 5.30 am the Brigade* [19] *was assembled in the area to the north of Jaune-Bois Ferme* [sic = Jeune Bois, which is located just to the north of the N43 by the turn off for Caudry]. *About 8.00 am the Brigade was launched into the attack against Caudry to the left of 14* [Brigade]. *Kürassier Regiment 4 was on the left, then the order was 4th, 3rd and 5th Squadrons. The 1st Squadron was initially held back in a hollow with the led horses under Rittmeister* [Captain] *von Wachs. There*

Rittmeister Detlef von Kutze, OC 4, Ku.7, KiA 26 August 1914.

it had the job of keeping at bay the 'Sugar Beet Swine', that is to say small groups of British soldiers who were holding out in sugar beet fields behind our front and picking off our led horses, causing serious casualties. [In all probability these were British stragglers, rather than stay-behind parties.] *The Regimental staff, with Oberstleutnant von Albedyll, Oberleutnant Freiherr von*

Weichs and Leutnant Freiherr von Salis, took up positions in accordance with the peacetime practice on a hill immediately in rear of the firing line. Major von Madai did not have the patience to stick it out idly with the staff. Moving upright he shifted, just as he had in the south west, along the firing line from man to man, adjusting sights and discussing each man's target with him. When we commented that he should not expose himself unnecessarily to heavy enemy fire, he replied that it was not appropriate for an officer to lie down; he must move upright amongst his men, giving them an example of courage.

It was the mission of the 9th Cavalry Division to hold the position at all cost until relieved by II Army Corps [sic]. *During the battle we came under enemy flanking fire from Bertincourt* [sic] [This must refer to Béthencourt] *from our left. The Regimental Commander ordered the 3rd and 5th Squadrons to turn to face the new enemy and directed that the soldiers of the 1st Squadron should prolong the left flank of the 5th Squadron which was hanging in the air. Oberleutnant Freiherr von Weichs was directed to carry this order to the 1st Squadron. Having carried out this order, he returned and, standing up, brought his hand up to his helmet in salute. At that point he was hit in the middle of the forehead by a bullet and fell dead at the feet of his commander. The regiment had lost its tireless and faithful adjutant.*

In the meantime Leutnant Freiherr von Salis was ordered to explain to the soldiers of the left hand squadron the prolongation of the line by the men of the 1st Squadron. On the way forward he met up with the commander of the left flank platoon, Leutnant Freiherr von Berchem, who was kneeling down behind some sheaves of corn. As he was briefing him on the situation, Leutnant Freiherr von Berchem was shot through his open mouth and left cheek. The remarkable thing was that Berchem did not let his monocle fall out, which cheered everyone up, despite the seriousness of the position. Whilst Berchem was being attended to, Salis took over command of his soldiers. As a result of their fire, the British soldiers pulled back from hasty positions they had produced to our front. Oberleutnant Graf [Count] *von Westerholt, the senior officer of the flanking squadrons of the regiment, gave the order for immediate pursuit, during which the men had to endure a great deal of frontal and flanking fire. Graf von Westerholt was just about to lead his men down into dead*

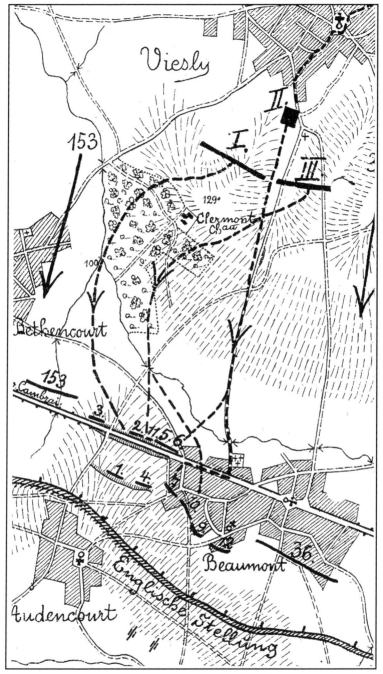

Map 12. German advance on Beaumont and Audencourt.

A German firing line is resupplied with 7.92 mm rimless ammunition.

ground, when he was hit and severely wounded by a bullet. We pulled him down into a depression. Enemy fire increased, but apparently the British did not dare to advance, having overestimated the size of Westerholt's little band. The approximately forty strong detachment, which was led by Leutnants Freiherr von Salis and Freiherr von Wambolt, lay there for about four hours, utterly cut off and unable to move left or right. Freiherr von Salis directed that the helmet covers be removed, so that the sight of the shiny helmets would prevent our own troops from firing too short. Finally, after a long time, the soldiers of 14 Brigade appeared. Four Kürassiers carried their brave commander, Graf von Westerholt, through a hail of bullets to the aid post. During the process, Leutnant von Salis was wounded. Towards 5.00pm the British withdrew from their position. Graf von Westerholt died of his wounds on 29 August 1914. The following morning his burial took place in a simple, but dignified manner. The local priest met his coffin in front of the church. Two lightly wounded officers and six Kürassiers accompanied the cortège. Numerous inhabitants of the French village took part. In a message of sympathy delivered to the field hospital, the mayor wrote, "Victor Webremez, maire, salue messieurs officiers, habitants chateau et presente condolences occasion enterrement officer a lieu ce jour." [*sic* – either the mayor was not very literate or the Germans had poor French!] *The body of Graf von Westerholt was laid to rest next to the grave of the fallen Oberleutnant Freiherr von Weichs. Because the field post failed completely at the beginning of the campaign, it was not until 11th September that the regiment received news of the death of Graf von Westerholt, who was equally respected by his superiors and subordinates.'*

One anonymous member of *4th Squadron* has also left us a vivid description of the fighting viewed from ground level.

The 26 August was the day of Caudry. The regiment was located in Béthencourt. The order to attack arrived. We approached the summit of a hill. Freiherr von Landsberg mounted "Minister", because his horse "Salome" had become excited and uncontrollable. Now the bullets began to whistle past our ears. Hand signals were given: "Dismount! Stand by to fight on foot! Riflemen forward!" My faithful horse "Minna" reared up, having been hit on the neck by a bullet. Kürassier Scholz collapsed in front of me and I had to jump over him. Our Squadron Leader assumed command and Leutnants von Galen and von Davier command of the dismounted elements. Advancing in individual short dashes, we arrived at a farmyard. The sections were reorganised. Leutnant von Davier requisitioned bread and bacon there and distributed it amongst the men. Shrapnel rounds burst overhead. One at a time we squeezed through a hole in the barn, so as to emerge in a sunken road 800 metres from Caudry. My section was the last to leave the farmstead. By then the British were directing all their fire on the small exit. One, two, three, the sunken road was reached. Major von Madai leapt up, signalled direction with both arms and shouted: "One section advance in bounds to extend the flank to the left." "Go! Double march! Down!" My section took cover behind piles of straw. Enemy bullets drilled holes in the soft ground left and right of us. It was like watching mice. We dashed forward from stack to stack. One final dash and we inclined to the right and the extension of the line was achieved. We lay there in a shallow ditch. The music of battle made a hellish racket. Some telephone wires, which had been shot through, dangled down. Bleating, a herd of sheep wandered out into the road. The

British were well dug in in front of Caudry. We only caught occasional glimpses of them. Lying by a tree was Oberst Seiffert, our Brigade Commander, who had been first to advance. Hussars and Uhlans arrived as reinforcements. All the sections were mixed up. Lying next to me was a member of 5th Uhlans [14 Brigade], who told me some brilliant stories about the Rhineland. Along the line of riflemen came a message from Leutnant von Davier: "I have lost my monocle. Whoever finds it, give it to me later!" We had a good laugh at this critical order given at such a time. From time to time there was a definite lull in the battle and we could relax a little. Tiredness was overcoming any thought of fear. The word spread that the infantry would be joining the attack in twenty minutes, but these minutes became several hours. About 1.00 pm, the first heavy greeting was on its way to Caudry. Tensely, but happily, we watched the effect of these exploding shells. Our artillery concentrated on bringing heavy shells down on the factory. That evening the scenes in Caudry and around the factory were said to be dreadful. The battle died away gradually. About 5.00 pm we rallied. Our Regimental Adjutant, Freiherr von Weichs, had been killed. He had been hit by a bullet when he was standing next to our commander. Many men helped themselves to a British coat.

Unteroffizier **Arthur Loeser. 4. Ku.7, KiA 26 August 1914.**

There were a great many lying around and they were made of excellent material. We buried the dead by the farmstead, then the soldiers returned to their horses, which had been under heavy fire and had had to be withdrawn. The squadron losses were considerable. In the farmyard lay the seriously wounded. On a stretcher and moaning deliriously was Oberleutnant Graf von Westerholt from 5th Squadron, who had been shot through the stomach. He was to die three days later. I remained behind on guard with a few others. Graf von Galen, a cousin of the fallen adjutant, brought the horses forward. Despite his neck wound, my horse "Minna" was in quite good spirits. A lightweight cart arrived and we placed the body of the adjutant on it and took him to the cemetery in Beauvois. White shutters were removed from a house on the way and used to make a temporary coffin for the dead man. The *cemetery was located outside Beauvois. As evening fell, guards were posted around the cemetery and the gravedigger dug a grave. The grave was ready and the body was lowered slowly down. The grave digger then resumed his duties. We took off our helmets to pray, gathered around the heap of freshly dug earth. In the distance we could see the muzzle flashes of the guns and the flames of Caudry lit up the night sky. Moving away from this place of the dead, we continued, with God's help, the battle for King and Fatherland.*

The centre of the 3rd Division: 8 Brigade.

It was the very late arrival of the 3rd Division that, perhaps, more than anything decided Smith-Dorrien that a further withdrawal would be impossible because of the exhausted condition of the men. 8 Brigade held the ground (developing more partly dug trenches, prepared by French civilians) to the east and north of Audencourt, with the line extended westwards to the railway line running south to the east of Caudry. Because of the considerable German pressure on Caudry (which formed a salient out of the British line), at about 8.30 am two weak companies of the 2nd Royal Irish Regiment were brought up immediately to the east off the railway line, where they were within 7 Brigade area.

The Germans started shelling the Brigade lines rather later than 9 Brigade's; the firing was almost coincidental with the advance of German infantry down to the Cambrai road. The infantry's machine guns only came into action at about 9am. At about 1.30pm German infantry advanced against the junction of the Royal Scots and the Gordon Highlanders, but made no progress, not least because they were enfiladed by the fire of the left company of the Gordon Highlanders.

About 3.30pm 8 Brigade received orders to retire, but communications with most of the Gordons, some of the Royal Scots and the two companies of the Royal Irish did not get through; the rest of the Brigade made good its retreat. At 2.30pm Audencourt had come under a most severe bombardment, which destroyed the Brigade transport as well as the vehicles and horses of the Headquarters. The German infantry advanced at about 5pm and came under effective fire from the units, consisting of about a thousand men, that had been left behind. At 6.45pm and again at 8.30pm heavy fire was directed at Audencourt, which of course by this stage was completely deserted.

The situation for these remaining troops became awkward. The second in command of 1/Gordons was Brevet Colonel William Gordon, VC – senior in army rank but junior in regimental rank to the CO, Lieutenant Colonel Neish; and because the force was now a mixed one, Gordon took over command – as the regimental history so diplomatically puts it, 'apparently to the displeasure of the commanding officer'. At 12.30am the force marched off through Audencourt, reached Montigny at 1.30am and by 2am the head of the column had reached the cross roads south west of Bertry. Coming under fire, it was decided to return towards Montigny, but the wrong road was taken (towards Clary) and eventually the British became trapped by German troops and guns between that village and Bertry. After about an hour or so the force surrendered and the Gordons alone lost about five hundred men – some escaped however and eventually got back through enemy held territory and reached England via Antwerp. A month later the Battalion was almost back to full strength, but it was a terrible fate. Colonel Gordon was exchanged and returned to the UK in January 1916, a good eighteen months and more before Colonel Neish.

During the follow-up in the early evening, the units of *Infantry Regiment 153* moved through the area which the Gordons had been occupying:

Around 5.00 pm the regiment advanced in a single formation towards the enemy positions. The national road [presumably the N43] *was one tangled mass of torn up trees, telegraph poles and shot-down wires, which had been caused by the effect of German artillery fire. Its edges had been used as an advanced position by the British. In the skilfully constructed main defensive position – which had been camouflaged with torn-off sugar beet leaves! – located on the summit of a flat-topped hill to the south of the road, were the bodies of many men of the Gordon Highlanders. They were strangely attired in Scottish national dress. The short womens'-style short skirts and bare knees looked repellent on the dead. An excellent topographical map was found on the body of a fallen officer. It showed the area of the Franco-Belgian border. It was an improved version of a 1:80,000 French general staff map, overprinted in English and bearing the marking, "Printed at the Ordnance Survey Office, Southampton 1909". This was yet another illustration of the long-established secret preparations for joint operations in the current theatre of war. We did not come across any more wounded. The enemy had evacuated all of them.*

Infantry Regiment 165, 14 Brigade, 7th Infantry Division which had not been involved in any of the fighting earlier in the day, was called forward under its new commander, *Oberst* von Dassel, at about 5.00 pm to begin the pursuit, but the men of this regiment were also exhausted from previous exertions, so it was not until the early morning of 27 August that the march began in earnest:

> *The march took us through burning villages full of wounded British soldiers and via Bertry to Gouy. Everywhere we came across evidence of the rapid British withdrawal. The route was littered with dumped weapons and equipment, abandoned ammunition wagons, dead horses and burning ration wagons. It was a scene that reminded us of the line of retreat in Belgium. More and more prisoners moved past us heading for the church in Bertry. It was this that above all demonstrated the scale of the success of the previous day to the soldiers. The numbers increased so rapidly that arrangements for their onward movement had to be made immediately. By order of 14 Brigade, 7th Company under Hauptmann Petiscus was given the task of arranging the movement to the rear of the prisoners. They took over twenty six officers, including Colonel Gordon from the famous Scottish Highlander Regiment [sic] and 1,200 men in the church at Bertry. By that evening the company, which was reduced to two platoons, reached Troisvilles, where the night was spent in the church. The biggest problem was the provision of rations, because most food was being obtained at that time by requisitioning; not until much later did the supply of food through official channels begin. Hauptmann Petiscus therefore arranged for some wagons filled with enormous cauldrons to accompany the party. These provided the only means of feeding the 1,400 strong party. Hauptmann Petiscus made special mention in his report of the outstanding support in the maintenance of good order which he received from the British officers in general and Colonel Gordon in particular.*

4th Battalion Middlesex Regiment [4/Middx]

4/Middlesex had fought a hard battle at Mons and had suffered some dreadful losses; at roll call on the evening of 23 August it had only 275 men, but over a hundred of the 'casualties' reappeared over the next few days. It is likely that the strength had crept up to about 350 or so by the time that they reached Audencourt, with stragglers rejoining by then.

The Battalion reach Audencourt soon after the thunder storm had passed over; having set off at 5am that morning, the men had had a march lasting over twelve hours. Fortunately they were not called upon to find the outposts for the Brigade position, which was centred on this small hamlet. These were provided by the Royal Scots (on the right) and the Gordons (on the left). In the morning the trenches were improved, two weak companies of the Royal Irish moved to the left of the position, beyond the Gordons, whilst its two remaining companies were in reserve in the sunken road that ran through Audencourt in a north south direction. 4/Middx had one company in the front line, prolonging the line of the Royal Scots and connecting up with the neighbouring 9 Brigade; one company was in rear of the Royal Scots, capable of firing over their heads at the enemy; whilst the remaining two companies were in reserve in the eastern corner of Audencourt.

At about 6am the picquets, which had been positioned north of the Cambrai road, fell back in good order; the initial shelling by the Germans did very little damage and the men were able to continue working on improving the trenches. In the early stages the British artillery was able to keep the Germans at bay, the infantry acting as interested observers. At about 9am the machine guns of both the Royal Scots and the Middlesex fired on Germans who were attempting to cross the Cambrai road. This happy situation, whereby 4/Middx were hardly affected by proceedings, continued until about 4pm. The Battalion withdrew, at about 5pm, without incident towards Vermand, though it had lost all its transport and horses to shell fire which had destroyed the farmyard where they were being kept. There is no record of the casualties suffered by the Battalion – in fact the War Diary entry for the day comes to the princely total of thirty six words!

2nd Battalion Royal Scots (2/R Scots).

Once it became clear that a stand was to be made in the early hours of 26 August, the CO, Lieutenant Colonel McMiking, sent a platoon to man the high ground between Inchy and Béthencourt, north of the Cambrai road; they were to act as a screen for any British cavalry that still remained beyond the British line. It returned safely before the Germans opened fire on the position. The men of the Battalion

Moving up in good order to stem the Geman advance.

showed initiative by stripping the garden fences of Audencourt of their barbed wire and fringed the forward edge of their trenches (which overlooked Beaumont and Inchy from the south west) with it. The companies were situated in a line, right to left, A, B, C and finally D, on the left; with Battalion HQ behind D's trenches. Two years earlier the Battalion had purchased its own field telephone system, which worked admirably and kept contact with the companies until it was destroyed by shell fire. Because of the need to push the Brigade line some five hundred yards to the right, towards Caudry, a platoon from D was shifted to cover the gap created on the left and took up a position on the right of A Company.

8 Brigade front was bare and flattish, and therefore the Germans were slow to advance towards it, concentrating instead on the exposed position of 7 Brigade in the Caudry salient. An attack launched against Caudry at 2pm was combined with one against the inside flanks of the Gordons and the Royal Scots, but the latter attack was easily seen off. The utter destruction by shell fire of Audencourt took place in the afternoon; amongst other casualties there were the pipes and drums of the Battalion. At 4.30pm the withdrawal commenced, with the whole Battalion getting away except for the two platoons closest to 1/Gordons. However, the withdrawal, in full view of the enemy, meant

111

that the casualties were heavy – Captain Shafto DSO (D Company) was killed – he is buried in Caudry British Cemetery; and several others were wounded or missing, including the commanding officer. D Company was reduced to seventeen men, though stragglers did augment the numbers; two platoons were, of course, caught up with 1/Gordons.

1st Battalion Gordon Highlanders (1/Gordons).

1/Gordons' position gave them a front of about a thousand yards. There were a few times in the day when the Battalion's fire power came into action – at about 9am, as mentioned above and again at 2pm when the Germans attempted to advance to the right of the Battalion, an attack seen off by the combined firepower of the Gordons and the Royal Scots. At 5pm the Germans tried again [note that this was after most other units had left the field], surging forward in close formation; 'though they displayed great bravery and persistence, they once more failed to make progress'.

The Brigade ordered a retirement at about 3.30pm; for whatever reason, the order never reached the Gordons, the two companies of the Royal Irish and a platoon of the Royal Scots. The regimental historian, Cyril Falls, noted dryly that the situation as to who was in command of the remaining force was 'a complication which only the British service could have produced'.

Again for unknown reasons, the Gordons and the remnants of the other two battalions were only gathered together for the withdrawal at midnight. The subtext in the histories (both Official and regimental) suggest there was a considerable *frisson* between the two colonels. The bare bones of what happened next has already been given above; but Falls provides fuller details of the final minutes before the surrender:

> *At 2am the head of the column was fired on south west of Bertry. The column – certainly its advanced guard – extended and returned the fire. As it appeared to be suicidal to attempt to fight a way through in darkness and against opposition of unknown strength, thoroughly on the alert, the troops were ordered to fall back on the Montigny road. Instead of turning off right handed by the way they had come, they kept straight on south westward to Clary, a mistake which, even in darkness, seems inexplicable except by extreme fatigue.*

German gunners struggling to bring their guns to bear.

Suddenly they found themselves facing a field gun trained to fire down the road, which was nearly straight. The gun was seized before it could be discharged, but the rear of the column at once came under fire from the south. It extended and returned the fire whilst the head made a desperate attempt to force a way out of the trap by breaking through Clary. A ferocious fire fight followed, lasting an hour, but it was so one-sided that the end was inevitable.

> *Various little parties of stragglers must have joined the column at one point or another, for a German account states that ten regiments, including artillery, were represented among the 700 prisoners taken. Of these approximately 500 were Gordon Highlanders.'*

Amongst the officers killed, only two have known graves – Lieutenant APF Lyon in Bertry Communal Cemetery and Lieutenant JK Trotter in Caudry British Cemetery. All that remained of 1/Gordons was the transport and three platoons, which had withdrawn from the battlefield in time.

> We are fortunate to have a memoir of 1/Gordons in these first few days of the war, *Wounded and a Prisoner*, written by Major MV Hay of the Special Reserve, 3/Gordons (at the time of Le

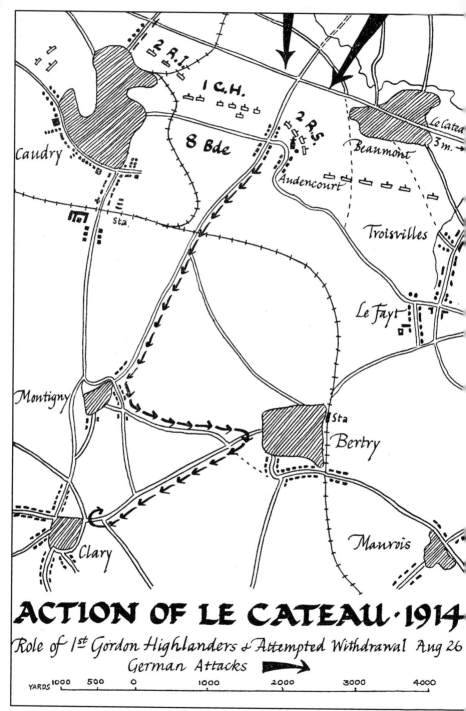

Map 13. 1st Gordon Highlanders at Le Cateau.

Cateau he was a subaltern).

'In the chill light of dawn trenches were being dug outside the village...the position of No 13 Platoon [his – part of D Company] *was about half way to Caudry, close to a small square shaped plantation. The rear of my platoon had just cleared the wood when a shell burst overhead, and we had the unpleasant experience of digging trenches under fire.*

He suggests that the Germans already had a battery placed behind Petit Caudry, which was east of Caudry on the Cambrai road, and that their observer was probably in the church tower at Béthencourt; the latter saw the troops coming out of the wood and therefore signalled the guns to open fire. In fact the guns were soon driven off by an attack from the British coming out of Caudry.

The platoon established range marks; the Cambrai road, then lined with poplars, provided an easy one, at a distance of 350 yards. 'At the edge of the village [Béthencourt], on the ridge of the hill, the gate post of a small paddock was our second range mark – 900 yards.' A third, at 1200 yards, was indicated by telegraph poles in a beetroot field on top of a hill to the right front.

Our trench was dug in a stubble field where the corn had just been stooked and it was now our business to push the stooks over. This gave occasion for a great display of energy and excitement. When the stooks had been laid low we made a very poor attempt to disguise the newly thrown up earth by covering the top of the trenches with straw, which only seemed to make our positions more conspicuous than ever. The trench was lined with straw and we cut seats and made various little improvements. Then our guns began to speak.

At the corner of the village of Béthencourt there stands (or stood that morning) a farmhouse. In the adjacent paddock two cows were peacefully browsing. The first shell burst right above them. They plunged and kicked and galloped about, but soon settled down again to graze. Several shells hit the church tower; the fifth or sixth set fire to a large square white house near the church on the right. Our gunners made good practice at the two cows and shell after shell burst over or near their paddock, from which they finally escaped to gallop clumsily along the ridge of the hill and disappear into the wood, no doubt carrying bits of shrapnel with them.

About 9am the German artillery got to work. Many attempts have been made to describe the situation in a trench when an artillery duel is in progress, but really no words can give any idea of the intensity of the confusion. On both our flanks machine guns maintained a steady staccato. All other sounds were sudden and nerve-straining, especially the sudden rush of the large German shell followed by the roar of its explosion in Audencourt, where dust and debris rise up like smoke from a volcano, showing the enemy that the target had been hit.

The Huns evidently suspected that the little wood on our right rear is being used to conceal artillery, for they dropped dozens of shells into it, doing no harm to anything except the trees. The noise of the shells bursting among the branches just behind us was most disturbing. Sometimes these shells pitched short of the wood; they were then less noisy but far more unpleasant in other respects. Just when the uproar was at its highest a scared face appeared over the back of my trench and stated that four ammunition boxes lay at the far corner of the wood at our disposal, please. The owner of the face, having delivered his message, rose up and returned whence he had come, doubled up yet running at great speed.

...Gradually the number of our own shells grew less and less as our batteries were silenced or forced, or perhaps ordered, to retire. As this went on it became evident – far more evident than at Mons – that we were up against overwhelming odds. The rush of shells reached a maximum, and then for a space there was silence. Pipes and cigarettes, up to now smoked only by the fearless ones, for a short time appeared on every side, and conversational remarks were shouted from one trench to another.

The Germans now concentrated their artillery on the trenches, having used a spotter aircraft to identify them. Some infantry advanced across the beetroot fields where the telegraph poles gave the 1200 yards range mark; these were dealt with by machine gun.

It was not long before we had a chance of getting rid of some ammunition. German troops, debouching from the little wood where the cows had taken refuge earlier in the day, now advanced across the stubble field on top of the hill, moving to their left flank across our front. My glasses showed that they were extended to not more than two paces, keeping a very bad line, evidently very weary and marching in the hot sun with manifest disgust.

The command, "Five rounds rapid at the stubble field 900 yards," produced a cinematographic picture in my field glasses.

116

German dead scattered across a battlefield early in the war.

The Germans hopped into cover like rabbits. Some threw themselves flat behind the corn stooks and when the firing ceased got up and bolted back to the wood. Two or three who had also appeared to fling themselves down remained motionless.

The enemy, having discovered that we could be dangerous at even 900 yards, then successfully crossed the stubble field in two short rushes without losing a man, and reinforced their men who were advancing through the beetroot fields on our right.

Great numbers of troops now began to appear on the ridge between Béthencourt and the little wood. They advanced in three or four lines of sections of ten or fifteen men extended to two paces. Their line of advance was directed on to the village of Audencourt and on the low plateau on our right, so that we were able to pour on hem an enfilade fire. They were advancing in short rushes across pasture-land which provided no cover whatever, and they offered a clearly visible target even when lying down. Although our men were nearly all first class shots, they did not often hit the target. This was owing to the unpleasant fact that the German gunners kept up a steady stream of shrapnel which burst just in front of our trenches and broke over the top like a wave. Shooting at the enemy had to be timed by the bursting shell.

We adopted the plan of firing two rounds and then ducking down at intervals, which were determined as far as could be arranged by the arrival of the shell. But the shooting of the Battalion was good enough to delay the enemy's advance. From the 900 yard mark they took more than an hour to reach their first objective, which was the Route Nationale [Cambrai road], 400 yards from our nearest trench. Here they were able to concentrate in great numbers, as the road runs along an embankment behind which nothing but artillery could reach them. This was the situation on our front at about three o'clock in the afternoon. I happened to look down the line and saw Captain Lumsden looking rather anxiously to the rear. I then saw that a number of our people were retiring. There was not much time to think what this might mean as the enemy were beginning to cross the road; we had fixed bayonets and I thought that we would have little chance against the large number of Germans who had concentrated behind the embankment. For a long time, for nearly an hour, the British guns had been silent, but they had not all retired. With a white star-shaped flash two shells bust right over the road behind which the Germans were massed. These two shells must have knocked out forty or fifty men. The enemy fled right back up the hill up to the 900 yard mark followed by rapid fire and loud cheering from all along the line.

The Germans were now reforming on the hillside and a machine gun hidden in the village of Béthencourt began to play up and down our trench. The bullets began to spray too close to my left ear, and laying my glasses on the parapet I was about to sit down for a few minutes rest, and indeed had got half way down to the sitting position, when the machine gun found its target.

Recollections of what passed through my mind at that moment are very clear. I knew instantly what had happened. The blow might have come from a sledge hammer, except that it seemed to carry with it an impression of speed. I saw for one instant in my mind's eye the battlefield at which I had been gazing through my glasses the whole day. Then the vision was hidden by a scarlet

German Maxim 08 machine guns in improvised firing positions. Each infantry regiment had six of these grouped into a specialist machine gun company.

circle, and a voice said, "Mr H. has got it." Through the red mist of the scarlet circle I looked at my watch (the movement to do so had begun in my mind before I was hit); it was spattered with blood; the hands showed five minutes to four. The voice which had spoken before said, "Mr H. is killed".

A soldier with him in the trench, Private Sinclair, made him as comfortable as he could and by digging under the parapet made a shelter for Hay. He had periodic bouts of consciousness – for example he was aware that Sinclair was trying to protect his face from shrapnel by covering it with his hands. Eventually the order came to move at midnight.

Sinclair and the other occupants of the trench lifted me out, this operation coinciding with a fusillade from the enemy, who from their position on the road were firing volleys into the night – a great waste of ammunition. Still, the bullets must have been close overhead, for the men put me back into the trench, jumped in after me, and waited till all was quiet.

The second attempt to get me out was more successful. I was laid on to a greatcoat and lifted up by six men. It is probably not easy to carry along such a burden in the dark, and they made a very bad job of it. Some one suggested that a substitute for a stretcher could be made with three rifles, and the suggestion was at once adopted with most painful results. I still remember the agony caused by the weight of my body pressing down on my head and the small of my back, while my head, just clearing the ground, trailed amongst the wet beetroot leaves. The distance to the little wood was not great, but to me the journey seemed to take hours.

There Hay lay for some hours; attempts to find a stretcher failed and eventually the two soldiers who had stayed loyally by him were ordered to move off, having left him as comfortable as possible. Interestingly enough, Sinclair got separated from the Battalion and took shelter for a while – an indeterminate number of days – in Caudry, sheltered by French civilians; and then decided to head for home. He must have succeeded, for according to this account Sinclair was a sergeant by the end of the war.

In the morning a straggler from the Royal Irish Rifles came across him and moved him into the sunken road leading from Audencourt to the Cambrai road, which emerges west of Beaumont. Hay was concerned about the possibility of being hit by stray shells whilst he was out in the open.

In full daylight he started observing people passing by. Some French 'peasants' came along but steered clear of him – understandable in the circumstances. He then saw a a small group of Germans sweeping the ground in extended order; one saw him. 'They all came and stood on the road in a circle. Their attitude was distinctly sympathetic, but I was too far gone to struggle with their language.' As time went by he saw more and more German troops and cavalry, transport wagons and machine guns.

For some inexplicable reason I now tried to get away. By seizing a tuft of grass in the left hand (his right arm and legs were paralyzed) I could move along a few inches at a time. After advancing in this manner about a foot along the edge of the road, I collapsed from exhaustion, and drew the greatcoat over my head. I do not know how long I had been thus covered up when I heard a shout and, peeping through one of the holes in the coat, saw a German soldier standing on top of the bank. He was gesticulating and pointing to his revolver, trying to find out if I was armed! But he soon saw I was past any further fighting.

He offered me a drink from his water bottle and pointed to the Red Cross on his arm. I can never hope to convey to anyone what a relief it was to me to see the cross, even on the arm of an enemy. The man asked me if I could walk, tried to lift me up, and when he saw I was paralyzed said he would go for a stretcher. "You will go away and leave me here," I said. "I am of the Red Cross," he replied; "you are therefore my Kamarad and I will come back and I will never leave you."

The soldier went off and some time later a small group of French civilians came along, searching for wounded. They put him on a stretcher – 'to lie on the stretcher after the hard ground was inexpressible relief to my tired limbs'. About to set off, his German friend reappeared, with others, joined in due course by an Uhlan officer (all German cavalry seem to be described as Uhlans!). There then followed a heated discussion as to which stretcher Hay should be taken away on. The officer eventually settled the matter by addressing Hay: 'Choissez'. I answered him with a smile, 'J'y suis, j'y reste'.

The German Red Cross soldier came up to my stretcher and took my hand, "Adieu, Kamarad". The young German officer leant over and offered me a bit of chocolate. "Why have you English come against us?" he said; "it is no use. We shall be in Paris in three days. We have no quarrels with you English."

Hay was taken to a house in Caudry and nursed by a French family through the crisis of his illness (during which the Last Rites were administered); and from there he went to a hospital in Caudry, where he made a reasonable recovery.

The left of the 3rd Division: 7 Brigade, in the Caudry Salient

The Brigade had formed the rear guard for the 3rd Division on the 25th. There had been considerable problems with German probing in the area of Solesmes, which was not finally resolved until late in the evening, and in the confusion numerous men became lost; the result was that the Brigade was highly disorganised and very under strength when most of it turned up at various stages well after dark into Caudry (for example, 3/Worcs did not get there until about midnight). Indeed

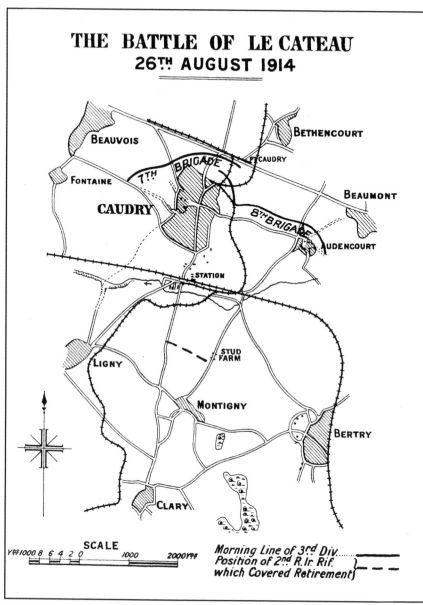

THE BATTLE OF LE CATEAU
26TH AUGUST 1914

BETHENCOURT

BEAUVOIS

7TH BRIGADE

FONTAINE

PT CAUDRY

BEAUMONT

CAUDRY

8TH BRIGADE

AUDENCOURT

STATION

STUD
FARM

LIGNY

MONTIGNY

BERTRY

CLARY

SCALE
YDS 1000 8 6 4 2 0   1000   2000 YDS

Morning Line of 3rd Div.
Position of 2nd R. Ir. Rif.
which Covered Retirement

Map 14. 3rd Division's Front

122

2/Irish Rifles, the rearguard of the Brigade on the 25th, had completely lost contact and eventually turned up at about 2am at Le Cateau; and from there was ordered to move immediately to Maurois (on the Roman road, south east of Reumont) with 41 Battery (which the Battalion had collected near Amerval). The Battalion had marched forty five miles in forty eight hours and had fought a battle on the 23rd.

The battalions were disposed as follows: 1/Wilts to the right (north east) of the town; 2/S Lancs (which had suffered some 300 casualties in the Mons fighting) and 56 Field Co. RE to the north of the town, beyond the Roman road and to the left of the road running north to Quiévy; and 3/Worcs the remainder of the line to the north and north west of Caudry. A divisional reserve, especially in the absence of the Irish Rifles, was formed of men from the First Line Transport, signal sections and any others available.

No order, it appears, reached the Brigade with the decision to hold the line; in any case, the German attack here came before any scheduled move. By 7am German troops were advancing against both flanks of the town with some commitment, the Worcesters in particular getting close attention. It should be noted how great the open gap was between 7 Brigade on the 3rd Division's left and 11 Brigade on the 4th Division's right. To help to ease the situation, at 8.30am two weak companies of 2/R Irish Regiment were borrowed from 8 Brigade and placed in a railway cutting to the north east of the town; in due course these moved back into the 8 Brigade line (on the extreme left) and 2/S Lancs took their place.

2/Irish Rifles turned up at about 9am and were promptly sent to hold a rear position a kilometre or so south of the town, near Tronquoy, a small settlement based on a large stud farm; 41 Battery took up a firing position to its right rear.

The *Official History*'s account says simply that things in Caudry went along more or less fine until about noon: 'Until noon the 7th Infantry Brigade contained the Germans without difficulty, and they gained little or no ground'. Lieutenant Johnston's account below will tend to throw a different light on things, but it as well to remember that, in the great scheme of things, and relative to events on other parts of the battlefield, the *Official History* is not inaccurate. The *History* suggests that the German's relative inactivity was probably due to a policy of waiting for the pressure on the flanks to have their effect on the whole of Smith-Dorrien's position.

From about noon German shelling eased, and half a company of the Royal Irish Rifles was sent into the town to bolster the defences. Then the guns opened fire with a far greater intensity at about 1.40pm, directed, at least at first, principally at Caudry. It was at this time that German infantry made their failed attempt towards Audencourt. The result of the frightening shelling of Caudry was that the town was effectively abandoned, and by 2pm German infantry were occupying much, if not all, of it. However, by about 3pm 3/Worcs had launched a counter attack and regained much of the town, with the exception of the northern-most part. The (albeit temporary) loss of Caudry had a knock on effect on 11 Brigade, as will be explained in the next chapter. The situation at Caudry was not helped by the fact that 7 Brigade's commander, McCracken, had been temporarily disabled by a shell; it seems likely that McCracken ordered the retirement from Caudry, which was an error: his military career did not prosper. Command fell on Colonel Bird (he was told by General Hamilton soon after 3pm), commanding 2/R Irish Rifles at Troncquoy; he was instructed to withdraw 7 Brigade, which he had achieved by 4.30pm, when the last British troops left Caudry, not to see it again for over four years (unless, of course, they were taken prisoner in intervening battles to the west). 2/R Irish Rifles suffered thirty four wounded and sixty killed or missing.

The *Official History* is silent about 2/S Lancs and 1/Wilts; the regimental history of the Wiltshire Regiment, not a very big tome in any case, has very little to say about Le Cateau. The war diary is succinct in the extreme: *Wilts held NE edge of Coudry* [sic] *the whole morning, were heavily shelled and attacked by infantry and suffered 80 – 100 casualties*. Johnston was scathing about the behaviour of many of the troops in Caudry; as indeed was Corporal John Lucy of the Royal Irish Rifles. He was attached at the time with the transport of his battalion, and therefore had arrived late at Caudry, whilst the bulk of the rest of the unit was considered as definitely lost – it will be remembered that it finally turned up at about 9am. He gives a vivid description, from a soldier's perspective, of the battle around Caudry in his book *There's a Devil in the Drum*, published in 1938 and reprinted in 1993 by the Naval and Military Press. It is a quite outstanding account by a pre war regular soldier who had a fascinating career during the war, eventually being commissioned into his own Regiment (and Battalion), a singular honour.

2nd Battalion South Lancashire Regiment was in a very weakened state after the severe casualties it had sustained during the fighting at Frameries, south of Mons, on 24 August and its rearguard actions in conjunction with 1st Battalion Wiltshire Regiment at Solesmes the previous evening. The battalion transport had become separated from the main body during the withdrawal, but thanks to the immense energy of the quartermaster, Lieutnant Sidney Boast (one of three Boast brothers who served with the Battalion during the Great War) it was withdrawn under artillery fire and under the very noses of the German cavalry. The war diary has almost nothing to say about the fighting at Le Cateau, but it is known that the companies, some of whom did not arrive into position until the early hours of 26 August, were dug in just to the north of Caudry and that they held their positions from early morning, not finally withdrawing until 5.00 pm. Such was the confusion that one party of 140 men under the command of the RSM, TV Roberts, after a series of adventures and skirmishes, did not finally rejoin until the battalion was at Chartres on 5th September. The casualties of Frameries and the Retreat from Mons amounted to five officers and 149 OR killed with seven officers and 301 OR wounded and exceeded those suffered by the regiment throughout the Peninsular War.

Alexander Johnston was commissioned into the Worcesters in 1903; he spent 1907 – 1910 serving with the West African Frontier Force. At the time of Le Cateau he was based at Brigade Headquarters and was a lieutenant in command of the signal section. By September 1917 he was a brigadier general; he was soon afterwards severely wounded and took no further part in the war. During his convalescence he wrote up the diary he had kept, making sure he did not change entries with the benefit of hindsight. It is a very important memoir and he a respected observer – for example a chunk of his diary can be found with the War Diary of 7 Brigade for these early months of the war. Johnston was also a brave man – he won two DSOs and an MC. His diary (when he was a brigade major) has already been extensively quoted by Nigel Cave in Vimy Ridge in this series. The diary has been published very recently.

Johnston gives us an interesting description of the retreat during 24 and 25 August.

24 August: *We started our march back to Bavai, some thirteen miles distant – rather stiff after a long morning's fight, on a very hot day, and in retirement too. One got a slight idea of what a terrible thing defeat in war may be. Wounded men had had to be left behind in the chateau at Ciply, others were in the ambulances, others bandaged up tried to march along, men were scattered all over the place, very tired after the morning's long and anxious fighting, while the road was very hard, dusty and hot. However the men stuck to it well and were not the least bit* *demoralised. At first 2/South Lancs, who were rather disorganised, could only muster about a hundred men and the Battalion (3/Worcs) only some 400 etc., but as we got on small parties joined in and battalions began to look more like battalions again. But what a catastrophe might have ensued if there had been no-one to cover us, and if the Germans had been able to follow up closely and attack us when the men were so exhausted! A long weary march back and reached Bavai myself about 3 pm. Found the place crowded with troops of all kinds, mostly transport, Staffs and L of C* [Lines of Communication] *troops etc. When I was there the remnants of 2 Cavalry Brigade came in: they seem to have had a fearful doing, had had to charge a large force of infantry and guns, and consequently had lost heavily. Had a talk with Grenfell of the 9th Lancers who said that our fellows were more than a match for the German cavalry where the numbers were reasonably equal, but that in the big engagements the Germans seemed to have enormous numbers to employ. Our Brigade was put into a field preparatory to going into billets, but we had hardly taken off our equipment when we heard that the 5th Division was in difficulties and it was therefore necessary to move out and help them. Though the men were dog tired and had had nothing to eat all day, they stuck it well and they marched till dark. As we were not required to fight, I presume the 5th Division were able to get clear. Ended up near a place called Wargnies where I at last got a meal and had a sleep in the barn with some of 2/Irish Rifles. Lost four of my men, but I expect they will join later on. The days' operations have been very disappointing and difficult to understand. It seems that we were up against a force a lot stronger than our ourselves. It is a pity that after continually endeavouring to foster the spirit of the initiative and attack, that we should immediately have at once had to act on the defensive and, more particularly, that after trying to dig oneself into defence as strongly as possible, a retirement should have had to be made so early. We certainly ought to have reconnoitred and commenced work on a position the first day we arrived at Ciply, and 2/South Lancs' trenches were undoubtedly badly sited.*

25 August: *Started the day badly as I got no orders from the Brigade Major or information as to the movement of the different units and it is obviously impossible to keep communication if one does not know the position of the troops. However, after having*

"The Retreat".

a fair breakfast on bread and jam at 4 am, went direct to the place which I knew the main body must pass which proved right. Again I could do little as the General would never stay in his place for more than a minute. We continued our retirement which went on without incident for some time. The heat was awful and the march seemed endless. A certain number of the men began to tail off and straggled in an appalling manner. A retirement certainly seems to have a vast demoralising effect, discipline seems to relax, little attempt seems to be made to keep the ranks, and men fall out to get drinks or food or to lie down. One soon learnt if one did not know before which were the best disciplined battalions, and one did not see so many stragglers from 1/Wilts and 3/Worcs. The country people are kindness itself and give the men refreshments all along the line: it is misplaced, as the more a man drinks, the more he wants it later on, the worse his thirst gets and the more exhausted he becomes. We heard during the morning that the French had been pushed out of Valenciennes and that Namur had fallen. We had not been worried in the rear at all, and it was obvious now that the danger was to our left (eastern) flank. We therefore stopped taking up a series of positions, closed up the column and pushed on as far as possible, leaving 2/R Irish Rifles as rearguard. No incident for a bit except that the straggling was bad and the intense heat of course made things worse. Just after passing Romeries, the Brigade got checked on the high ground above Solesmes, which is in a deep hollow with steep and narrow streets resulting in the transport etc. getting blocked. Every minute's delay was making things more serious, our cavalry could be seen in action on our left – very interesting – and stragglers from a French Territorial Regt. which had been cut up by the Germans came pouring in from that direction. Yet there we waited right out in the open along a road that could be seen for miles, the artillery and infantry in column of route affording an excellent target to the enemy's artillery should they spot us: this they eventually did and promptly sent over some shrapnel which luckily did no harm.

General Allenby, commanding our cavalry, came up and spoke to General McCracken [7 Brigade commander] *to say that he was afraid he could not cover us any more. 1/Wilts then extended and took up a position while he, after a certain amount of galloping about with messages on my part, placed 2/South Lancs where required. These were to cover the retirement of the rest of the Brigade, helped by a couple of batteries who I am told did splendid work later, firing off every round they had though the Germans had got close up to them, and then coolly and in perfect order limbering up and trotting off as if on parade. The General then said that he must find out where 2/R Irish Rifles were, so I rode out through Romeries rather anxious lest I should get caught by the German cavalry. I went about a mile beyond the village when an old man stopped me and told me that there were some Germans around the corner, and as I could hear no infantry fire it was obvious that 2/R Irish Rifles had left the main road, no doubt because the Germans were threatening their left rear and probably had sheared off to their right a bit. I then rode back to the village and struck out east, came upon one of our cavalry patrols who knew nothing, however, about the movements of 2/R Irish Rifles. I then made my way back to Solesmes where there was a stiffish fight going on, the rearguard trying to hold the Germans back until the guns and the transport could be got through the town. 2/South Lancs retired too soon and men of my Signal Section were pushed up into the firing line to give a helping hand: several of them I've not seen since, including Sgt Rouse* [he appears to have survived this encounter]*: his is an irreplaceable loss and I am still hoping against hope that he is not killed, may have slipped off somewhere and will rejoin me somewhere: he was an excellent fellow in every way. The General then told me to go with him into the town and try to get the guns etc. through. On the way we met Haslam, Wandby and Neame of the 18th Hussars who said that they had been having an awful time of it, but had managed to get through unhurt so far. The confusion in the town was appalling, the place being packed not only with our fellows but with civilians and the remnants of the French Territorial Regt., and the traffic was continually being blocked. If the Germans had driven in our rearguard and got onto the hill above the town sooner, they would have had us at their mercy. As it was as the stuff was being pushed through there was something like panic* *amongst the less stout hearted, they with guns, carts etc. trotting to the rear as fast as they could. I was then detailed to go and try and find 2/R Irish Rifles once more. I had a fearful ride all by myself over miles of country in the pitch dark and the drizzling rain, never knowing when I might not run into a German patrol, and of course finding it very difficult to keep my bearings in the strange country. At one place some cottagers very kindly revived me a bit with a drink of water with a touch of brandy in it and gave poor old Broncho (my horse) a drink. I came across French Territorials making their way to Le Cateau, and men in the 14th, 8th and 9th Brigades, but not a sign did I get of 2/R Irish Rifles. I had had practically no food since four in the morning and by now must have covered quite some sixty miles altogether, both myself and my horse (which had cast three shoes!) were dead beat. However an officer with a picquet of 1/Dorsets, who at first thought I was a Uhlan patrol approaching, revived me with a little bread and butter. I eventually got into Caudry, a largish town, about midnight, where the confusion was awful, guns, wagons and troops crowding the streets and trying to find out where their units were. Could only find two men of my Section! Reported at the Town Hall to say that I could not find 2/R Irish Rifles, got some food at an adjacent hotel and went to sleep in the stable.*

3rd Battalion Worcestershire Regiment (3/Worcesters).

Of all the Great War regimental histories, arguably the most magnificent production is that of the Worcestershire Regiment, written by Stacke. It truly is a labour of love as is shown by the detail in the text, the profusion of illustrations and the quite extraordinary number of detailed maps; whilst the original, very large, volume was produced to the highest possible publishing standards. It certainly does not fail to live up to expectations as regards the actions of 3/Worcesters at Le Cateau.

It was nearly midnight when 3/Worcs entered Caudry. When the troops marched in they were somewhat astonished to see shops still lighted and people sitting at the little tables of the cafés; but all ranks were too tired for such wonderment. The Battalion came to a halt in an open space at the northern end of the town. There the Battalion transport was parked. The companies were told off to billets [in the Rue de Bruxelles] *and the troops were hospitably received by the inhabitants.*

Outposts were established along the line of main road [the Cambrai road] north of the town, and it was learned that preparations had been made for defence. Positions had been selected in the vicinity and had been entrenched by local labour. It was not possible to reconnoitre those positions in the darkness, but the company commanders were informed, and arrangements were made for local guides to lead the companies from their billets to the prepared trenches. As yet nothing was known as to the general plan. It was uncertain whether the Brigade was to fight the next day or was to continue the retreat.

Dispersed in their billets, the tired troops slept heavily for some two hours. Then came a sudden alarm [about 2.30am]; an outpost on the main road had observed suspicious movements in front. The platoons were roused; boots and puttees were donned. Still half asleep, the troops struggled out of their billets and the companies assembled in the darkened streets.

The orders to hold and stand did not reach the Brigade before it came under enemy fire.

3/Worcs were disposed on the north and north western outskirts of the town, with D in reserve [see map]. There was some difficulty in finding the relevant trenches in the dark and then the trenches were found to be shallow and weak, so that the troops had to do the best they could to improve them with their entrenching tools.

See map p.139

The soil was muddy after the recent thunderstorm. The troops worked for some time with their entrenching tools. No attack had as yet taken place. Presently their digging slackened off and the tired soldiers dozed over their rifles. With the first grey light of dawn came a sudden bark of field guns close at hand to the north west. Shells hurtled overhead and burst over the houses.

The trenches held by B Company had been sited to face south west, apparently to command the little valley that runs up to Caudry from Beauvois. Consequently the enemy's guns took the company in enfilade. The position was puzzling at first, but when the situation was realised B Company wheeled back into a new position in the firing line (B2). There again the company was enfiladed, for German machine guns opened from Guizette Farm. To avoid that fire B Company withdrew a few hundred yards and found good cover in a sunken road on the outskirts of the houses (B3).

130

The spreading daylight revealed German cavalry and guns in the wooded valley north of Beauvois. The Battalion machine gun section was ordered up to engage them. But before the machine gunners could come into action, a section of the RHA (two guns of I Battery) unlimbered at the northern end of the town and opened fire. The enemy's guns stopped firing and shifted position and the German cavalry withdrew to a safer distance. By that time the two other battalions of the Brigade had turned out and had occupied positions on the right of 3/Worcs; but all units were intermingled and one company of 1/Wilts took up position between C and A companies of 3/Worcs. D Company was then sent forward by Colonel Stuart [CO 3/Worcs] *and took up a position close to the Wiltshire company. Small parties of the enemy were seen moving at different points along the front and several German machine guns opened fire. The British platoon answered with sharp bursts of musketry and presently the enemy's fire died down.*

A lull in the fighting then ensued, and the Battalion transport, still parked at the northern end of the town, set about preparing breakfast for the troops [although no supplies had come from the Divisional train, the second in command and the Quartermaster had obtained food locally]. *As yet no special orders had been received and it was assumed that the retreat would be continued. But before further orders had been received a fresh and heavier bombardment began. The enemy had brought up additional artillery, and shells burst in rapid succession all over the northern end of the town.*

The line of the main road north of the town afforded an easy ranging mark, and the shelling along the road became so severe that [the OC of C Company] *ordered his platoons back to new positions on the edge of the town close to the positions occupied by B Company. Further to the right the two forward platoons of A Company likewise fell back from the line of the road to the position of the remainder of the company, on the northern outskirts of the town. D and the company of 1/Wilts for a short time remained isolated, and then by mutual arrangement fell back in succession along the western outskirts of Caudry to new positions north of the railway.*

The German artillery was not unopposed. Three batteries of British field artillery (XXX (Howitzer) Brigade) had taken up position behind the ridge south east of Caudry and were engaging every available target. In order to provide an escort for those guns the Brigadier ordered one company of 3/Worcs to be sent back. A Company was selected and marched back at about 8am through the streets. Its progress was much impeded by the terror-stricken inhabitants crowding southwards out of the town, but eventually the company got clear of the houses and took up position on the high ground [A2]. There it lay for some time, watching the shell fire but seeing no good targets for musketry.

B and C Companies were more hotly engaged. From 6am onwards strong forces of the enemy came in view beyond Jeune Bois. German machine guns were again brought into action as the enemy advanced. By 8am firing was general in every direction. The shooting of the Worcestershire platoons was rapid and accurate, and such of the enemy as came south of the road were severely punished. Most of the German bullets were high and the enemy [dismounted German cavalry] *made no great attempt to come to close quarters. The two companies had not suffered heavy losses when, about 9.30am, orders came for them to fall back to a fresh position* [B3, C3]*, on high ground west of the town. The reason for the move was because of the pressure on the 4th Division on the left and the not inconsiderable gap between the flanks of 11 and 7 Brigade.*

British 4.5 in howitzer in action.

The withdrawal of the two companies was followed by a retirement of other troops from the northern end of Caudry. No very definite orders as to the length of their resistance seem to have reached the front line. All ranks knew vaguely that a general retreat was in progress. Moved by that knowledge rather than by pressure from the enemy, various units of the defending troops fell back from the northern to the southern side of the town. In doing so several units became disordered and there were many stragglers. Lieutenant Johnston...rallied stragglers of all units in the main square of the town, organised them hastily as a fighting force and led them out to a new position on a spur to the westward.

Lieutenant Johnston's account of proceedings thus far was as follows,

26 August: *Up at 3 am and tried to find my men, eventually succeeded in collecting about ten of them but Sgt Rouse was not among them. My spare horse, both pack animals, and my cart with all the equipment and also my personal kit on it, were still missing. In spite of the crush in the town, nothing much seemed to be doing and as far as one could see no arrangements made for settling on a scheme of defence – I suppose because we thought we were going to continue our retirement. Suddenly heavy firing was heard quite close. Rode out with the General to try and choose a defensive line. Had a busy time collecting various small units and posting them: it seemed that our left flank was the dangerous one, but we had some cavalry out that way. I then went back to the market square where the Brigade HQ was situated. There was a little confusion getting the gunners out of the street onto their positions. The Germans were coming on quick all round us, so every man, including transport men, the remainder of my section etc. were pushed up into the firing line. I was then sent up to the right [sic] of the line to find out the situation where 3/Worcs were. There was a lot of shell fire and a couple of slugs hit a wall within a couple of inches of me. Then went back to the square and got busy collecting reserves, issuing ammunition etc. Was next sent up to the centre where things were much the same, pretty heavy shell fire but not much rifle fire. The German was obviously acting up to his principles in his text books in which he always advocated having lots of guns near the head of his columns. There were a lot of men making their way back in a disgraceful manner, even NCOs. I managed however to stop them quite easily and to get them back into the firing line*

133

without trouble. Returned to the square and spent most of my time stopping stragglers and taking them up into the firing line. It makes one sad and anxious for the future to see Englishmen behaving like this, and the fire was not really heavy nor the losses great. Of course there were only the bad men or men whose officers had been hit and were therefore 'out of control', and one always found plenty of splendid fellows holding on gamely even if their officers had gone. Eventually it got so bad in the centre [about 9.30am], owing to the Germans having started to shell a brick house near a gasometer which our fellows had been holding, that I collected some men from about five different regiments and ran forward to get them in front of the buildings where we would not be easily seen and where we would avoid the German fire, which was mostly directed on the buildings. The position otherwise was not a very good one and there was not a good field of fire, but I thought from the point of view of 'morale' alone that it would be a good thing to get some men pushed forward. As a matter of fact I ran over fifty yards in front of the firing line before any of the men would follow me, possibly because hardly any of them knew me, and then about a dozen came along amongst whom I remember a couple of excellent Gordon Highlanders and some of my own Regiment. We lay out here [J] in the turnips about a couple of hours and had a very hot time of it. There was a heavy shrapnel fire chiefly aimed at the horses behind us so that the shells were mostly just over us: all the same there were several short ones and some fell within a few feet of me. There was continuous rifle fire at us but

British infantry firing from a field ditch.

the German musketry struck me as being poor and most of the shots were going high. However a poor devil near me was hit in the arm but managed to make his way back to the rear and then one or two of the other men [were hit] and so there were not many of us left. Next a Maxim was turned on to us, it had got the range exactly and I had a very terrifying couple of minutes with almost every bullet hitting the ground within a yard of me: however for some reason or thank goodness the Maxim never opened on us again; but it had knocked out two more of my men. After a while their artillery opened on us again but this time with the right range. I felt a sharp blow straight over the heart and later in the day actually found the bullet hole in my coat and the shrapnel bullet itself in my left hand breast pocket: it was a spent bullet which could just penetrate my coat and no more, but what an escape! A minute or two later I got a blow on the side from another bullet which had hit the ground in front of me and ricocheted on without much force, again no more harm than a big bruise though it made me feel a bit sick. I then got wounded higher up in the thigh, nothing much but hurt a bit and cut out a biggish piece of flesh. By now Corden, the Quartermaster of 1/Wilts, had made a line on the outskirts of the buildings, and I felt that we had done what was required of us and kept the men in position behind us for a long time, so I gave the order to the men to crawl back. Personally I preferred to rush some 200 yards to a deep ditch or stream, but directly I started I went over like a shot rabbit as my right leg, which had been hit, refused to work! I tried again, but once more came down after the first stride, expecting to be shot every moment as I was now in full view. At the third attempt I had better luck and got down to the ditch which was in dead ground. And along which I made my way into the town where I joined the Brigade Major (Hildyard) again.

Stacke continues:

Battalion Headquarters of 3/Worcs moved from the north of the town to a new location in a building near the railway embankment. There came disaster. A big shell hit the building and burst, killing or wounding many of the HQ personnel, including the 2 i/c and the adjutant, badly wounded. Many of the signallers were killed and for a time communication with the companies broke down.

The movement back became more definite. The field batteries south east of the town limbered up and moved off. A Company guarding the ridge above them was told of their movement. No further orders had been received, but Major Milward saw the other troops marching south and assumed that his company ought to conform to the general movement; so A Company formed up, marched in fours down the hill to the road and then turned southwards. It tramped through the arch of the railway embankment, halted on the further side and lay down on rising ground to await orders. The Divisional Commander [Hamilton] rode up. Milward explained the situation and was directed to take his company back into Caudry; it was not intended that the town should yet be abandoned. The Company fell back in again and marched back under the railway arch.

By that time Caudry was empty of troops. It had been heavily shelled and the retreating British troops had fallen back to the high ground to the south east and south west of the town. B and C Companies of 3/Worcs were by then south west of the town, shooting at such of the enemy as showed themselves in the open on their front. D Company had been ordered back to the southern side of the embankment (D3) and then had been directed to move to the eastward to protect two batteries in action near the station (D4). The Battalion was therefore much scattered and when orders reached Colonel Stuart to deliver a counter-attack and retake Caudry it was not easy to assemble the necessary force. Eventually Colonel Stuart organised details from B and C Companies and part of A Company (as well as a collection of stragglers from other units) into a temporary command and led them himself back into the town. Such few of the enemy's advanced troops as had followed up the retirement were driven out with the bayonet. The southern part of the town was reoccupied as far as the main square. Advanced posts were pushed forward, but the shelling was severe and further advance was countermanded. On the right flank the remainder of A Company had co-operated in the advance ad had reached the station, which was occupied and held without difficulty.

That vigorous counter stroke had the effect of paralysing the enemy around Caudry; but further to the west the position was not so favourable. 11 Brigade had at last withdrawn from the ridge south of Fontaine au Pire. The enemy there had been reinforced and was attacking with fresh energy; soon afterwards came definite orders that Caudry was to be abandoned.

Between 3 and 4pm the troops of 7 Brigade fell back from

Caudry, first to the line of the railway and then to the height above Derrière le Tronquoy. There the companies of 3/Worcs were sorted out and reorganised…at Caudry the enemy had been hard hit and the German cavalry made no attempt to cross the railway line. Musketry fire died down and presently orders came to continue the retreat. The battalions of 7 Brigade assembled and marched off in fours down the road to Montigny. The enemy did not pursue, and as darkness fell the sound of firing died away.

Johnston gives his account of events:

They then started shelling the town with high explosive 5.9" shells: they make a most awful report and in buildings do a fearful lot of damage – almost the first shell pitched in the square and destroyed the house we were near, wounding Hildyard (very slightly), Hopkins of the RE and four others who were standing by: again I was in luck and came off without a scratch. The town was now mercilessly shelled, but it seemed to me to be very wicked the way in which the Germans destroyed part of the town not occupied by troops at all: the church was hit several times and a house in the square demolished with some women and children in it. This high explosive shell has undoubtedly a most unnerving effect amongst buildings, and to this may be attributed the fact that we eventually withdrew from the town though the enemy's infantry had really advanced very little. A crowd of stragglers of all regiments seemed to find their way into the square; Hildyard and I began to stop and collect them to send them back to the firing line when the General came along and ordered a retirement. We therefore made our way back to the high ground behind: picked up my horse by a great stroke of luck, a shell had burst near him, not hurting him though hitting the groom; being frightened for the moment he had galloped down the road (fortunately the right one!) for a bit and had then stopped and grazed by the side of the road until I picked him up! I feel that we ought to have stuck on to the town somehow. The German infantry showed no inclination to assault, there had been a considerable lull in their fire until they commenced their high explosive shell fire, which I believe was a last resource, and our infantry – except for the stragglers – were holding on well. Reinforcements (French) were said to be coming up and our left was not being so heavily attacked. I think we had only got to stick it out for a bit and the Germans would have had to give it up for the moment, though of course one does not know what is happening elsewhere. Poor Clarke was killed [Lieutenant M Clarke, buried in Caudry Old

137

Communal Cemetery, Grave A7] *and Beresford and Chichester were badly wounded, all of my Regiment, also Charley from 2/Irish Rifles, who had rejoined the Brigade from near Le Cateau during the morning. On reaching our next position behind Caudry I saw De Salis with his company, they were well in hand and everything seemed to be going on in a very orderly way: General Sir Hubert Hamilton rode up and said we were to form a new line here. By this time I was feeling pretty rotten and as there was nothing much to do for the moment and as we had got all the wounded away, I got into a passing ambulance and was taken to a Dressing Station* [almost certainly in Montigny].'

3/Worcs suffered about a hundred casualties of all ranks, far fewer than was at first thought, but certainly no light loss.

Johnston has his own description of the withdrawal:

Here I was given a cup of soup and lay down on some straw: after a bit somebody put his head through the door and said something about having to leave us out, I suppose through being dazed I did not pay much attention at the moment. Later I noticed that the place was quite empty and, on looking out of the window, saw a stream of people making their way to the rear. I learnt afterwards that this was the result of the disaster to 8 Brigade which had been caught by the German artillery when crowded in a village near by. It was an awful sight, a perfect rabble of men of all ranks and Corps abandoning their equipment and in some cases their rifles in order to get into safety in the rear. No doubt the RAMC had thought that I was one of the severely wounded who would have to be left behind: if I had stayed behind I would undoubtedly have been taken prisoner fairly shortly. I went out into the road at once and met Colonel Geddes who said that his guns had no escort. I therefore collected a motley gang of men of all sorts of regiments, including some of the 5th Division who seem to have taken rather a knock in the Le Cateau direction, and did escort to his guns during the retirement. Luckily the Germans did not seem to be following very closely and I had no fighting in consequence, which was fortunate with the men in their present state. Very tiring march and my leg was hurting. Went round the wrong way which of course caused an appalling block at the crossroads; guns take up an enormous amount of space so we had to wait for hours. It was most anxious work as one expected the German cavalry to be on us at any moment. On getting on to the right road met Bertie Gilmour with his company so we went along

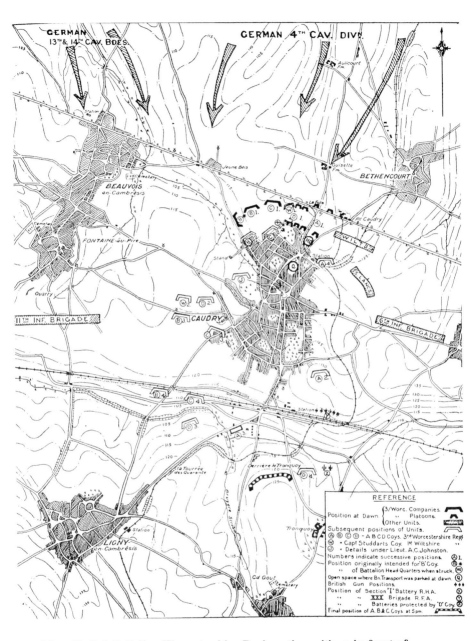

Map 15. 3rd Battalion Worcestershire Regiment's positions in front of Caudry, 26 August 1914.

139

together until we joined the rest of the Battalion. We then had a long wearisome march to Beaurevoir which we reached about midnight, thoroughly dead beat having been fighting and marching all day without any food whatever.

Following up that evening, *Vizewachtmeister* [Staff Sergeant] Genzky of *3rd Squadron Husaren Regiment 10*, the regiment which provided close reconnaissance for *IV Corps*, passed through Caudry on his way to a bivouac in Bertry, about five kilometres to the south east. He recalled later:

Dead and wounded British soldiers lay everywhere in heaps in the trenches. Some of them still had their eyes open. In amongst them were more than forty captured guns. Complete villages were destroyed and some were in flames. The inhabitants searched around trying to salvage their possessions. At 11.00 pm we arrived in a small place called Bertry and bivouacked on the street. The paymaster, the armourer and I made ourselves comfortable in the house of a chemist, whose inhabitants had all fled. We helped ourselves to a change of underclothes from the stocks of the man of the house. We folded our dirty items neatly and placed them in the cupboard. Day dawned. We had had only a few hours sleep, when suddenly we heard rifle fire, which quickly died away. We leapt quickly out of bed and asked what had happened. Apparently the British had tried to ambush us, but had been driven back by our troops. We had no idea how close we had come to danger. When we later crossed the scene of battle we saw a large number of dead and about 800 captured Scots, which bore witness to the scale of the fight. The Scots in their colourful uniforms, with bare knees and short skirts made a remarkable impression on our men. Before our departure the chemist had reoccupied his house. I had discovered him cowering in the courtyard with his wife. In fear, they had spent the entire night outside in the garden and had probably fled when they heard us knocking on the front door. Now the wife came up to us, begged us to spare her and her family and said that she would do anything for us. At that we got her to brew up good strong coffee. It must have come as a shock when she found our dirty underclothes in her cupboard, but it was only a joke.

Chapter Three

THE LEFT OF THE LINE: THE FOURTH DIVISION.

The Division had only arrived in France during 23/24 August, disembarking at Le Havre, Rouen and Boulogne. By the 25th eleven battalions of infantry and a brigade of artillery had arrived at Le Cateau; the Division was ordered forward to Solesmes to cover II Corps' retirement. Subsequently it was ordered to cover the left of II Corps on the Le Cateau position (indeed this was the original plan, and Snow had selected a line – somewhat longer than his final one – with Divisional HQ in Esnes Chateau). On the evening of the 25th it moved to a new line, Fontaine to Wambaix, ie about three miles in length. 11 Brigade (left) and 12 Brigade (right) were to hold the line whilst Brigadier General Aylmer Haldane's 10 Brigade was held in reserve about Haucourt. The remaining battalion and some more artillery (but minus the Heavy Battery) had meanwhile arrived and joined up with the Division in the new position, The move to it started at 9pm, but 10 Brigade could not shift from its location until after midnight.

GOC 4th Division commander, Major General TD'O Snow.

At this stage the Division did not come under II Corps, but at 5.30am Snow, on receipt of a message from Corps HQ, agreed to cover the left flank. Dispositions were amended, so that 11 Brigade was to cover from Le Coquelet Farm (to the south of Caudry) on the right, the line continued by 12 Brigade to Moulin d'Esnes, north west of Esnes.

The 4th Division was in a strange predicament. Although it had all its infantry and field artillery, it lacked its cavalry, cyclists, Heavy Battery, field engineers, signal company, train (ie supply column), ammunition column and field ambulances. For reasons that are unknown, GHQ had 'impounded' these troops at St Quentin. It therefore lacked its 'eyes', was severely lacking in communication, was short of transportation and medical support, including evacuation,

Men of 4th Division taking advantage of a stop in their railway journey to the front.

and had no engineers. To these shortages might be ascribed in large part the responsibility for the heavy losses in prisoners that the Division suffered during the battle.

The right of the 4th Division (Major General T D'O Snow) – 11 Brigade before Fontaine au Pire.

What follows is a summary of how the *Official History* saw the action; the regimental histories usually record a far more complex picture.

The rear guard of the Brigade continued engaging shots with the enemy to the north of Beauvois until about 6am and then gradually withdrew through the area of Fontaine au Pire, taking up positions at the head of the valley which separates Fontaine from Ligny and Haucourt to the south. Some Germans who were imprudent enough to come through Fontaine were seen off by men of 1/Hants. The line was held, from right to left, by 1/Rifle Brigade, 1/Somerset LI, 1/E Lancs and 1/Hants.

Initially things proceeded quietly enough; but the problems on the left suffered by 12 Brigade (see below) and the distance from 7 Brigade in Caudry gradually made the position more and more difficult (for whatever reason, 4th Division did not extend as far to the east as seems to have been originally intended; but given the length of front it had to defend this is at least understandable). Although the field of fire was quite good at the centre, the right and the left provided a good means of approach for the Germans. More and more German artillery was employed, although not generally supported by infantry assaults. When Caudry was evacuated in the early afternoon (at least for a part of it, only temporarily), Brigadier General Hunter Weston decided that the time had come to withdraw his Brigade from an increasingly dangerous situation, especially as there was the threat that the Germans might come around the left flank of 12 Brigade on his left. The problem was that the battalions would have to cross the open valley between their positions and the new line before Ligny. Part of 1/RB was left as a rearguard whilst the other battalions withdrew at about 3pm into the low ground of the ravine; which they did under a 'perfect tempest of shrapnel' (OH). As they moved up the far slope of the valley to Ligny, the withdrawing battalions once more came under very heavy fire and suffered considerable casualties. When the

Brigadier General Hunter Weston.

rearguard withdrew from the 'Quarry' (in fact gravel pits) the German infantry leapt into the attack. These in turn suffered considerable casualties from the British guns which Snow had had dug in in front of Haucourt; regardless of loss they continued to press home the attack and started to advance against Ligny before 11 Brigade had been reformed. Hammered by artillery, the attack faltered; but once it was reinforced the attempt was made again, though this time the infantry were also able to contribute effective rifle fire against it. This attack also failed and, some time about 4pm, the 4th Division was left in undisputed control of Ligny.

It was about this time that General Sordet's French cavalry corps made its fortuitous appearance on the left flank of the 4th Division. In fact it had been in the vicinity for some time (part of it had billeted on the night of 25 August near Esnes), but the Germans were unsure of its whereabouts and when it opened up with its artillery on the Germans at Wambaix it provided the security that Smith-Dorrien so urgently sought for his left flank. As the Germans were unsure about its intentions, its presence served as a considerable disincentive to attempt rash action in pursuing the British, especially on the western flank.

The German troops advancing against this part of the battlefield were drawn from elements of HKK [Senior Cavalry Command =

Jäger in dismounted attack.

Corps] 2 under *Generalleutnant* von der Marwitz. As has been seen the regiments of *Generalleutnant* von Garnier's *4th Cavalry Division* became totally committed to the fight for the centre ground around Caudry, so it fell to the *9th Cavalry Division* under *Generalmajor* von Bow and *2nd Cavalry Division*, commanded by *Generalmajor* Freiherr [Baron] von Krane, to attempt to locate the British left flank and to engage the men of the British 4th Division. The only German infantry available in this sector were the *Jäger Battalions 3, 4, 7, 9* and *10* in support of the mounted regiments. There was sharp fighting on this

German cavalry watering their horses in a farmyard in northern France.

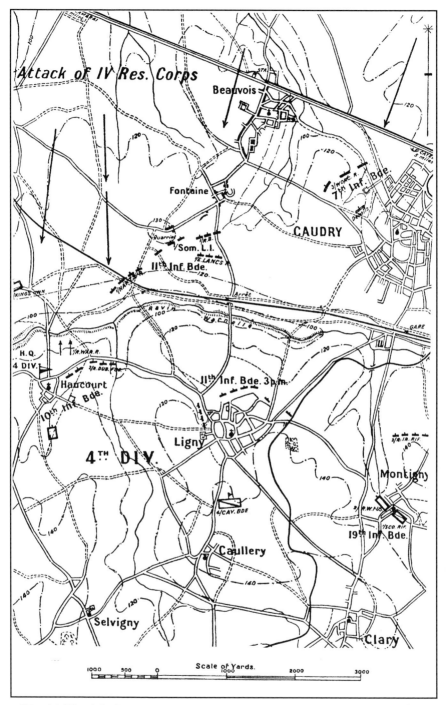

Map 16. The right flank of the 4th Division.

flank as the day wore on, but due to the lack of infantry and the distance to be covered to the west, it was not until late in the battle that the German army succeeded in really building up pressure on the British 11 Brigade. Indeed, it is far from certain that the German army had a clear idea about the precise location of the left flank of the British II Corps at any time during the battle.

After a very short period of rest on boggy ground on a rain-soaked bivouac during the night 25/26 August, the cavalry headed off at 4.00am to resume the pursuit. Spurred on by tales of victory at Maubeuge and Givet, all were anxious to press on, but the sodden routes forward delayed the advance considerably. The *9th Cavalry Division*, supported by *Jäger Battalions 3, 9* and *10*, was directed towards Beauvois-Prément. The advance guard was provided by *19 Cavalry Brigade*, with *Dragoon Regiment 19* leading *Uhlan Regiment 13*. *2nd Squadron* under *Rittmeister* [Captain] von Galen was in the lead and point troop was under command of *Leutnant* von Dittfurth. Unusually the formation employed by the advance guard departed from the normal. *Major* von Kaehne of *Dragoon Regiment 19* later noted:

> *It had annoyed me during the past few days that the divisional advance had tended to be interfered with by nuisance fire from enemy detachments concealed in houses along the route. I determined, therefore, to split the leading squadron; that is to say, to direct one half to advance to the right of the road, along which we were advancing, and the other to the left. My idea was to concentrate all my resources forward, in order that I could swiftly deploy the artillery, in particular, to take on possible fire missions. The splitting of the leading squadron and dispersal in long columns of the follow-up forces reduced the ability of enemy patrols to report on our movements. In the event, the division of the leading squadron meant that it was able to deal with fire coming from the houses and to put a stop to it. Everything remained fluid and there was plenty of momentum to the movement.*

The leading squadron came under fire from Beauvois. *Vizewachtmeister* [Staff Sergeant] Strühwind reported:

> *With six troopers, I had the task of maintaining liaison between the advance guard and the regiment. Suddenly we came under a hail of fire from Beauvois. My groom, Dragoon Boldt, was shot through the neck, but it was a lucky shot.'*

1st Battalion Rifle Brigade (1/RB).

The Regimental History provides not only a detailed account of the action of its 1st Battalion at the battle but provides a very detailed examination of the events at higher formation level, most interesting reading in itself, but for which there is no space here.

Initial contact was made with the Germans at about 4am (ie a couple of hours earlier than on the right of II Corps' line).

By about 2am on 26 August the Battalion was bivouacked to the north west of Fontaine au Pire on a track that runs down the forward slope towards Cattenières and Estourmel; C Company was ordered into Cattenières to form an outpost line. The move to the position from Briastre, near Solesmes, had been a nightmare:

> *Earlier in the day a heavy thunderstorm had broken and the rain still continued. The downpour and the heavy volume of traffic had combined to convert the road into a quagmire of such consistency that most of the signallers' bicycles, with their wheels immovably clogged by mud, were of necessity carried a considerable part of the distance. The mere effort of walking on such a surface was a trial of endurance. And the road was still thickly congested with groups of stragglers in addition to vehicles and horses.*

Bear in mind, also, that the movement was being conducted at night and the maps were also woefully inadequate – the map boxes opened up at the station so eagerly in the early hours of the 25th at Le Cateau station were full of those for Belgium.

The outpost line fell back to the main body, which was drawn out in extended order across the glacis to the west of Fontaine; it held off the Germans coming from the direction of Cattenières and from the north. Two companies of SLI went through Fontaine to the southern limits of Beauvois to cover the withdrawal of the Brigade transport. Meanwhile the other two battalions of the Brigade took up position on and behind the Quarry position, with 1/Hants' left flank across the railway line. Brigade HQ was by the railway bridge, with elements of 1/E Lancs and 1/SLI nearby, on the other side of the Warnelle Ravine.

The Battalion made its way on to the main Quarry position. Parts of it had to be shifted so that it did not come under enfilade fire – for example, I Company shifted to a position on the sunken road that runs from Fontaine to Ligny; and it was here that the CO, Lieutenant

Colonel Biddulph, established his HQ and added two platoons of B Company to the reserve.

In due course, what had been a reserve position became part of the front line as 1//SLI and 1/Hants on the left and right respectively were gradually pushed in on the position:

> *By now the enemy was seen to be massing as if for an attack. The artillery, machine gun and rifle fire increased. Major Rickman's* [the second in command and in charge of the forward troops] *companies fixed swords* [the Rifle Brigade does not have bayonets but swords – actually the same thing] *and prepared to meet the attack half-way; but no attack developed.*

Meanwhile things were degenerating on the left, where 12 Brigade had been forced back off the commanding high ground above Esnes; whilst matters were equally precarious on the left, with a threat from Caudry. C Company on one occasion had to move forward to re-establish the line before the Quarries as other troops felt the pressure of the German attack.

At 1.30pm, during a lull in the fighting, all the battalion commanding officers happened to be at Brigade HQ, though Hunter Weston and his brigade major were away in the front line. They considered the possibility of a counter-attack, as 12 Brigade was in the process of doing just at that time. This failed, and by 2pm German artillery fire once more opened up, with greater intensity. The one good thing was that the German gunners had decided to concentrate their fire on a line of poplars parallel to and two hundred yards behind the sunken road on the Quarry Knoll.

Now attacks developed along the left; with 12 Brigade out of the way, there was nothing to hinder the Germans. Caudry had been evacuated, albeit temporarily. In fact the previous evening it had been realised that there was a gap between Caudry (7 Brigade) and the right of 11 Brigade; the latter was ordered to extend its line to cover the gap, something like a mile in width, but the order never arrived. Thus, by 2pm, 11 Brigade was in a salient, coming under fire from the flanks as well as the front.

Hunter Weston ('who had spent the day in the most reckless disregard of danger') arrived back at his HQ soon after 2pm, where he met his COs and were joined by a Divisional staff officer. He was authorised by the latter to withdraw his troops to the Ligny position if the line became untenable. Any idea of a counter-attack was abandoned and Hunter Weston decided, at about 3pm, that he would withdraw his Brigade. What he would have done if he had known that

3/Worcesters were reoccupying the west of Caudry at just that time is purely speculation – there had been no communications with 7 Brigade all day and the Germans were already between the two brigades.

1/E Lancs and 1/Hants were instructed to move off first (part of 1/E Lancs was already on the other side of the ravine). The initial move could be done in concealment, but once the troops started to climb the hill to Ligny they would come in full view. The idea was that 1/Somerset and 1/RB would move off as these latter came into view of the enemy. However, these orders did not reach the forward companies, a mixed group of various battalions.

The enemy could clearly see the retreating elements of 11 Brigade and reacted accordingly. The enemy was closing in and Major Salmon, commanding in the front line, including three companies of 1/RB, had to decide what to do, having received no orders. [Major Rickman had been mortally wounded at about 2.30pm; he is buried in the communal cemetery at Fontaine.] There remained only a gap of about four hundred yards through which the men could make their escape. Captain Prittie was ordered, with his men, to open 'five rounds rapid' whilst the remnants bolted and made for Ligny as best they could, hotly pursued by the Germans.

Major Rickman's grave at Fontaine.

The regimental history does not give details of casualties, but they cannot have been insignificant. About 5pm the evacuation of Ligny got underway, with the Brigade moving towards Malincourt.

Jäger Battalion 3

Although *Jäger Battalion 3* belonged to *10 Infantry Brigade* of the *5th Division*, like the bulk of the other *Jäger* battalions it found itself subordinated to the cavalry during the invasion of France to bolster the fire power of the mounted cavalry regiments. On 26 August its main role was to protect the 'heavy radio transmitting station' [i.e. Heavy Wireless Station 1 of the German *2nd Cavalry Division*] to the west of Beauvois. *Oberleutnant* Claus-Just von Lattorf wrote later:

> *Excitement mounted when we heard that we had the British opposite us, because we were thirsting for the blood of this most hated of all enemies. We heard heavy small arms fire from our right where the 10th Jäger Battalion was already engaged in heavy fighting. Despite our earlier superhuman performances, suddenly all weariness disappeared. The first rounds were fired at 6.00 am. The point of the battalion came under fire from the*

direction of Beauvois and our battalion was directed against that place.

The 2nd Company *under Hauptmann Freiherr* [Baron] *von Rechenberg, the* 3rd Company *under Reserve Hauptmann Reimnitz and the* 4th Company *under Hauptmann von Mühlen deployed. Initially the* 1st Company *under Hauptmann Freiherr von Werthern and the Machine Gun Company under Hauptmann Freiherr von Wangenheim remained in reserve behind the battalion right flank. We attacked, with 10th Jäger Battalion on our right and dismounted cavalry on our left. Moving over open ground we closed to 800 metres from the enemy position, almost as we would have done back home on the Majoransheide...Not for nothing were the elite British troops that opposed us called 'Rifles Brigade'* [sic]. *They were battle hardened professional soldiers, who had fought on every continent. They were a tough, callous lot, who maintained an extraordinary calm, even when wounded. Their marksmanship and fieldcraft on favourable terrain was of such a high order that even for Jägers it was extremely difficult to draw a bead on them. Added to that was poor observation of the fall of* [artillery] *shot on the soaked and soft ground, the rolling ground and mist which was late to disperse. Despite all this, we advanced so determinedly that Graf* [Count] *von Schmettow, commander of 9 Cavalry Brigade to which we were subordinated, had to order our battalion commander about midday not to advance any further. The next few hours were to show how right this order was and how difficult it would be for us to carry out the further order to hold our positions at all costs... Small arms fire increased by the minute. Reinforcement of the Battalion right flank was called for at 10.00 am and the Machine Gun Company was deployed there; the guns being rushed forward in bounds. This made the gunners sweat freely, because they had to carry their heavy guns and heavy ammunition boxes up over the hills and across a deep railway cutting, forcing a way down twenty-five metres through dense undergrowth, before negotiating a steep climb through thick acacia bushes under enemy fire on the far side. The first platoon was commanded by Oberleutnant Freiherr von Wrangel; the second by Oberleutnant Mackensen von Astfeld and the third by Reserve Leutnant Heller. Reserve Vizefeldwebel* [Staff Sergeant] *Schmidt, commander of the reserve gun, moved with 1st Platoon. Vizefeldwebel Mütze led the Machine Company*

Machine-gun team in the opening phases of the war when the German army was sweeping through Belgium and France.

vehicles forward across the main road to the Ferme du Fraineu. It was impossible for the mounted battery of our cavalry division to meet all the demands placed on it by the width of the sector and limited ammunition. Nevertheless it supported us significantly, in that it kept the British reserve columns under fire. That evening we were able to observe its success. These reserves were located by Reserve Leutnant Griesemann, who had climbed a tower. From there he was able to observe the fire extremely efficiently until he was relieved by an artillery observer. At the start of the battle he had been ordered to take a few Jägers and sweep through the brewery and its surrounding buildings, because shooting was coming from there. Soon the situation of our firing line, which was only very thinly occupied, became extremely critical. The enemy had certainly abandoned

151

its positions around Beauvois, but he had excellent fields of fire from his main position on the hills to the west of Fontaine au Pire. His enfilading machine gun fire, upon which enemy artillery fire was superimposed, had a painful effect on us. At certain places along our line the shells were causing such problems that, for example, the 2nd and 3rd Companies, on their own initiative, moved forward. In so doing they avoided further casualties and improved their positions. A light rain was falling, which made observation even harder. Our firing line began to run short of ammunition. All reserves were loaded up with machine gun ammunition and sent forward. Even the horse holders had to carry ammunition. Griesemann's platoon carried packages of ammunition forward right across the battalion frontage and company commanders sent Jägers back to fetch additional rounds.

Of the crew of the first machine gun which was deployed in the area of 3rd Company, only Gefreiter Krägenbrink was still manning the gun. The gun commander Oberjäger [Corporal] Arndt and Jäger Stadt had crawled to the rear to fetch ammunition. Shortly after that the gunner, Gefreiter Gastmann, and Jäger Meyer were wounded. So Krägenbrink put the gun on his back and, taking up a water container and a box of ammunition, went forward alone. Suddenly shots rang out around him, so he had to take cover. He immediately drew his pistol and spotted three British soldiers, who had crawled the wrong way and found themselves overtaken by the advancing Jägers. The first Tommy spun away, hit by a well-aimed shot to the head. The second attempted to disappear behind a cornstack, but was shot through the knee and collapsed. The third, a strong-looking man, threw his weapon away and surrendered, shocked into silence and trembling like an aspen leaf.

The longed-for reinforcements eventually arrived at 3.00 pm. Our artillery, which had also been replenished with ammunition, could open up once more and really pound the enemy position. We observed the way this fire sent things spinning up into the air. Now the 10th Jägers on our left could advance, which enabled us to move forward too. Reserve Leutnant Klingender and his platoon stormed forward on the flank of the 10th Jägers and captured 240 British soldiers [this is almost certainly a considerable exaggeration]. The Battalion attack was pushed forward across the railway line from Cambrai-Le Cateau. The *enemy had abandoned his hedgerow positions along the line of the railway embankment. Dismounted cavalry on our right supported our attack.*

The 2nd Company and the Cyclist Company advanced across the railway to protect the artillery that had moved up. Now we were able to see what a superbly favourable position the enemy had occupied behind folds in the ground and the railway. The enormous quantities of weapons and ammunition that we came across showed very clearly that the enemy had had the intention of defending the position very vigorously. Near the estaminet "Rendezvous des Chasseurs" in Fontaine au Pire two stacks of straw, which the enemy had been using as observation posts, were ablaze. The Jägers who were marching by them appreciated the warmth they gave off, because the cold, wet weather had worn them all down. In a sunken lane by the entrance to a gravel pit close behind the railway embankment the fallen British soldiers lay in heaps. Here our artillery had simply scythed down the British reserves. The ground was strewn with countless cartridge cases, knapsacks and items of clothing. These last had obviously been taken from the wounded because they were soaked with blood. We were full of amazement at the superb quality and practicality of the British equipment. Their belts and web equipment was all of one uniform grey-green colour, which was barely distinguishable from the ground. Every man had spare underwear, tea, ample supplies of tinned rations and, which was an especially wonderful sight to we grubby, bearded, front line soldiers, an excellent razor. Whilst in the position, they had enjoyed meals of biscuit, jam and other tinned foods. This food was very welcome to us, because we had not seen a field kitchen for twenty four hours. The British were armed with rifles which were somewhat shorter than ours and which had wooden furniture right up to the muzzle. Each had a hole in the side, which officially had a practical use, but in reality, as we discovered, was there to enable the tips of bullets to be broken off – Dum-Dum rounds! [this statement, variations on which appear throughout the literature, is based on the mistaken identification of the magazine cut-off catch].

Our pursuit was hindered by heavy enemy artillery fire...That day the following sealed their oath to Kaiser and Reich with their death:

Reserve Leutnant Hunsdörfer 4th Company

Einjährig – Oberjäger *Marseille*
Einjährig – Gefreiter *Dittmann*
Jägers Moritz, Busch and Brackhahn (3rd Coy) *Mix, Erich Meyer, Wuschke Gerstmann and two further Oberjägers and four Jägers (MG Coy).*

Two officers, five Oberjägers and thirty-six Jägers were wounded.

For all the fallen the words of the old soldiers' song are particularly apt: "There is no finer death in this world than that which befalls he who, struck down by the enemy on the green sward of a far-off field, hears no wail of lamentation."

1st Battalion Somerset Light Infantry (1/SLI).

Working under the original orders of the 4th Division, after arriving at Fontaine at about 2.30am on 26 August, the CO, Lieutenant Colonel Swayne, took two companies to a position about 800 yards north west of Ligny, leaving C and D Companies (along with the machine gun section) with the rest of the Brigade, temporarily resting in Fontaine. His Battalion's duty for the following day was to provide the rearguard for the Brigade for the continuing retirement. The two companies in Fontaine,

were told off to the southern end of the village to hold off the enemy should he advance from the north east. They were also to ensure the safe passage of all wheeled transport to the east and then southwards, the rain having made impassable the direct roads south from the halting place.

At 4.14am, just as 11 Brigade was about to move off from Fontaine in order to take up its allotted positions on the left of II Corps, rifle, machine gun and shell fire were opened on the outposts west of the village of Beauvois, ie on 1/RB. The two companies of Somersets, at the southern edge of Beauvois, also came under shell fire, though up to this point they do not seem to have suffered any casualties.

Eventually 1/Hants and 1/E Lancs were safely withdrawn to the ridge (of which Carrières [the Quarries] is the centre). I/Hants then opened rifle and machine gun fire on the enemy, under cover of which the Rifles and Somersets also moved off and retired to the ridge and Quarries south west of Fontaine: all transport having previously been sent back.

The change in orders by 4th Division at 5.30am were somewhat academic to the men on the ground, as is clear from the account above.

At 5.30am heavy hostile artillery fire was opened on the Quarries position, which was very exposed and entirely unentrenched. Here C and D Companies had taken whatever cover was possible, the surrounding country being very open. A glacis-like slope, which provided the only fair field of fire, led up to where the companies were extended, but the enemy was too cautious to advance in that direction, his attention being turned to the flanks of the position.

By 6.30am masses of Germans were advancing from the main Cambrai-Le Cateau road, west of Beauvois. They were supported by their artillery in action near the road. Their

Lieutenant Colonel Swayne.

machine gun detachments, which had worked their way around Fontaine and through the village, now opened very heavy flanking fire on the right of 11 Brigade [this was one of the consequences of the gap between 7 and 11 Brigades], *and casualties amongst 1/SLI became severe. Major Compton was hit in the shoulder, Major Thoyts* [C Company] *in the neck* [he subsequently died – no known grave], *Captain Broderip and Lieutenant J Leachcroft in the head* [the latter was kia on the First Day of the Somme and is buried at Redan Ridge Number 1, Beaumont Hamel] *and Lieutenant Philby in the leg; many other ranks had also become casualties.*

A and B Companies, south of the railway, were then hurried up to reinforce C and D. They advanced in extended order, under heavy shell fire. As they reached the firing line German skirmishers were seen about 700 yards away, advancing and taking cover behind the corn stooks that dotted the fields. From Fontaine the enemy's machine guns now enfiladed the line, the rain of bullets clipping short the grass along the crest of the hill. But at the enemy's infantry there were fewer opportunities of firing…his troops were careful to expose themselves as little as possible.

Shortly after 8am the Quarries became untenable. Both flanks of the position were exposed, 7 Brigade on the right and 12 Brigade on the left having been forced back by heavy pressure and intense machine gun fire. Measures were therefore taken to withdraw to the railway embankment that ran along the valley between Ligny and Fontaine. Just previous to the decision to retire, a German patrol, waving a white flag evidently meant to invite the Somerset men to surrender, endeavoured to work around the right flank of the Battalion. "The men asked me what to do. 'Fire on the beggars, range 500 yards.' Germans drop hastily" [the future Lieutenant Colonel W Watson, kia in May 1917 whilst commanding 2/5th KOYLI at the Battle of Arras; he has no known grave].

So, leaving a single platoon behind under Lieutenant Taylor, the Battalion in short rushes retired south of the railway, towards Ligny. But neither the platoon nor its commander escaped; Lieutenant Taylor was wounded and fell into the hands of the enemy [not officially declared missing until 25 September, as was the case for a number of other 1/SLI officers]*; the fate of the platoon can only be conjectured.*

In Ligny 1/SLI reorganised and took up positions at the eastern end of the village. Casualties were collected and placed in the church. Unfortunately the Divisional Field Ambulances...had been held back by GHQ and were at St Quentin. The wounded could not be evacuated, though Captain Holden RAMC managed to collect a few carts in which he placed some of the worst cases and despatched them southwards towards St Quentin. For some inexplicable reason these carts were turned back to Ligny under the direction of a staff officer. All these wounded subsequently fell into the hands of the enemy.

1/SLI remained at Ligny and formed part of the defence of that place against the German attacks that followed in the afternoon. The fight at Le Cateau had cost it approximately twenty killed, 150 wounded and 100 missing. It is notable how this account differs from that of 1/RB above – for example, was the CO of 1/SLI present at Brigade HQ at 2pm as stated in 1/RB's account?

1st Battalion Hampshire Regiment (1/Hants).

The Battalion reached Le Cateau station at about 4am on 25 August; during the train journey from Le Havre it had suffered its first casualty. The adjutant's groom, trying to control the frightened charger in passing through a tunnel, was kicked out of the train and killed. On the 25th it formed a cover for II Corps, along with the rest of the Division, north of Le Cateau, in its case around Briastre. The Battalion eventually all arrived at Fontaine between 2am and 3.30am and shortly afterwards moved out to the north west, B Company joined part of 1/RB to cover the move; on arrival there B Company came under artillery fire and suffered several casualties. In the confusion caused by the arrival of the Germans in the vicinity of Fontaine, the machine gun section got separated from the rest of the Battalion, but joined up with that of 1/RB to the south of the ravine.

The rest of 1/Hants took up a position roughly facing north west towards Cattenières and astride the railway line. Major Hicks had time for a hurried reconnaissance and placed A and D Companies and set them digging with their grubbers – but hardly before they came under artillery and machine gun fire.

The Regiment's historian, CT Atkinson, notes the consequences of the lack of the Divisional Signal Company. Its 'absence was probably on the whole the biggest handicap from which the Division suffered and was responsible for losses which, with proper means of communication, might have been averted.' He cites the Brigade's own experience:

Being without a Brigade Signal Section, the Brigadier kept in touch with his forward troops by riding freely about: his charger having been shot from under him, he borrowed B Company's charger which also was hit and with it were lost the Field Conduct sheets in a wallet on the saddle.

It is doubtful that any soldiers lost much sleep over the loss of these sheets!

1/Hants position was separated from that of 12 Brigade by a wide gap, but not so wide that the enemy could advance into it without coming under effective fire.

The country, though under cultivation, largely with beet and clover, not yet harvested as other crops had been, was open, with few trees and hedges, and gave a fair field of fire, particularly to D Company, north of the railway, as the Germans found when they tried to advance, British rifle fire soon discouraging them and checking efforts to work around towards our left. Accordingly, against 11 Brigade they relied mainly on shell fire and machine guns...

After the Brigade had taken up its position the covering parties were able to fall back. B Company had been quite sharply

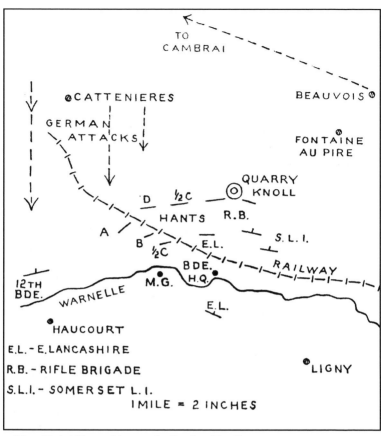

Map 17. 1st Hampshires at the Battle of Le Cateau.

engaged and had several casualties. As they fell back one detachment had the satisfaction of wiping out a platoon of Jäegers who had incautiously emerged from Fontaine au Pire in pursuit. Half the Company, under Captain Baxter, became separated from the rest and joined 1/SLI, alongside whom they fought until that Battalion had to retire to Ligny. [Baxter was badly wounded and taken prisoner.] *The rest of B, under Captain Harland* [kia on 30 October 1914 and buried in Ploegsteert Churchyard], *was now placed in reserve behind D, who had to endure the main ordeal of the German shell fire. The line here, on top of the ridge, was very much exposed, though a sunken lane leading down to the railway bridge gave the supports some shelter. However, Captain Connellan* [kia 20 October 1914, as a major, and buried in Pont de Nieppe Communal Cemetery] *brought two platoons of C up to reinforce, and he and Captain Palk set a splendid example of leadership and coolness, encouraging the men to endure the ordeal and keeping them ready to take advantage of any targets which presented themselves.*

Captain Palk, indeed, is said to have read Scott's 'Marmion' aloud to his men; which was worse for the men, this or the enemy's fire, is not recorded. Palk was killed commanding 1/Hants on 1 July 1916 and is buried at Sucrerie Cemetery.

About 9am D had the satisfaction of seeing Germans coming forward in large masses. Reserving the fire of his left half company [ie closest to the railway line] *till the enemy were quite close, Lieutenant Halls* [subsequently taken prisoner] *then opened rapid fire with great effect, the surviving Germans falling back to a ridge nearly 300 yards away; but after that very few such targets were given again, and the Germans, apparently dismounted cavalry, merely maintained a desultory fire at a very respectful range. South of the railway line the left company (A) had rather better cover, thanks to sunken lanes, and its men dealt very effectively with efforts to creep forward along the line. Some Germans, creeping up under cover, got near enough to call out "Retire", which for the moment deceived a few men, but they gained little from the ruse.*

1/Hants was also able to assist elements of 12 Brigade as it retired across the Warnelle valley at about 9am. Two platoons 'rushing forward a little got a good target in a battery which had unlimbered in the open near Cattenières, shooting so effectively at a range of over 200 yards that it was forced to limber up and get away.'

Targets for the infantry were generally few, but,

The best marksmen of D Company were able to pick off some of the machine gun crews and occasional officers who marked themselves out by carrying drawn swords, and the men were very steady and fired with good effect. One German machine gun was put out of action and the efforts of their infantry to cross the railway line or advance along it were effectively checked while, heavy as the artillery fire was, much went high and our casualties were less than might have been expected from such a volume of fire. At one moment a battery got the range of a hedge along the railway cutting with disastrous results, Lieutenant

Kent and Second Lieutenant Cowan [both with no known grave] *and several men being killed and many wounded, but this was, luckily, exceptional. Later on, however, when infantry were pressing forward against 12 Brigade, now back between Ligny and Harcourt, parts of A and C Companies tried a counter attack to take this advance in the flank, but their move drew down on them so fierce a storm of shrapnel that the Brigadier had to stop the advance and bring the men back to their line, several casualties having been suffered.*

Sometimes the men were shelled out of positions, but reinforcements from the Warnelle Ravine ensured that they were reoccupied. When the decision was made to withdraw the Brigade, 1/Hants and 1/E Lancs were the first to go. As they moved off 'it seemed as if every gun and rifle in the German army had opened fire' (from a letter by Lieutenant EJ Dolphin, subsequently kia on 7 November 1914 and buried in Ploegsteert Churchyard), but the men were soon in dead ground. They came under fire again as they went up the valley's southern slopes, though the men were 'well extended and the losses were not heavy'.

By this stage (about 5pm) all the units of 11 Brigade were jumbled up, a situation exacerbated by the lack of Signals, which made the controlling of troops all but impossible for the Divisional and Brigade commanders. When the orders came to retire at this time, they failed to reach several detachments, amongst whom were about 300 of 1/Hants. The adjutant came back to Ligny at about 6pm to order these, too, to move out – whilst another group, under the CO, hung on in Ligny until about 7pm.

The machine gun section had an unfortunate experience as a result of this confusion. It had remained in position until dark,

Then started to retire as all other troops near were doing. It had some difficulty in getting the limbers along a bad track but after a time met a Frenchman, who offered to guide it to Clary, where he said the English were concentrating. [This was not true.] *When the party, increased by stragglers to a dozen, reached Clary, it was to run into Germans in force and to be taken. The two machine guns, left for a time in a courtyard, were discovered there by a civilian, M Fernaud Lerouf, who concealed them so successfully that the Germans never found them. Eventually, in 1921, the then Mayor of Clary informed the local military authorities of the existence of these guns and Captain Le Hunte (the machine gun officer) had the satisfaction of going to Clary to recover them for the regiment and to express its thanks to M*

A posed photograph of a British infantry firing line. Even by 1914 standards the men are too tightly packed together.

Lerouf for their preservation, who had risked his life for them.'

1/Hants had lost ten officers killed, wounded or missing, forty six other ranks killed and missing and 126 wounded: D Company, unsurprisingly, having suffered most severely

The *jäger* battalions of the German *9th Cavalry Division* were supported by the shell fire of Field Artillery Regiment 10 from Hanover. *Hauptmann* Fritz Schneider later recalled:

It was still pitch black on 26th August when the 9th Cavalry Division mounted its horses. The order was, "Maintain contact with the enemy at all costs". In the grey dawn contact was made with enemy infantry within and to the west of Beauvois. The 1st

Mounted Battery, which advanced from the southern edge of Bévillers, engaged them. They were British advanced posts, covering to the front of the main positions that ran along the line Cambrai - Le Cateau - Landrecies. Once Beauvois was cleared, 2nd and 3rd Mounted Batteries were moved forward to the western edge of Beauvois, south of the main road Cambrai - Le Cateau. There they took up positions facing Fontaine au Pire and the hills south west of it. As soon as they crossed the road and went into position, the batteries came under heavy small arms fire, as a result of which Einjährig-Freiwilliger Schaper of the 3rd Mounted Battery was so seriously wounded that his leg had to be amputated later. Whilst our Jäger Battalions 3 and10 deployed to attack, we brought the enemy infantry under heavy fire. In the same way the British counter-attacks were repeatedly broken up. It was clear to see that the enemy had suffered heavy casualties. This was later confirmed by the jägers.

In the meantime the 1st Mounted Battery went into position about 1.5 kilometres south of Bévillers, facing Caudry. Here it came under heavy enemy artillery fire itself. Hauptmann Freiherr [Baron] von Wangenheim and Vizewachtmeister [Staff Sergeant] Muß were wounded. By command of the Abteilung [artillery battalion equivalent], Oberleutnant Freiherr von Bothmer, who had previously been commander of the ammunition column, took over command of the 1st Mounted Battery. Until he arrived, Reserve Leutnant Kauffmann continued to direct the fire. He was fortunate enough to spot the muzzle flash of an enemy gun and to put it out of action.

Around 1.30 pm the jägers called for support near Fontaine au Pire. Major von Wangenheim immediately ordered the two batteries on the right to gallop forward to Fontaine au Pire via Beauvois. We could see the result of our fire during the morning by a cemetery on the southwest exit of this place. Numerous British soldiers had been killed by our fire. Here was a team of horses lying dead in front of their ammunition wagon. Over there was a horse crumpled up in front of a two wheeled wagon. It was so shattered that it looked like a dog lying between the traces. In the middle of this battlefield lay the weak jäger company which had called for assistance. Because of enemy superiority in numbers, they were hard pressed. There was no time to lose and no really suitable fire position could be found in a hurry, so Hauptmann von Uslar ordered the guns of the 2nd Mounted

Battery to be unharnessed in the village and to be pushed into individual open fire positions along the road to Cattenières. Enemy infantry in front of Ligny were swiftly brought under fire, as were dismounted cavalrymen to the west of it, who suddenly appeared out of the dust and smoke. Suddenly we observed a British attack. Dense lines were advancing against the weakened jägers. It was taken in the flank at close range and halted with bloody losses. Despite coming under heavy fire from enemy artillery, which had spotted the battery in its exposed positions, fire continued to be brought down on the retreating infantry until they went to ground. Only now could Hauptmann von Uslar take on the enemy artillery and then only with a few rounds. He had to cease firing due to shortage of ammunition. In order to minimise casualties, he ordered the gunners to leave their guns and to take cover in the protection of the houses. The Battery suffered five men wounded. Gradually the fire died away and it was possible to pull the guns back without further casualties. The mission had been accomplished; the jägers received the support they needed and were now much better placed to continue...Our Mounted Battalion look back with pride on the Battle of Beauvois (officially it was called the Battle of Le Cateau). The 26 August is a glorious day in its history. The British also fought bravely. That must be recognised. Despite heavy and bloody losses, they held their positions, as we were able to confirm when we advanced later. When, later that evening, we found ourselves on the road in Beauvois a group of forty to fifty prisoners was being led past. They were all tall, well-built men, whose bearing and clothing made an outstanding impression. What a contrast to the short, pale and anxious Frenchmen in their grubby coloured uniforms, who we had captured two days previously in Tournai!

1st Battalion East Lancashire Regiment (1/E Lancs).

As for much of the rest of the Brigade, 1/E Lancs did not reach Fontaine until after 2.30am. It was bivouacked in 'a rough field which was surrounded by wire and had obviously been tenanted by cows'.

In the morning, Major Collins prepared the Battalion to move off; the CO, Lieutenant Colonel Le Marchant, was away for a conference that Hunter Weston had called. Unfortunately he had been

The East Lancashires on parade before war had taken its toll.

instructed to go to Divisional Headquarters (in Haucourt) instead of Brigade HQ and so he got no orders until he received them second hand via the CO of 1/Hants. He got back to his Battalion at 5am and gave out the new instructions, which had it sited on the Carrières ridge, 'the centre of which was marked by a knoll and a quarry'. The CO went off to reconnoitre the position, the Battalion 'halted with A and B Companies on the southern slope of the ridge and C and D Companies on the crest and northern slope'. In this time heavy firing broke out in Beauvois. Majors Collins and Green decided to deploy the men, not wanting the Battalion to be caught whilst ready to move off, and dispersed them on the ridge facing the north west and the west. 'At the same time A and B Companies, with two platoons of D, took up a position on the slope south of the Warnelle Ravine.' C Company was on the left, with 1/Hants left of it.

Germans in Fontaine were dealt with by Major Lambert, using the machine guns and the personnel of the transport (minus the drivers, of course). The situation was eased by these men and elements of 1/RB and 1/SLI, described above, though not before there had been quite a brisk action, including some fighting in the streets.

'As soon as the transport was clear away, 1/RB and two companies of 1/SLI retired to Quarry Ridge, under cover of the fire of the troops already holding it.' The companies from 1/SLI and 1/RB were placed in and east of the quarries. 'Some men of both regiments, retiring in small groups, appear to have got into the position held by C Company, causing some congestion.' The machine guns were also posted with C Company for a while, but were then sent 'to a hollow in the rear'.

As the attack developed at about 6am, A and B Companies were sent forward to the railway embankment north of the Ravine, whilst D was sent to Haucourt to cover the left flank. Major Green, its commander, found Haucourt already satisfactorily held and returned to Brigade HQ, then in the ravine.

164

The German attack increased in intensity.

Eventually, about 10am, C Company less one platoon, in a most exposed position on the left, was forced to retire to a position on the railway in the southern slope of the ridge where A and B Companies were already posted, More casualties were inflicted during the retreat and amongst them was Major Collins, severely wounded. [More will be said about him at the end of this Battalion's account.] *He was the last man to leave the position and exhibited exceptional gallantry and power of command on*

withdrawing the Company. The platoon left behind was commanded by Lieutenant Hopkinson, who was with 1/RB at the south west corner of the quarry. 1/E Lancs was now in close support of 1/RB.

Shortly after noon an attack was made on 1/Hants on the left and two platoons of D Company under Lieutenants Chisholm and Richards were sent to reinforce it. The attack was repulsed and the two platoons were then sent by Major Green to clear the scrub, along the railway, through which the enemy were advancing.

When Hunter Weston ordered the Brigade to withdraw to Ligny he ordered in person,

Lieutenant Hopkinson's party and one company 1/RB to hold the sunken road along the south side of the quarry to cover the retirement. The remainder of the Brigade withdrew to the bottom of the reverse slope of the ridge, where it was reorganised to a certain extent under cover of the bank

Lieutenant Hopkinson.

of a road. During the withdrawal there were many casualties, and on continuing the retirement over the wide open slope to Ligny the Brigade came under a hail of shrapnel and small arms fire. There were more casualties, the most serious of which were from small arms fire, for the German shrapnel burst very high and, though nearly every man was bruised by shrapnel bullets, very few serious casualties were caused by them.

The Brigade organised Ligny for defence and were able, with the aid of field guns, to see off German attacks, concentrated in particular on the east side of the village.

In the meantime Lieutenant Hopkinson's party and one company of the Rifle Brigade, which had not retired with the rest of the battalion, had been completely isolated and were very hard pressed, especially on the left, which was held by C Company's platoon. Casualties were very heavy and the left flank could not have been held but for the gallant men of the Rifle Brigade company. By 5pm – or thereabouts – the ammunition of both parties was nearly exhausted, the Germans had advanced to within one hundred yards and were encircling both flanks. The two senior officers decided that it was time to go and, after firing the ammunition in one burst of rapid fire, the survivors – a mere handful of men and four subalterns, two of whom were wounded – bolted for the cover of the Warnelle Ravine. The last burst of fire gave the party some hundred yards' start, but the last two hundred yards were swept by rifle and machine gun fire.

On reaching the dead ground in the valley the survivors re-formed and retired in extended order towards Ligny; the Germans followed them to the crest of the quarry ridge, but were meet by a hail of shrapnel from the artillery of the 4th Division between Haucourt and Ligny, which completely stopped the advance.' '...less than a hundred survivors of the rear party which had held up the German advance for over two hours reached Ligny.'

The move off from Ligny was confused: in fact the Battalion ended up in three distinct parties, the infantry in two bodies and the transport making its way separately: they did not combine until 2am on 30 August.

Major E Collins, 1/E Lancs

Major Collins commanded C Company during the battle, until he was severely wounded. He was taken prisoner, but wrote a number of letters and an account of the 26th and what happened to him subsequently. I am grateful to the Regiment for giving me access to these.

From a letter, written on 25 September whilst in hospital in Halle:

It will be a month tomorrow since I was hit, early in the day, after about four hours fighting a series of rear guard actions. My Company happened to be placed so as to engage the enemy at daybreak. It was about 9am, as I was beginning to be hard pressed, that I decided to retire through my supports and take up a fresh position so as to cover them. I got all my wounded men away except the very serious cases I was bound to leave behind and was the last to leave the position. Getting some 300 yards clear and over a slope that hid me from the enemy, but over which bullets and shells were passing, as luck would have it, just as I thought I was safe, I was

Major E Collins.

struck on the right arm, as though I had been hit with a sledge hammer, and was twisted half round, falling backwards towards the blow. The pain was awful and I felt quite frantic. I had the sense, however, to put my thumb on the artery and keep it there until a man passing came to my assistance and put my field dressing on. I then found that the artery was not injured. I tried to get up but my arm would not come with me and, unfortunately, I had sent the man away. Things were getting hot and no one came my way, so with a great effort I seized my right wrist with my left hand and managed to get up and run back to my supports; they turned out to be Somersets. They carried me to a place of safety. I now began to feel the effects of the wound and severe thirst. Soon after the doctor came [Lieutenant Flood] and redressed the wound, reset the arm temporarily and told me it was badly broken and gave me a dose of morphia. I was much more comfortable after my arm had been put into its right position and the morphia began to take effect.

This is the sanitised version of the medical attention. In a full account of the day he is rather more graphic.

[Flood] *sat beside me, talking, and suddenly seized my arm and*

167

gave it a sharp twist and placed it at right angles to me. I gave a most frantic yell and kicked in my agony, telling him that if I had my revolver I would have shot him. He merely laughed and said that he was sorry, but in carrying my arm I had twisted it like a corkscrew, that a sharp piece of bone was almost bursting through the skin and that as he knew I would never let him touch my arm, the only thing he could do was take me by surprise and put it straight before I made it worse by moving it. He gave me some morphia and went off to look for a piece of wood to use as a splint and then dress it properly. The pain he gave me made me pour with sweat again and awfully thirsty.'

Collins' letter continues:

While I was lying there Lambert (second in command) came to see me. He is the last man of the Regiment I have seen, barring a boy of the 3rd Battalion who was wounded and in hospital with me at Ligny. I lay where I was for some hours. I saw the Regiment retire. Four men came to me and carried me down to a wood and laid me on a slope, quite safe from the fire. They wanted to take me on but I would not hear of it. Fortunately so, for the Regiment was heavily shelled and they would all have, probably, been hit and myself also. As they went away they left four other wounded men with me. One belonged to the Somersets and the other three to my Regiment. The last of the Regiment I heard was Green's voice ordering a wide extension, because of the heavy fire to which they were being subjected. ... I lay where I was with the others and in about an hour the remainder of the Brigade retired under heavy fire. [In his account, Collins gives much fuller details of the retirement, noting his very considerable surprise at how few casualties the hail of German artillery fire caused as the men moved across the valley in extended order up to Ligny.] *The German guns and machine guns advanced on either side of the wood but did not enter it. About an hour after dusk tremendous shelling from our side commenced, shells of all sorts fell around but none came into the wood. This silenced the German fire and I think they withdrew, probably being only outposts. I then sent one of the men with a note to say that we were much in need of help, but he never returned. I afterwards ascertained that he managed to reach Ligny and that a wagon was sent out to bring us in, but it returned on being fired upon.*

Eventually, when it was dark, he and a corporal in the Somersets

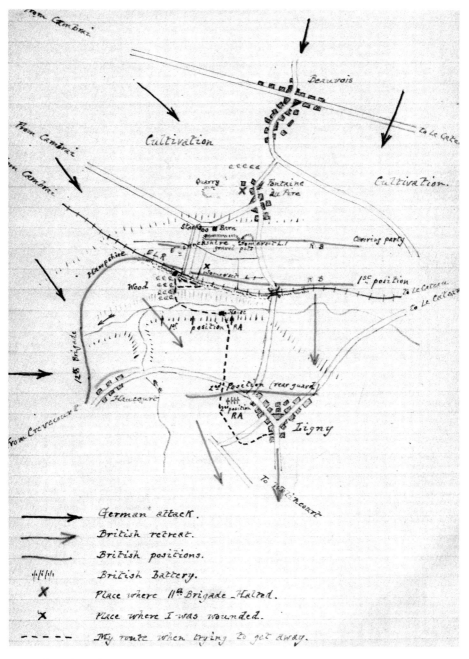

Map 18. Major Collins's sketch map.

Front row from left to right: 2/Lt GHT Wade, Lt CEM Richards, 2/Lt K Hooper, 2/Lt TH Matthews, Lt EC Hopkinson, Lt WM Chisolm, Lt Flood (RAMC).

Middle row from left to right: Captain Walker (ASC), Captain EE Coventry, Captain G Clayhills DSO, Lt FF Belchier (Adjutant), Major TS Lambert, Lt Colonel LStG Le Merchant DSO, Major FR Collins DSO, Major JE Green, Captain GT Seabrooke, Lt R Longstaff (QM).

Back row from left to right: 2/Lt WA Salt, 2/Lt RY Parker, Lt FD Hughes, Lt HT McMullen, Captain AStL Goldie, Lt EMB Delmege, Lt JF Dyer, Lt WF Dowling, LT LA Leeson, Lt HW Canton, 2/Lt WR Tosswill.

Of the twenty-six officers in this photograph, nine were killed and twelve wounded.

decided to try and get some help themselves. They got mixed up in some intermittent shooting and actually moving was laboriously slow and painful: 'I walked ahead reconnoitring and carrying my right arm in my left hand, stopping about every fifty yards for the corporal [who had been hit in the wrist and by shrapnel in the foot] to overtake me and to take a short rest, for he could do little more than crawl. 'It took them twenty minutes to negotiate a barbed wire fence and eventually got to a cottage at about midnight. Having spent twenty minutes trying to get in, 'in our desperation we broke a window, for we were both quite done. This, luckily, produced the occupant, who opened the door and finding that we were wounded Englishmen, took us in and at once administered to each of us a strong dose of brandy and water, and not too soon, for we were in a sad state of exhaustion.' His wife and young child then appeared, they were fed and given mats to sleep on the floor. When one looks at the position of the house on the map, it is quite surprising that there was much of a house left, let alone windows! Woken at Collins' request at 3.30am, and fortified by more brandy and makeshift crutches for the corporal, they set off once more for Ligny and reached there about dawn.

Here we met a number of villagers going out to search for wounded soldiers. I told them where we had left three in the wood and of one we had seen in a field. I found later that they brought in all these and found several others in their search.

It is worth mentioning here that this activity was not without its dangers: the priest at Haucourt was shot by the Germans for helping wounded British soldiers.

I gave the corporal in charge of one of the villagers, begging him to take him direct to the hospital and then proceeded with others who took me to the hospital. The first they took me to was full of wounded officers and men, lying on straw mattresses. [In fact he met Flood outside the church, full of the less seriously wounded – the critical cases were in the school.] *All were bad cases, many dying during the day or the next night. Among them was poor Chisholm of my Regiment. He was too far gone to recognise me, though I did my best to find if I could be of use to him.* [Elsewhere Collins gives a fuller description: 'Flood told me he was dying, shot through the body with a rifle bullet. He died on the following morning. He was Green's most promising subaltern and Australian by birth, who received his commission through the military college there into the regular army. He was buried at Ligny and was the first officer of the Regiment who fell in the war (and the first Australian).']

For fuller details about Chisholm, see *Cambrai: the Right Hook* in this series.

I left the school and was taken by Flood to the schoolmistress's house, which adjoined the school, and was put in a room upstairs where four or five beds were being prepared for officers. I was put to bed at once as they would not take off my coat and shirt, but merely propped me up with pillows. I was so exhausted that I fell asleep in spite of the noise that they were making in the room... When I woke up [about two hours later] *I found a*

German officer in the room and four more [British] officers. The
German was collecting any arms, glasses, maps and papers we
had. He was quite polite, a young infantry captain. ... When he
came to me I only had a map to give him. To get at it my pocket,
which was under my bad arm, had to be cut open.

Collins comments on his fellow occupants, one of whom 'nearly lost
his sight as a result of shell shock'.

Collins' account goes on to describe the medical care offered, the
tremendous work of some of the local inhabitants and the fate of some
of the wounded who had been left out for several days:

One was hit in the head and his brain exposed. He was raving
mad when found in a turnip field, with maggots in his brain. He
died soon after. Another with broken legs had been dragging
himself about a potato field, living on raw potatoes for three
days. He got tetanus and died soon after he was found.

From Ligny Collins was removed to Cambrai on 8 September and
thence to hospital and imprisonment – for the duration (he was
repatriated in December 1918) – in Germany.

Left of the 4th Division – 12 Brigade before Haucourt and Esnes.

The 4th Division moved through the night from its position covering
the retirement to Le Cateau and attempted to locate its new position,
Fontaine au Pire to Wambaix, with its reserve around Haucourt, on the
left of the Corps. The first in the area were Divisional HQ and two
companies of 2/Inniskilling, which had previously been at Ligny; they
arrived at Haucourt at about 1am and then the companies went on to
form the divisional flank guard at Esnes. The Battalion's other two
companies had been detached to form a flank guard before Beauvois
and Bévillers; these latter remained there until 3am (they had some
contact with the enemy) and were then ordered by the Brigade
commander, Brigadier General Henry Wilson (not to be confused with
his more famous namesake), to Longsart. Two companies of 2/Essex
reached Longsart at about 3.30am, shortly followed by 2/Lancashire
Fusiliers. They set about digging in to the north and west of the village.
1/King's Own arrived at the eastern end of Haucourt at about 4am and
stopped there (mixed up as they were with elements of French cavalry),
and then moved up to positions on the Cattenières road; about 5am the
other two companies of 2/Essex came up to Haucourt and finally the
two remaining companies of 2//Inniskilling got in to Longsart at about
5am. Haucourt must have presented a picture of complete confusion,
as the reserve brigade (10) also came in to Haucourt at about 5am,

having arrived at Caudry just as dawn was breaking. A French cavalry patrol reported that the ground ahead of 12 Brigade was clear, and the Division, of course, had no cavalry of its own (or even cyclists) to throw forward and check the situation. The *OH* describes the ground held by the 4th Division as 'a dreary boggy moor, soaked by the rain of the previous night, and in many places churned into deep mud by the passage of men, horses, guns and vehicles'. He should know; Edmonds, the author of this volume, was the G1 (senior operational staff officer) at 4th Division's HQ.

Up to now Snow had not been able to communicate with his brigades about the orders he had received at midnight – all of them had been on the move when the orders arrived. Staff officers were sent off to establish contact with the troops in their new positions and orders readied, once this had been done, for the retirement to be continued as possible. But also at about 5am came the orders to hold fast and the request for the 4th Division to cover II Corps' flank. New orders were prepared to be sent out as soon as possible – but before this could be done the officers who had been sent out earlier came back to report that fighting was already well under way.

1/King's Own came under completely unexpected machine gun fire at 6am just as it was assembled *en masse* before beginning entrenching. It was caught in the open and became a tangled mess, with many of the men unable to open fire because they were packed together too densely. This initial attack was devastating, with over eighty men killed (including the CO) and two hundred wounded. Although the German machine guns were seen off, at least for a while, a couple of German batteries then brought them under fire from open ground between Wambaix and Cattenières. The sadly depleted ranks of 1/King's Own took shelter in a nearby sunken road. An attempt by two companies of 1/Warwicks (10 Brigade) had only limited success in assisting 1/King's Own by coming up from Haucourt; they were themselves swept by German fire as they came over the crest and were forced back, at great cost, into the Warnelle Ravine. Eventually 1/King's Own stabilised the situation, but at a cost of about 400 casualties; whilst some of those who had headed for shelter on the reverse slope of the valley made their way back to the line.

The Germans then turned their attentions on 2/LF; when the direct approach failed, they began to attempt an enfilade attack from the left flank. By this stage the two companies of 2/Inniskilling at Longsart had been sent forward with a company to either flank, thereby extending 2/LF's line, as was a company of 2/Essex. It was becoming apparent, too, that the situation to the north and west of Esnes was far from satisfactory, and that the risk of the outflanking of the west end of II Corps front was a very real threat.

Although the Germans were held up for some time – at least until 8.30 - the threat of being taken in the flank meant that Wilson decided to withdraw his forward line and bring it back to the line Esnes – Ligny. 1/King's Own came away first, assisted by another two company attack by 1/Warwicks; this helped with the extrication of 1/King's Own, but it again caused 1/Warwicks heavy casualties. The last to leave were the men of 2/LF and 2/ Inniskilling.

Crucial in the defence of the new British line was the artillery, whose performance here as elsewhere on the battlefield was outstanding. Aided by their covering fire, 12 Brigade was able to reorganise and 2/LF saw off convincingly a German attack on the line. By 11am this had become a relatively calm sector of the battlefield. Brigadier General Haldane of 10 Brigade took 2/Seaforths out of his reserve line (now becoming the front line) and moved them to a ridge south east of Esnes to provide flank cover for what had now become a two brigade position, with all the composite units extraordinarily mixed up with each other. This was to lead to real problems in communications and the subsequent loss of troops as prisoners because messages were not received.

About 5pm the brigades got their orders to retreat; 10 Brigade was to form the rearguard. This was easier ordered than acted upon, but the Seaforth Highlanders were more or less intact and, along with part of the Royal Irish Fusiliers, were able to cover the first part of the withdrawal from contact. Others made their escape – 2/Essex and two companies of 2/Inniskilling soon after 5pm; 2/LF and part of 1/King's Own soon afterwards; the rest of the Inniskillings slipped away in small parties from Esnes as the Germans began to enter the western side of the village. Much of the artillery was also withdrawn, though orders were given for the guns of 135 Battery (which had done such sterling work in front of Ligny in support of 11 Brigade) to be abandoned. In fact four of the six guns were got away. The other two battalions of 10 Brigade, 1/Warwicks and 2/Dublin, were scattered – some still in Haucourt, others carrying out a variety of functions, such as gun escorts.

The bulk of the troops left at Haucourt after the main body had retired consisted of two companies of 1/Warwicks and two of 2/Dublin, and some of 1/King's Own, for the most part situated east of Haucourt. At about 11pm the remnants of the King's Own made good their retreat. Major Poole of 1/Warwicks led a mixed group (joined at dawn by a platoon of 2/Dublin at Caullery) on the track of the 4th Division; but the 2/Dublin group had a much more adventurous time. It lost touch with the other group in the darkness and eventually found itself in Ligny at about 2am, where the men fell out and slept. The men continued towards Clary, but came under heavy German fire and made their way back, in small groups, to Ligny. There were now about 200 men in this collection of troops, 'comprising soldiers from nearly every battalion of the 3rd, 4th and 5th Divisions – and even two men of the 1st Division [which Division was miles away] … under Major Shewan. Finding his way to the south blocked by Germans, Major Shewan led his men on an extraordinary odyssey through France, periodically engaging in fighting the Germans, and ending up, after days behind enemy lines, with seventy eight officers and men in Boulogne, the rest being killed or taken prisoner.

Dragoon Regiment 19

Earlier in the day, *2nd Squadron Dragoon Regiment 19* and the *10th Jäger Battalion* had launched a quick attack on Beauvois, capturing it after a short, sharp battle. In the meantime the remainder of *19 Cavalry Brigade* had pushed forward somewhat to the west via Estourmel and, in conjunction with the other regiments of the division had deployed its dismounted element against the heights around Fontaine-au-Pire. For hours they were engaged in a hot fire fight with the British, who were about 800 metres away. *Oberleutnant* von Oechelhaeuser, one of the troop leaders, later reported:

> *Our troopers found themselves in a very unfavourable position, because they were greatly outnumbered by the British who also had the sun at their backs. I was in the firing line with Major von Kaehne and frequently observed the fact that groups of up to forty men with rifles and hands raised launched themselves repeatedly at us as though they wished to surrender. Our troopers, observing the rules of war, did not fire at the assaulting infantrymen. These men, however, made use of these unfair tactics to gain ground. They then took cover once more and continued the fire fight. In order to remain masters of the situation, the regiment then gave the order not to take prisoners – the British attack was beaten off completely. Towards 6.00pm as pressure built up due to the arrival of infantry from IV Corps, the enemy withdrew from its positions. The regiment remounted and rode off at the head of the division towards Cambrai via*

Estournelles. Reserve Leutnant Thörl, 2nd Squadron, forced his way into the town, but came under fire and had to withstand a wild street battle. Displaying great determination, these courageous men evaded capture. The regiment veered off in the direction of Escoudoevres, three kilometres northeast of Cambrai, and spent the night there. Troopers Ziehm and Fedemar of the 2nd *[Squadron] were killed. Troopers Henkelbehrens and Wurm of 5th Squadron were wounded.* Major *von Kaehne received a head injury and had to leave the regiment. Reserve Leutnant Kulenkampff and his horse took a heavy fall and he had to leave the regiment as well. In a report he was described as 'an extraordinarily reliable patrol officer'. It was a victorious battle for the Cavalry Corps; General von Poseck declared 26 August a day of honour for the cavalry.*

1st Battalion King's Own (Royal Lancaster Regiment) (1/King's Own)

Much of the details about this Battalion have been given above in the overall account of 12 Brigade. The men had had an exhausting day on the 25th. In fact their entire three days up till then had been one great whirl of activity. The Battalion had disembarked at Boulogne at 6am on 23 August, and then marched up one of the steep hills surrounding that town to St Leonard's Camp for a rest before returning to the town and entraining by 9pm – the Battalion numbering exactly 1,000 men. The men arrived at Bertry at 10am and then moved on to Ligny – where they bivouacked north of the village until nightfall. They would be back to a position nearby just over a day later. The Battalion marched to the Viesly area in the dark, forming part of II Corps' cover, and came under shell fire in the afternoon of the 25th. By the time the men got to Haucourt in the early hours of the 26th they must have been utterly exhausted. After a short rest there, a move was made to the position to be held on the west side of the road to Cattenières, whence they arrived at about 5.45am and then prepared to deploy to dig in, extending earthworks beyond those that 2/LF had already commenced for them. The men were in a root field and were proceeding to pile arms and dress ranks when they came under fire.

The attack at about 6am, which left the CO, Lieutenant Colonel Dykes, dead and so many of his men casualties, effectively wiped out C Company. Attempts to restore the position at 8am failed, and the Battalion then formed part of the defence of the Haucourt-Ligny line. When the time for withdrawal came part of it made its way to Selvigny and then Gouy; the rest failed to receive the withdrawal order and came under German attack at about 9.30pm. Some Germans gained entry to the village but were driven out. The remaining remnants of the Battalion, under Major Parker, managed to make their way through the Germans and rejoined their Battalion on the 27th. The War Diary records six officers killed, two missing, four wounded and 431 other ranks killed, wounded or missing. The only officer with a grave is Captain H Clutterbuck, a forty year old veteran of the South African War, one of some forty men buried at Haucourt Communal Cemetery. The only other known grave there is that of CSM William Sharp, of C Company. The rest of the men were almost certainly buried in a mass grave, probably by French civilians acting under German orders.

2nd Battalion Lancashire Fusiliers (2/LF).

The Battalion War Diary described this action under the title of the Battle of Ligny. The Battalion arrived, according to the Regimental history (*The Lancashire Fusiliers 1914 – 1918*, Major General JC Latter, 1948), 'in pitch darkness at about 3.45am'. As soon as it was light enough to see, trenches were sited and Brigadier General Henry Wilson came up to give further directions as to the siting of the line. By 5.45am there was some sort of shelter for everyone, with B Company in reserve on the Esnes road and the transport at Longsart Farm. D Company was on the left of the position, A in the centre and C on the left. Once the Germans had shattered 1/King's Own, their guns were turned on 2/LF. The Battalion machine guns, sited between D and A Companies, were rapidly brought into action, but one jammed and had to be removed from the line.

As the fighting progressed, and especially as the threat from the left flank increased, contact was made with B Company of 2/Essex by Captain Roffey.

The enemy, having a greater number of machine guns, had begun to work around the battalion's left and enfilade it. Captain Ward [D Company] *had therefore withdrawn his company a short distance. Roffey considered that a further retirement was imperative; but as he was crossing over to the Essex to arrange it with them, Captain Vandaleur* [B Company, 2/Essex] *was killed* [he is buried in Esnes Communal cemetery] *and Roffey was so seriously wounded in the neck and mouth that he was not recognised a few hours later by Sergeant H Bibby, the Officers' Mess Sergeant. As he lay wounded at the bottom of the Essex trench, German jäegers arrived and lined the outer edge of the parapet. He saw a German crawl over the parapet, come right up to him, take his revolver from his case and fire at him twice. Nevertheless, Roffey managed to crawl away into a field of corn stooks and later in the day was helped along by the adjutant and some men of the Essex.'* [Roffey was killed in April 1918 whilst commanding 2/5th Lincoln and is buried in Bailleul Communal Cemetery Extension.]

It was now about 8am and Ward's company and Cross's platoon (A Company) were being seriously harassed by machine gun fire from behind, which Lieutenant Boyle and Cross tried to correct. Very shortly after, Ward and Boyle, two devoted friends, were killed instantly. Casualties were mounting; D Company was without an officer; Lieutenant CH Bass was seen to be lying wounded in the open and Corporal Walsh disappeared in a fruitless effort to bring him in. [Bass is the only officer from the Battalion in this action with a known grave; he is buried at Naves CCE along with a large number of 'unknown' men from the Battalion and 1/King's Own; Walsh seems to have survived the war.] *The Germans were creeping around the flank and a retirement became necessary. A and D Companies (the latter*

commanded by Captain Sidebottom) withdrew to the cover of a
hedge, suffering in so doing. Sidebottom gathered as many men
as he could, but fell with many wounds. Privates Bannister and
Hanson tried to recover his body, but the enemy was too close
and the former was dangerously wounded. In the meanwhile
Second Lieutenant Humfrey was carrying back part of the
surviving machine gun when he stopped to help a wounded man
and fell mortally wounded. Sergeant Roch, who was carrying the
tripod of the gun, was hit in the wrist. Both of the Battalion's
guns were lost that day and the Battalion was without machine
guns until nearly the end of September.

Later in the day, after several gallant counter attacks made by
small parties with some success, the whole of this part of the line
fell back by Brigade orders, across the stream running behind
the original position, to a saddle back ridge running south west
from Haucourt. Closely pursuing Germans, firing as they
advanced, were seen off with the assistance of two companies of
2/Essex. *The holding of this new line was assisted by the fire of*
the artillery; but the enemy had pushed ahead all of their
artillery of IV Reserve Corps, which joined with that of the
Cavalry Corps [HKK2] in heavily shelling this line and the plain
behind it as far as Selvigny, to which the bulk of the Brigade was
ordered to withdraw. The shelling caused some dispersion and
mixing with 2/Inniskilling.

A hospital had been set up in Haucourt (in the church, amongst other
places) and Lieutenant Stuart, killed a few days later, went there and
'advised all men able to walk to leave at once, as the enemy were
beginning to shell the village'. He put Sergeant Whittaker (who had
been hit in the head) on a borrowed horse and with others left the
village, being picked up later by lorries. In the meanwhile, various
parties of the Battalion had been assembling under Major Griffin on
the main road leading to Selvigny '... and arrived at Vendhuille at
about 10pm.' This march was not made any easier by the fact that,
whereas officers were well laden with maps of the area east of Mons,
there was only one copy in the Brigade of the map of the country
traversed by the Retreat – and that a hachured, uncontoured and French
map on a 1:80000 scale.

A party of about a hundred was left at Haucourt; this group attached
itself to Major Parker's group, leaving Haucourt at about midnight and
rejoining the Brigade, after an exhausting twenty-two mile march, on
the afternoon of the 27th. It had been an appalling day for 2/LF:

Losses were six officers and an uncertain number of NCOs and men killed; three officers and eighty six other ranks wounded; and six officers and 402 other ranks missing. Of the latter, three officers rejoined a few days later and 143 NCOs and men on 9 September, having in some cases being taken by lorry to French barracks at Compiègne and thence by train to Coulommiers.

The German 2nd Cavalry Division.

Due to the distance to be covered, battle was joined on the extreme left flank somewhat later than elsewhere on the battlefield. Operations against the British 12 Brigade were launched by units and formations of 2nd Cavalry Division, supported by *Jäger Battalions 4, 7* and *9*. As the *jägers* pushed forward from Cattenières, they immediately spotted strongly–held British positions on the heights to the north of Longsart, beyond the Cambrai-Le Cateau railway line, which ran about 600 metres to the south of the village. *Generalmajor* Freiherr von Krane ordered an attack and the *jägers* shook out, *Battalions 4* and *9* on the left, advancing beyond the railway, whilst *Battalion 7* took a wider sweep round to the right, just skirting Wambaix.

All the concentrated machine gun companies and one battery of *Reserve Field Artillery Regiment 35* were galloped forward as a first move. Once across the railway they went into open fire positions and, despite the lack of cover, blazed away to their front. Reasonably swift progress was made and the dismounted troopers of *5 Cavalry Brigade* (*Dragoon Regiment 2* and *Uhlan Regiment 3*) were inserted into the firing line to reinforce the *jägers* further. A quick attack launched by *Jäger Battalion 4* succeeded in rushing the British positions. Casualties were caused and prisoners were taken. For the time being, however, a further advance was out of the question because British resistance was increasing; its artillery, in particular, having a serious effect on the unprotected German troops in the open. According to the history of *Jäger Battalion 9*,

> *The word went quickly from mouth to mouth. "Make sure you choose good cover. The British shoot well and they hit their targets!" This warning was entirely justified. The British fired a mean bullet; quite different to our previous opponents the Belgians and the bearded French territorials from Tournai.*

Jäger Karl Dithmer, a member of the *Machine Gun Company* of *Jäger Battalion 9*, left us a detailed account of

Kurasier Friedrich Schlue. (see p. 250)

181

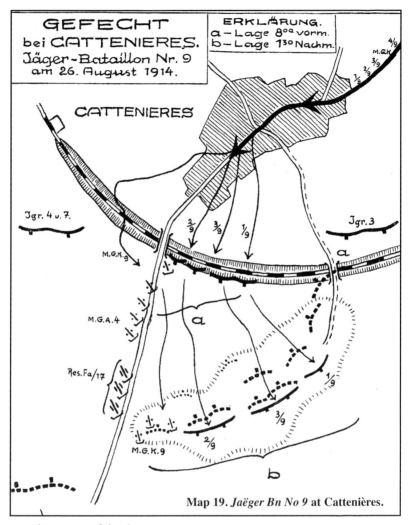

GEFECHT bei CATTENIERES.
Jäger-Bataillon Nr. 9
am 26. August 1914.

ERKLÄRUNG.
a – Lage 8⁰⁰ vorm.
b – Lage 13³⁰ Nachm.

CATTENIERES

Map 19. *Jaëger Bn No 9* at Cattenières.

the events of the day.

On 26 August we were up and away early to continue our advance. Our screening cavalry was out to the front. About 9.00am a patrol of hussars came to us and reported that the enemy was dug in on a hill behind Cattenières. The Machine Gun Company galloped past the battalion and men from the rifle companies shouted to us, "Pin them down!" Once we had reached the village the guns were prepared for action and we advanced along a railway embankment until we reached a bridge. An officer of the General Staff standing alongside shouted at us, "God be with you, Jägers!" Generalleutnant von der Marwitz [Commander HKK2] *was standing behind a concrete parapet on the bridge and as we marched at attention past him he called to us, "Lads, shouldn't you be taking cover!?" Our company commander, Leutnant Lorenz, quickly looked for suitable fire positions and we were inserted in the firing line between some cavalry engaged in a fire fight and other machine guns...We then opened fire. It was a hard-fought battle, because the British were well dug in on a hill, but they could not counter the massed fire of twenty-four machine guns. Holding sheaves of straw, the British soon pulled back. Suddenly we received the order, "Machine Gun Company start the pursuit!" Our vehicles arrived and we galloped forward. Once we had covered five hundred metres we came under a terrible fusillade from riflemen to our left. It was so bad that we had to take cover behind our vehicles. Our company commander rushed over and said, "Lads it's no use. Make the weapons ready! Vehicles about turn! Move!" My own commander was shot through the arm just as I was passing him. We prepared our gun carefully. We had not yet taken up a fire position when the company commander began to shout, "Where is the driver?" I looked and saw our vehicle about thirty metres to our front. I leapt to my feet and raced after it. I had half-turned when our horses were hit several times and set off at a gallop with me, until it ran over a hussar. I tripped over his long riding boots....Bullets were flying through the air and because two of my mates, who had already been shot, were already lying on it, our company commander, who was also wounded, raised himself up, turned half to his left and soothed them with the words, "Lads stop moaning!" He had hardly spoken the final syllable when he was hit for the third time through the right hip. When my gun commander, Oberjäger Rundeshagens, saw this, he fired back in the direction the shooting had come from. Once he had fired fifty to seventy-five rounds, the British fire suddenly stopped. Thereafter there was only the occasional shot and we were able to mount our equipment on the railway embankment. But first Leutnant Badinski, a mate of mine and I carried the severely wounded Leutnant Lorenz into cover. Everything was black before my eyes and I could do no more. We took a short break then we carried our equipment into the village which was under constant artillery fire. Once our company was reassembled, the Feldwebel checked who was missing. There were three killed and several wounded. The following morning the company paraded to the final resting place of our company commander who had succumbed to his serious wounds. Our Divisional Padre Streckenbach and our battalion commander, Hauptmann Herbig, said a few words, then our Leutnant was lowered into the earth in a groundsheet. As our battalion commander remarked, there was not a dry eye in the place.*

2nd Battalion Essex Regiment (2/Essex).

A and B Companies of 2/Essex were the Advance Guard of the Brigade on its move to the Esnes-Ligny position; they arrived at Longsart at about 3.45am. C and D Companies arrived at Esnes (where they were ordered to act as reserve) at 4.30am. When passing through Ligny it had been necessary for the men to proceed in single file through the town, as it was full of guns and troops, many of whom were trying to cook themselves a rudimentary meal. At Esnes a troop of French cavalry offered them morning coffee, whilst during the march through Haucourt other French cavalrymen had been seen reconnoitring to the north.

The Essex Regiment was most fortunate in its historian; the 2nd Battalion has its own volume: *Essex units in the War 1914 – 1919*, Vol 2, JW Burrows 1927.

There is an excellent description of the battlefield (viewed from Battalion HQ, south of the Esnes – Haucourt road) which has changed hardly at all in the intervening years; even the road near to the HQ is still pavé, though the Sugar Factory is probably much bigger than the one there in 1914 (and has been derelict for some years now).

The most prominent feature of the landscape … was the clear outline of the ridge, which bent inwards towards Esnes. A small ravine-like hollow scored the side of the ridge and to the right was the farm of Longsart embowered in trees. Yet a little further to the right … was a sugar factory, also surrounded by luxuriant foliage. There was a clear view to the right as far as Haucourt and in the distance Ligny could be seen, whilst to the left the rolling country beyond Esnes was also visible. The ground in front of the units of 12 Brigade on the ridge was so open that it was possible to see down to the railway line running to Cattenières.

The events on the Ridge, involving A and B Companies of the Essex up there, has been covered. The sound of gun fire heard in Esnes

Essex resting in Norwich Market Place.

resulted in C and D Companies being stood to arms. Informed by a French trooper that 12 Brigade was being driven back, the CO, Lieutenant Colonel Anley, moved D Company to a position just south of the Haucourt road, with its right opposite the sugar factory, whilst C Company was over to its right, straddling the track – now marked by a water tower – leading up to the ridge. As the two forward companies of the Essex fell back, A Company formed up on the right of D and B on its left [after Wilson had ordered the retirement from the ridge 'at 8.45am']. 'The preparations to resist attack were calmly and methodically made. For instance, the range-finder of D Company (Corporal Bloom) prepared and handed to each platoon a range chart, which was found extremely useful when the Germans sought to press their advantage further. …'

> Shortly afterwards the Germans appeared. C and D Companies immediately opened destructive fire at the extreme range of 1,300 yards and checked their advance, which had died away by 11am. The CO, who was watching the operation from higher ground, later stated that the fire of the Essex was most effective on the enemy supports, which were not observable by the former from their position in the valley, but which were moving forward in close formation.

The Essex moved some five hundred yards further back to improve

185

their field of fire.

About 1pm an advance was made to Longsart Farm, the enemy having apparently evacuated the hill. Many killed and wounded were found there, but as the Germans reopened a heavy fire, the troops were ordered to retire again to the Haucourt – Esnes road. The [German] shelling was maintained, but did little damage at this time, as the missiles passed over the heads of the Essex lying in the valley. Suddenly, about 3pm, a number of German guns appeared on the ridge north east of the farm, and a moment afterwards the air was thick with shrapnel, especially upon Haucourt village.

CO 2/Essex, Lt. Col. Gore Anley, pictured here later in the war, when he was a Brigadier-General.

An officer wrote:

The Brigade was lying down in a long line on the forward slopes of the low hills south of the road. In front of us and dominating our position lay the ridge from which we had been driven in the morning, except for a company [sic] *of Inniskillings, who were still gallantly maintaining their position on the extreme left. Through my glasses I saw the German guns gallop over the skyline, unlimber and open fire. The shrapnel caught the right of the Brigade and began sweeping along the line towards my position on the left flank. Unsupported to any extent by artillery fire and with the enemy's guns beyond effective rifle fire, the centre and right began to move. I told my company we should have to go back, but we should do so at a walk. The shrapnel caught us as we went off, certainly as a rule bursting too high, but putting a severe strain on men who had never been under fire before. Not a man attempted to run. We passed two of our guns, the only ones I saw that day, the subaltern in command explaining that he had "just time to give them a couple more rounds." About 5pm came the final withdrawal of 2/Essex. The march of two and a half miles across open country was a most difficult task, but when the men reached Selvigny village they formed up with absolute steadfastness.*

At 6.20pm the retirement continued from there to Vendhuille, which

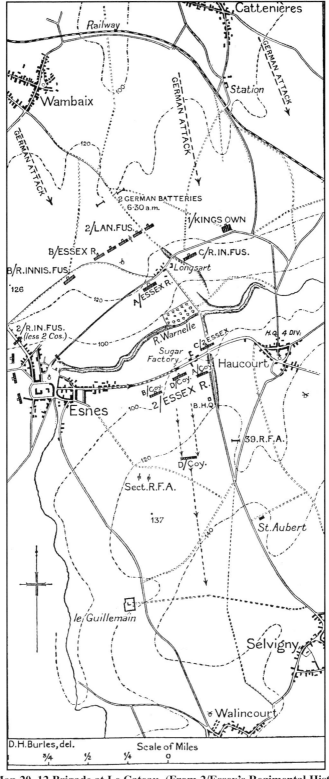

Map 20. 12 Brigade at Le Cateau. (From 2/Essex's Regimental History.)

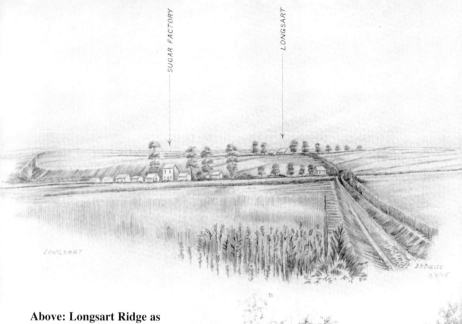

SUGAR FACTORY

LONGSART

LONGSART

B.H.OWLES
19.6.05

Above: Longsart Ridge as seen from Battalion HQ.

Right: On the lookout for the enemy. One soldier tries to draw fire by waving his cap on the end of his bayonet

Below: Longsart Ridge from just forward of the support company's position.

the advance guard of the Battalion entered at 10.30pm. As they were formed up there Colonel Anley asked one of the companies what sort of day they had had. A voice from the ranks replied, 'All right, sir, we can play this bowling easily' – a reply which caused general amusement.

The casualty figures were not so amusing – the Battalion suffered 141 – ten killed and forty men wounded [Lieutenant Round mortally; he died in the UK] whilst the remainder were reported as missing, killed, wounded or made prisoner during the retirement.

2nd Battalion Inniskilling Fusiliers (2/Inniskilling).

The role of 2/Inniskilling has to a large extent already been covered above. However, one or two individual stories of the fighting here appeared in the Regimental Journal, *The Sprig*. Some of the narrative is a little confused, but two companies were detailed off to guard the left flank at Esnes, under Lieutenant Colonel Hancox, the CO, whilst two others were pushed forward. B Company was positioned to the left of 2/Essex's B Company, whilst C was off on the right wing, to the left rear of 1/King's Own.

A platoon commander – a sergeant – sent an account of his doings on the day (almost certainly he was in C Company).

We halted at four at a farmhouse [Longsart] *near Ligny. The Lancashires were about to dig trenches and breakfast was being prepared when suddenly heavy Maxim fire was opened on our position. I was put in charge of a platoon and we filed out in extended order across fairly open ground. We advanced across a beet field, which was very heavy through rain, and had to discard what we could at the moment do without in order to accelerate our progress. The enemy was only about 1,000 yards off and was progressing. Nothing was audible above the crack of rifle and Maxim fire and the whistling of bullets as they tore through the beet and shrubs. How any of us escaped to continue the fight I cannot imagine! We took what cover was available and then returned their fire first at 1,000 yards, then at 600. At the latter range we could see them in big thick lines and seemingly bent on overwhelming us by mere force of numbers. My platoon had orders to retire to a roadway which was held by the Lancashires and the Essex. Some of us were able to double into the position, but others were so dead beat – among them myself – that we could just manage to walk.*

189

Near the roadway on the left was a trench almost vertical on to the direction from which the enemy were attacking [this would have been B Company's 1/Essex trench, prepared to face a threat from the west]. *We took up position there with the Essex and, seeing our danger and our thinned ranks, a captain of that regiment* [Vandaleur] *told us to get inside the trench. We had not been there long when a hail of bullets fell on us. The captain, who was at the end of the trench, and a young lieutenant* [almost certainly Roffey of 2/LF – see above] *were shot and fell where they stood. We held on like grim death, but soon recognised that, the trench being easily enfiladed, fresh cover would have to be found. ... A little to the right of the trench there was rising ground cover and we were quite unaware that there had been a partial retirement to the village. In the space we had crossed on the way to the trench there were many dead and wounded lying about. Before making the attempt to crawl out of the trench I discovered that the lieutenant of the Essex* [sic] *was only wounded. He asked me to remember him and get field hospital help as soon as I could. I promised him I would, but all the time feared I would never survive the ordeal with which we were faced. Anyhow, two of us crawled out to make the attempt. I was for making in the direction of our retirement. The man at my side said I would be killed for certain if I went that way. He had hardly said the words when he fell dead, shot by a German bullet. Apparently I was the only one left untouched in all that hot corner.* He managed to run for cover *('very meagre cover, it is true')* and stayed there until the British artillery forced a partial retirement by the Germans.

Afterwards he and a wounded corporal worked to help the wounded, amongst whom there were some Germans. Some of the wounded, who could not speak, were reduced to writing him notes, one of which said, 'Write mother and send Bible in base kit'. 'All the time we were at this work we were, as it were, between two fires, with the enemy preparing to advance again.' Eventually he made it to Haucourt: 'The inhabitants were fleeing – a pitiful spectacle, one of the most moving in all our experiences of war'.

Another recorded what happened when Lieutenant IFR Miller (of the regiment) was wounded. He was,

Shot in the leg, high up near the groin, and also in the shoulder. He told me that his shoulder wound was nothing but his groin wound hurt him... I carried him down to a farmhouse [Longsart]. *We were under heavy shell fire all the time. When we*

reached the farm I went on to tell the occupants, who were still inside [!], that I was putting an officer down in shelter of their wall and they must take him in when the shell fire abated. I then got my horse and rejoined my regiment, which was half a mile gone in retirement. ... From what I saw of Miller, if the German doctors got hold of him he ought to be all right. The sadness is that this was the message that went home to his family in Omagh. He died of wounds soon afterwards in a hospital in Cambrai and is buried in Porte de Paris Cemetery; confirmation of his death did not reach home until March 1915.

Finally there is the account of Drummer Parker's escape from the Germans. He was taken by some *Uhlans* but managed to escape when they were negotiating their way through some barbed wire. He evaded various German picquets and eventually arrived at a farmhouse.

The occupants were greatly alarmed at his arrival and did not seem anxious to let him stay in the place because of the vengeance which the Germans were executing on all non-combatants who harboured British soldiers. This was evident to Parker, who could not converse with the people. They did all they could, however, for him by giving him an old suit of clothes into which he changed, hiding his uniform. He concealed himself in a garret for a time, but during the day it was impossible for him to show his face, as the Germans were constantly visible. He had a scare when German officers and men searched the house: he concealed himself by lying on the side of a bed frame, pressed against the wall: although the Germans came into the room they gave it only a cursory look. 'He spent the next three days in the attic with very little to eat and on the third night resolved to clear out and do his best to reach either Boulogne, where he had landed, or the British lines.

Near Caudry he met a priest who gave him directions to the west.

He wrote a note asking any Frenchmen whom he met to facilitate him in his journey. The note was Greek to Parker, but it was his salvation, for it gave a list of the villages and towns for which he was to make. This note is still in the possession of Parker.

Disaster nearly overtook the wanderer again, for being ignorant of the country he found himself in the town of Douai, where there were some Germans. The French came to his rescue again and sent him on his way to Arras, one of the towns on the priest's list and, on arrival there, footsore and weary, he was immediately arrested as a German spy. An interpreter was sent for, but he could only speak a little English, and in the end it was Parker's identification disc which saved him and he was released.

At Boulogne he got a pass for a ferry to Folkestone (from the British Consul) and then reported to Shorncliffe, where there was a formal enquiry; and then he returned to the depot in Omagh.

What is particularly interesting from many of the soldiers' reports from various of the divisions is how many of them thought that Le Cateau was Mons – they came up with the name which they had heard about. By and large, the soldiers had very little idea of where exactly they were; and, quite frankly, in their situation it did not matter very much.

10 Brigade (Brigadier General Aylmer Haldane): 4th Division reserve, around Haucourt.

The activities of the four battalions of the reserve brigade have been described in outline above, and there is very little left to add. 2/Dublin and 1/Warwicks were on the right, to the east of Haucourt, and they were reinforced by elements from 1/Royal Irish Fusiliers, the Faugh-a-Ballaghs. Its regimental history says nothing of great interest of the battle, but an interesting memoir has come out recently: *Angels and Heroes*, A Moreno and D Truesdale, RIF Museum, 2004, which tells the story of Sergeant Hugh Wilson during the first months of the war. That battalion and 2nd Seaforth Highlanders spent the few hours – if that – of rest they had on arrival at Haucourt in the vicinity of the cemetery there. The bulk of these two battalions were moved to support the left flank, taking up positions around Point 137, south of Esnes, and despatching elements of the battalions as necessary to support units in the front line (most especially the Irish Fusiliers, where the better part of two companies were sent to reinforce troops in and to the east of Haucourt). Inevitably some of them got confused in the mass of infantry and dislocation of the line, but when the time for the retreat came these were the only two battalions that Haldane could safely consider to be members of his brigade.

The *jägers* of *Battalion 4* witnessed the move of the men of 10 British Brigade, which coincided with a considerable increase of British artillery fire on the hapless attackers at about midday. As the German soldiers watched the British advance over the hills to the east of Esnes and Haucourt, they had a problem. Their own guns had fired off almost all their first line ammunition and had fallen silent. Much

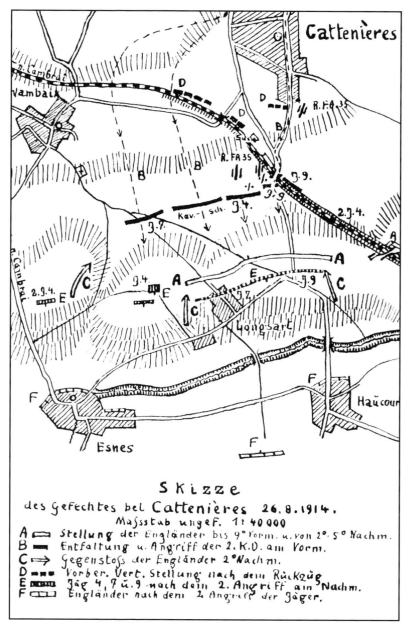

Map 21. Operations of *2nd Cavalry Division* around Cattenières 26 August 1914.

the same applied to the small arms ammunition, especially that required for the carbines of the dismounted troopers. Strenuous efforts had been made throughout the morning to keep the firing line supplied, but the intense fire fight had used up a great deal. The commander of *2nd Division* had no choice, therefore, but to withdraw his artillery into cover in Cattenières and to order his forward troops to withdraw from the heights and go firm along the line of the railway and the remainder to pull back. It was known that formations of *IV Reserve Corps* were marching forward and their leading elements were expected to arrive in about two hours.

These adjustments went quite well, despite the fact that a number of stretcher cases had to be left where they had fallen and the fact that the British units pushed forward once more onto their original front line. A number of the German wounded were then recovered and treated by British medical orderlies. The *jägers* commented favourably that when they advanced once more that evening, they came across their wounded, who had been bandaged expertly and given cigarettes and chocolate.

By about 4.30 pm the advancing troops of *IV Reserve Corps*, with *Reserve Infantry Regiment 36* of *7th Reserve Division* in the van, came under British small arms fire and *Jäger Battalions 7* and *9* took advantage of the fact to launch forward once more onto the heights around Longsart. Eventually units of *IV Reserve Corps* closed right up, pressing forward more or less coincidentally with the British withdrawal on the left flank. During the past three days, the *jäger* units had covered 110 kilometres and fought two battles in support of the cavalry. They had had almost nothing to eat during that time and hardly any sleep. That evening their field kitchens were still twelve kilometres away so, letting the men of *IV Reserve Corps* move forward to give them security, they crowded into houses and barns and slept the sleep of the dead.

An account describes, somewhat optimistically, given the experience related above, how part of the German army, at least, managed to feed itself:

> *In peacetime the marching performance achieved on this and following days would have been regarded as impossible. Not the least of the reasons was the excellent food produced on the new field kitchens. The* [presence of the] *'Goulash Guns' meant that the weary infantrymen could be served with a hot meal at every resting place, without the necessity for them to use up valuable time in food preparation. The staffs and the mounted units, who*

were not yet equipped with field kitchens, were also always grateful to be the guests of the infantry. There was no lack of meat, so the army high command was able to order an increase in the daily ration. On the march through constantly changing surroundings many a cockerel or chattering 'Guardian of the Capitol' [which must refer to geese] *gave a last sigh in the proximity of a German cooking pot. The field kitchens often displayed tell-tale decorations of feathers. There was such a glut of beef that the imprudent cooks frequently only made use of the best parts of cattle freshly slaughtered on the march and abandoned the remainder. Luckily strong drink was readily available to complement the excellent food. Large quantities of light local red wine were discovered, which was just as well in view of the poor quality of drinking water and the amount of fruit that the troop ate. It certainly kept everyone healthy and enabled them to march long distances with high morale.*

Brigadier General Haldane's experience is also well covered, as he wrote a short memoir after the war, *A Brigade of the Old Army, 1914*, 1920. In this he mentions how difficult it was to keep control of what was going on – he lost many members of his Brigade Signal section in the opening moves to halt the German onslaught that had hit 1/King's Own. He notes how he found it quite impossible to find the commanding officers of 1/Warwicks and 2/Dublin. Thus, when it came to the time to retire (which 10 Brigade did as rearguard at about 6pm), he writes,

I had, before leaving the vicinity of my two battalions on the right, observed what appeared to be them conforming to a rearward movement of 11 Brigade, and as I had not succeeded in getting into communication with them nor received any reports throughout the day, I trusted that their commanders would succeed in withdrawing them in safety.

Haldane's comments underline two significant points about Le Cateau: the poor communications and the way in which the line had to be thrown together, using troops already tired and disorganised and without time to establish a line, meant it was a battle in which the capability of the regimental officer was crucial. Initiative, reacting to events with very little idea at all of what was going on and where the enemy (and friends) were was essential. Steadfastness and leadership were elemental, given the conditions. Men trained in the South African War – and in minor conflicts since – showed their worth in a quite remarkable fashion at Le Cateau. The other point was the problem of communication, an early example for the British: poor quality communications became the hallmark of command and control (or lack of it) throughout the war.

Hauptmann Alfred Wirth, a German staff officer, wrote in his memoirs of Le Cateau:

> *It was like being on manoeuvres; one could actually still see the troops taking part. In the later fighting all that disappeared, and, in the three days' battle on the Marne especially, we experienced the truth of the "emptiness of the battlefield".*

Time off to pose for the camera during the German advance.

Chapter Four

THE TOURS

Introduction:

Le Cateau covers a much larger area than the usual **Battleground Europe** book. The northern edge of the British line, more or less, is marked conveniently by the Cambrai to Le Cateau road, the N43, commencing from Estourmel and finishing on the eastern outskirts of Le Cateau as the road continues on towards Catillon. This front comes to some ten miles. The battlefield is also deep, if the opening stage of the British retreat is included; whilst some advice is also given on touring the north of the road. Therefore it is essential that the tourer is equipped with at least the French IGN Green Series Map 4 (1:100 000), Laon Arras and preferably the two relevant Blue Series (1: 25 000) maps: 2607 O Cambrai est and Caudry; and 2607 E Le Cateau-Cambresis.

These are usually quite easily available at reasonable sized bookshops and newsagents (*libraire*) in Cambrai and Le Cateau and possibly St Quentin and Péronne.

Because so little of the ground has changed, many of the maps produced in regimental histories and the big battle map in the *Official History* can be used today, with a few notable exceptions. Of the centres of habitation, the most changed is Caudry; it is very difficult to get a full appreciation on the ground now of the situation to the north west of that town in particular; whilst on the east side a multi-laned road has (more or less) gone over an old railway line. Some marked roads or tracks are now no longer passable – though these are very few; or need a four wheel drive vehicle. In such cases this is, we hope, made clear in the text.

There are numerous CWGC cemeteries on the battlefield, but normally these contain very few – if any – casualties from the battle of Le Cateau in August 1914; they contain the large number of casualties from the heavy fighting in the area in October 1918, subsequent to the breaking of the Hindenburg Line; and numbers of wounded prisoners from other battles to the west who succumbed to their injuries.

The best time of year to visit Le Cateau is in the spring, but not much later than mid May; and in August, September and possibly October. The reason for this is the problem of crops – what you will see in your tour is a lot of landscapes as there are very few signs of the battlefield on the ground and many of the villages were destroyed or severely damaged in later fighting. However, because so little has changed in the size of many of these places, it is very easy to place yourself on the ground and to get an appreciation of what the soldiers saw in those traumatic hours in this, thankfully, relatively sleepy part of northern France.

We would suggest that a minimum of two days is needed to cover the battlefield well; to do it fully requires more time. On the other hand, it is also quite possible to do a simple drive around in a half day and get some feel of the situation on the ground. However, to do that misses one of the key problems faced by both sides, most particularly by the British. Account after battalion account makes the point that communications were very poor, that there was often minimal contact with the flanks and even between the composite parts of a battalion. A good look at the ground shows why this was so.

It may also seem that these tours are less full than some of those for other books in the series. The fact is that it is often very difficult to improve on the mapping that is provided in so many of the published accounts; with the relevant map and with the layout of roads and tracks so little changed, it is superfluous to add too many words. When an appropriate point is reached, the extracts from the regimental histories and the personal accounts can speak for themselves. Many readers will happily find their own routes and with the relatively light traffic, for the most part, will be able to saunter along without feeling too pressurised by the demands of other vehicles.

There are four tours offered in this book: three centred on each of the British infantry divisions involved and one for the area north of the Cambrai - Le Cateau road. All tours start on the assumption that the tourer is starting from Cambrai.

A final comment: these tours are directed at people in cars; a minibus should be able to manage, but please notice where we make a particular point about difficulties in turning around. Anyone bringing a bus tour would have to recce their route first. Of course, this is ideal country for someone to tour who has a mountain bike.

Tour 1: The Fifth Division Battlefield.

Start point: Le Cateau Military Cemetery

In some respects, this tour is the most difficult one to access. However, the tracks are generally good, though there are one or two 'sticky' places where one has to drive with caution. However, we have done all of these routes in a standard saloon car (though with reasonably high ground clearance) and came through unscathed, with perhaps the odd ominous sounding 'clunk'. Tracks can also be churned up, so whilst we are confident of the routes stated now, we cannot be sure what heavy agricultural machinery might do to them.

Assuming that the tourer is coming from Cambrai, then a good view may be had of the slightly rising ground to the right (south) of the N43 Le Cateau road (although be warned: traffic belts along here) along which much of the defensive line of II Corps was spread. Bear in mind that the N43 was more sunken in 1914 (frequent references are made to the 'banks' along it in contemporary accounts); and it was lined with poplars.

Looking to the north, one can also appreciate the problems that the German infantry had of approaching the British line over what seems such open terrain. There are a number of safe(ish) parking bays along this road, so advantage can be taken of them and maps consulted. Note any distinctive buildings: Inchy, for example, has a church spire that Walt Disney would have been proud to produce and church spires, indeed, along with different shaped or painted water towers, provide some of the clearest landmarks on the battlefield.

Le Cateau Military Cemetery (1) is well signposted off the road and there is reasonable parking near it. Views from the cemetery are not particularly good, but this is a most unusual cemetery, with casualties from a variety of armies buried in it – British, French, Russian and German. Established by the Germans in February 1916, many of those who died at Le Cateau (which became a hospital centre during the war) were buried here; although not a huge number, a high proportion of the fatal British casualties in this part of the line are buried here. If you walk to the rear of the cemetery (ie to the east) there are good views over the town, you can appreciate the covered approach that the Germans had up to the battlefield, Highland Cemetery (or at least the area of it) may be seen off to the south east and the embankment where the nine German machine guns brought their fire to bear on the men on the right of II Corps front can be identified, as well as the covered approach that the Germans had to that position. Walking carefully across the road from the Cemetery entrance gives you reasonable views over the British right flank, at least as far east as the Suffolk Hill area.

The cemetery was originally laid our during battlefield clearance after the 1914 battle, but the great majority of the burials date from 1918, when large numbers of German wounded died in nearby field hospitals, or during the defence of Le Cateau. In addition to 5,522 German soldiers, the cemetery contains the remains of 696 soldiers of the BEF, forty two Russians and eleven French soldiers. There is a mass grave here but, unusually, it contains only 140 men, of whom seventy seven are known. After the war, between 1921 and 1923, the French military authorities concentrated burials from fifty three communes here. This included 1,000 from the German cemetery at Maubeuge alone. The *Volksbund Deutsche Kriegsgräberfürsorge*, (*Volksbund*, for short), the charity responsible for the upkeep of German military cemeteries outside the Federal Republic, began planting trees and shrubs here in 1930. These were mostly limes and sycamores.

The Leib Kürassiers Mememorial, transferred to Le Cateau Military Cemetery.

At about the same time, a memorial to one officer and seven troopers of the *Leibkürassier Regiment Großer Kurfürst Nr. 1* from Silesia was moved here. It commemorates an action which occurred on 26 August 1914 about twenty-five kilometres east of Le Cateau. The *Leib Kurassiers* were part of *11 Cavalry Brigade, 5th Cavalry Division*. Their *5th Squadron*, under *Major* von Guise, was acting as part of a two-squadron advance guard and clashed with two squadrons of the French 10th Hussars. One officer and seven troopers were killed and seventeen were wounded. French losses were estimated at approximately twice as many. The inscription on the memorial translates as, *In memory of their brave comrades who are at rest here.* This statement is still largely true. The whereabouts of the graves of *Leutnant* von Raczeck and *Kürassier* Josef Lempa are unknown, but Sergeant Max Heimann, *Gefreiters* Josef Meissner and Paul Hauke and *Kürassiers* Karl Baumann, Anton Schelenz and Benhard Bittner all lie in the mass grave. In 1976 the old wooden crosses were replaced with the stone memorials seen today and at the same time the entrance gate was renewed.

Overall it would seem that there were comparatively few fatal German casualties during the battle of Le Cateau, but some regiments, notably *IR 93* which fought for Beaumont and *IR 66*, which advanced from Montay along the line of the modern D932, suffered comparatively heavily. Of those who were killed, undoubtedly a high proportion was buried here. As always, it is extremely difficult to provide detailed information about the men who were laid to rest in this cemetery. The *Volksbund* registers (where they survive theft and acts of vandalism) provide nothing that could help to connect the individual to a particular unit. In practical terms, therefore, the only chance of finding out this information is if an individual is mentioned in a regimental history, appears on an appended casualty list, or if he was included in one of the Rolls of Honour published by some towns and cities after the war. Examination of the histories of those regiments who fought on 26 August 1914 yields a mixed picture. Of the regiments of the *8th Infantry Division*, for example, the histories of *Füsilier Regiment 36* and *Infantry Regiment 72* provide complete casualty details, which can be cross-checked systematically with *Volksbund* records, but nothing but overall figures are to be found in the appendices of the histories of *Infantry Regiments 93* and *153*. This is particularly unfortunate, because *IR 93* lost 118 killed that day.

The haphazard, frequently cavalier, way in which the French authorities paid lip service to their responsibilities under Article 225 of the Treaty of Versailles, is another source of frustration. *Infantry Regiment 66*, which was subordinated to *13 Brigade* of *7th Infantry Division,* suffered some of the highest casualties on 26 August 1914, having four officers and seventy-five men killed in action. The regimental history provides an extremely detailed

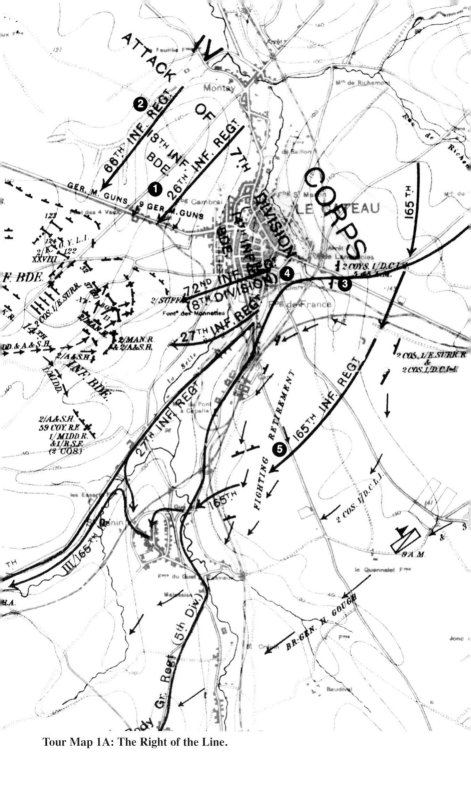

Tour Map 1A: The Right of the Line.

account of each man and we know, from contemporary photographs, that they were buried originally in properly marked graves; yet today only a mere handful can be identified. The most probable last resting place of the remainder is the mass grave in the German Cemetery in Caudry.

Despite these problems, it is possible to walk around the cemetery and visit the clusters of graves listed below, which relate to the battle. Where there are gaps in the lists, it may reasonably be inferred, providing the dates are appropriate, that many of the men named on the crosses are from regiments that also fought at Le Cateau.

Musketier Gustav Thieme 9th Company IR 72, born 30 Sep 1893 Atern (Sangerhausen) G 380

Musketier Willi Heimer 9th Company IR 72, born 12 Aug 1892 Trebnitz (Weißenfels) G 381

Musketier Heinrich Kulosa 5th Company IR 72, born 2 Jul 1893 Kalkowski (Grosse Wartenberg) G 383

Musketier Reinhard Herklotz 5th Company IR 72, born 19 Sep 1892 Heidesdorf (Freiberg) G 384

Gefreiter Hermann Zurleit 2nd Company IR 66, born at Berge G408

Vizefeldwebel Walter Grünewald 3rd Company IR 66, born at Schadeleben G439

Unteroffizier Willi Herrmann 8th Company IR 66, born at Schöneberg G442

Füsilier Albert Börner 3rd Company FR 36, born19 Mar 1892 at Sautzschen G 451

Einjährig-Freiwilliger Johannes Schwannecke 10th Company IR 36, born 2 Mar 1890 at Barby G476

Füsilier Kurt Rüdiger 12th Company FR 36, born 17 Oct 1888 at Roda G478

Füsilier Franz Kriehme 3rd Company FR 36, born 25 Aug 1892 at Wehlitz G 483

Füsilier Otto Krause 1st Company FR 36, born 23 Dec 1891 at Liedersdorf G485

Musketier Viktor Kusch 1st Company IR 66, born at Zawodzie G 488

Gefreiter Fritz Hundertmark 1st Company IR 66, born at Klostergröningen G494

Füsilier Wilhelm Fiedler 10th Company FR 36, born 28 Jun 1891 at Wippra G497

Gefreiter Ernst Uhlendorf 10th Company FR 36, born 6 Jul 1888 at Corbetha G498

Gefreiter Richard Beyer 10th Company FR 36, born 2 May 1891 at Keuschberg G500

Gefreiter Hermann Dönicke 10th Company FR 36, born 8 Jul 1892 at Halle G502

Einjährig-Freiwilliger Ernst Otto 2nd Company FR 36, born 28 Aug 1892 at Alt-Krüsow G512

Einjährig-Freiwilliger Otto Faulmann 2nd Company FR 36, born 10 Apr 1894 at Weißenfels G515

Füsilier Walter Magister 2nd Company FR 36, born 28 Oct 1891 at Oschatz G516

Füsilier Paul Schulz MG Company FR 36, born 6 Apr 1892 at Eiersleben G 518

Füsilier Otto Hartmann 5th Company FR 36, born 20 Jul 1891 at Zeitz G 527

Füsilier Paul Hilpert 3rd Company FR 36, born 22 Jun 1882 at Meuschau G 530

Hornist Johann Paschek 3rd Company FR 36, born 22 Oct 1891 at Zernitz G 531

Füsilier Hermann Grollmisch 3rd Company FR 36, born 17 Jan 1887 at Strelitzko G538

Füsilier Alfred Zech 3rd Company FR 36, born 22 Aug 1892 at Nißma G 539

Gefreiter Paul Giesemann 6th Company FR 36, born 25 Mar 889 at Riestedt G545

Füsilier Paul Dopke 7th Company FR 36, born 17 Ar 1892 at Labenz G546

Unteroffizier Franz Hoffmann 8th Company FR 36, born 28 Dec 1890 at Zörbig G547

Füsilier Hermann Stolz 8th Company FR 36, born 18 Feb 1892 at Hettstedt G548

Füsilier Kurt Hilpert 7th Company FR 36, born 11 Feb 1891 at Martinsrieth G555

Unteroffizier Friedrich Hecht 7th Company FR 36, born 28 Apr 1892 at Sandersleben G643

Gefreiter Karl Schrader 8th Company FR 36, born 27 Jun 1890 at Neudorf G632

Füsilier Karl Kirchhoff, MG Company FR 36, born 24 Dec 1891 at Stolberg G652

Reserve Oberleutnant Karl Bürger, born 28 Oct 1875 at Halle G653

Hauptmann Kurt Freytag, born 19 Sep 1875 at Rudolstadt died of wounds 28 Aug 1914 MG Company, FR 36 G659

Leutnant Walter Fricke IR 66 G661

Hauptmann Emil Frucht IR 72, born 2 Jan 1874 in Bremerhaven. G662

Major Eugen Hinsch 2nd Battalion FAR 75 Hinsch was killed by a stray rifle bullet near Rambourlieux Farm about midday 26 August, whilst his guns and observers were manoeuvring their batteries to bring flanking fire down in support of the attack on Inchy. He was the only member of FAR 75 to be killed that day. G 664

Füsilier Franz Blümling 10th Company IR 36, born 12 Jan 1889 at Argenschwenk G667

Gefreiter Karl Frühling 1st Company IR 36, born 8 Dec 1890 at Schlechtwitz G672

Block 2

Gefreiter Edmund Hubrig 9th Company IR 72. Born 3 Apr 1891 Prösen (Liebenwerda) G 651

Reservist (Musketier) Alwin Deckert 2nd Company IR 72, born 30 Jun 1891in Poserna, (Merseburg) G663

Unteroffizier Felix Simon 11th Company IR 66, born at Liebau G664

Musketier Walter Löwe 11th Company IR 66, born at Gommern G680

Musketier Georg Diebe 7th Company IR 66, born at Berlin G684

Hauptmann Heinrich Bonsac IR 66, buried Le Cateau Cemetery G 805

Block 3

Musketier Wilhelm Riemer 3rd Company IR 66, born at Tangermünde G 256

Kameradengrab

Gefreiter Franz Hoppe MG Company FR 36, born 2 Jun 1891 at Baasdorf

A notable British casualty of 1918 buried here is Lance Corporal JW Sayer of the Queen's Regiment (I B59), who won his VC at Le Verguier during the opening of the German Spring Offensive on 21 March 1918. He held out in his isolated post for a considerable period and caused numerous German casualties. He died of his wounds in a German hospital in Le Cateau.

Proceed another five hundred metres or so on the road to Montay and take the road on the left that is signposted to **Selridge Cemetery (2).** The road is pretty good, but take it carefully; after about one and a half kilometres, when the reasonable surface gives out and a track begins, the isolated cemetery is on your left. Almost certainly they are all October/November 1918 casualties, but as there are a few unknown it is possible that some are from the August battle. Go to the back of the cemetery and get as high as you can. The ground rises to the south of the cemetery, but there are still some reasonable views over the battlefield from Le Cateau to Inchy and beyond. Looking to the north gives one some idea of the German perspective. To the west, along the track and some 1500 yards away as the crow flies, is **Rambourlieux Farm.** This is the area from where German artillery was able to fire in enfilade on the British positions, in particular, of the battalions of the Fifth Division holding the area around Suffolk Hill. Note that the track becomes impassable shortly beyond the cemetery to practically all cars unless your four wheel drive has appropriate off road tyres.

Turn around and **return to the D932** and then to the crossroads on the N43, known at the time as the *Pont des Quatre Vaux*. At the N43 turning, turn left and drive through Le Cateau, keeping on the N43 (direction Cattilon). You will pass under a railway bridge (this line, towards Solesmes, has been dug up, but much of the bed remains) and then the road to Pommereuil is signposted to your left a few hundred metres beyond. Stop where it is safe **(3)** and then look back towards the town. It was here that the early shots took place, when 1/DCLI and part of 1/E Surrey were quietly preparing to move off and continue the retreat. Le Cateau was still something of a hive of British activity as troops were moving out, although thankfully (for the British) most of the units were clear. A few hours earlier and the Germans would have come to a scene of seeming chaos. Le Cateau had been a busy place in the days preceding the battle, as GHQ had been based here before the wise decision was made to move south, to St Quentin. Many of the soldiers of the 4th Division had also been detrained here on the 24th and early hours of the 25th.

Return into the town and take the next major turning to the left (it has traffic lights), the D21 to Busigny. After about two hundred yards there is a turning on the left, which is signposted with (amongst other things) *cimetière*. Proceed for about four hundred yards and **Le Cateau Communal Cemetery (4)** will be found on your left. Note that it is our experience that in any communal cemetery where there are CWGC burials there will be a small rectangular sign, in the familiar green background, white letters format, on the wall near (and sometimes on) the entrance gate. The burials in Plot III were carried out by the Germans, and there are some seventy of so casualties from the August fighting (most of whom succumbed to their wounds in the town's

German Memorial Le Cateau Communal Cemetery.

hospitals), most of whom are unknown. Until the early 1920s there were a number of Germans buried here; and the care shown by the Germans for the war dead of all nations is clearly illustrated by the memorial pillar in Plot III. Amongst other points of interest is the War Memorial to the sons of Le Cateau who were victims of various conflicts in the years preceding the Great War as well as during it, dating back to the Crimean War.

From the cemetery, turn around and return to the junction to the D21, and turn left. It soon bends to the left (at a meeting point of roads); some five hundred yards later there is a turning on the left to the station (*gare*), which you take. After a couple of hundred yards and almost immediately after a bend to the right, there is a turning on the left (the D12 to Wassigny), which almost immediately goes under the railway. Go up the hill and, about a kilometre after the turning, you will see **Highland Cemetery (5)** on your right. This cemetery consists entirely of 1918 burials. Proceed behind the Cross of Sacrifice and you will have grand views to the west over the right hand part of II Corps line. Looking to the north west, almost to the limit of views to the west of the cemetery wall, through some trees and by some buildings, the clump of trees that mark Suffolk Hill may just be seen; as well as much of the battlefield from Troisvilles to the rear areas as far back as Honnechy. One wonders what even

Suffolk Hill Memorial, taken from western edge of Highland Cemetery.

Suffolk Hill Memorial

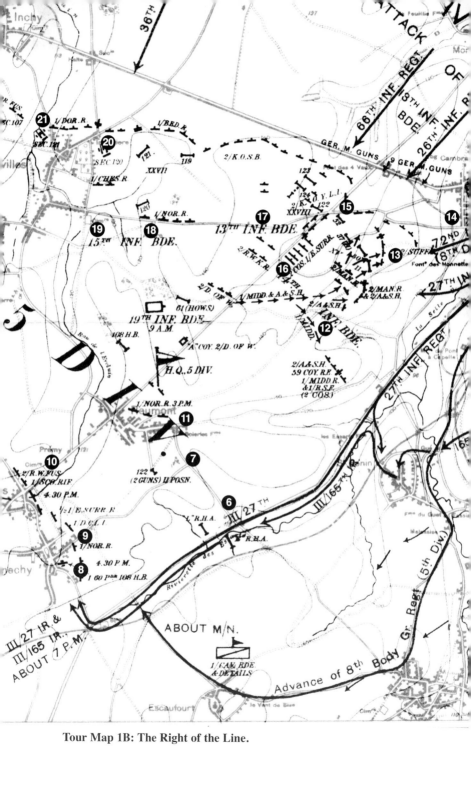

Tour Map 1B: The Right of the Line.

greater damage the German army might have achieved if they had brought up their artillery here during the day, especially as it was more or less vacant of British troops earlier on. It was along the ridge to the east of the road that the men of 1/DCLI and 2/E Surrey gradually retired; elements of the battalions crossed the road about a kilometre further on as they made their difficult withdrawal towards Reumont and Honnechy. Proceed along the D12 until you find a safe track which you can use to turn around; return towards Le Cateau and then back to the D21, turning left towards Busigny.

Continue along this for just over four kilometres; on your right, on the bank, you will see the small Quiétiste Military Cemetery, with some 60 or so 1918 casualties. [The name seems to relate to Fénelon, the saintly Archbishop of Cambrai who died in 1715, who was engaged in a running theological fight with Jansenism and its less extreme version, Quietism.] The cemetery marks the rough area where the German advance more or less halted on this side of the valley, the Germans coming under effective fire and lacking sufficient numbers to push forward.

A few yards further on there is **a minor road** on the right, which you should take. Proceed up this a short distance and stop **(6)** where it is safe – you will need to leap back into the car if another vehicle approaches. On the south side of the D21, at the crossroads, is a farm. Behind this was sited E Battery RHA and to the south east, within a hundred yards or so of where you now are, was L Battery RHA – though its exact location is a matter of some conjecture. They were tasked with covering the approaches of the Germans from Le Cateau along the valley of the Essarts, a tributary of the River Selle. Continue up this road and stop where **a track from the left** meets the road **(7)**. About two hundred yards to the west, in front of the water tower, a couple of guns of 122 Battery helped in the successful efforts to prevent the Germans from approaching the British from the right flank. Look to the right, where you are viewing towards the ground about 1,500 yards away which was covered by elements of 2/A&SH, 1/Middx, 1/RSF and 59 Coy RE. The tour will bring you closer to this ground in due course. Proceed to a suitable place for turning around. Return to the D21 (good views over E and L Batteries' positions) and turn right; after a couple of kilometres there is a turning on the right (the D115) to Honnechy; nearby was the old station for the village.

This road, running through Honnechy and Maurois to the Roman road (the D932), and the first part of the extension of it, which goes to Bertry, more or less marks the defended line, established at about 4pm, through which the forward elements of the 5th Division would retreat as the afternoon of the 26th progressed. As you come to the very first buildings of the village, 1/Norfolk (15 Brigade) was on the right, in the fields beyond the houses. The battalion had moved from its original position on the Roman road – Troisvilles road to a new position at Reumont (arriving at about 3pm) and then fell back to this line. As the road moves further into the village there is a coming together of streets, with the church high up on the left (there is a single, unknown British casualty buried there, a victim of Le Cateau 1914). Just before **the junction (8)**, on the right, was sited a 60 pdr gun of 108 Heavy Battery. Between the fire

Honnechy Church and below, Honnechy Cemetery.

of this gun and the rifles of 1/Norfolk, an advance by German infantry and artillery along the D21, which seems to have first been spotted at about 4pm, was halted.

Take the turning on the right, signposted to **Honnechy British Cemetery (9)**. The cemetery is most unusual, consisting entirely of casualties from the nearby hospital centre in the village (for both the Germans and the British) or of men transferred from German burial sites after the war. On the right of the road, some yards before the cemetery is reached, was 1/Norfolk. On the left was 1/DCLI and part of 1/E Surrey, with 1/Scottish Rifles taking the line to the Roman road and 2/RWF prolonging it to the other side. All these battalions would have had outposts forward to screen this reverse slope position, and it is an easy matter to drive up to the communal cemetery further up the road and get excellent views across to the north, west and (less good) east from this well sheltered position. Despite the incredible confusion as the men of the 5th Division poured down the Roman road, these rearguard battalions moved off quite safely, more or less unhampered by German troops following up the abandonment of the battlefield.

Return to Honnechy and turn right; the village melds with Maurois after a time. Michael Gavaghan's *Le Cateau* gives most useful information on the trials and tribulations of the British medical units across the battlefield, not least here in Maurois, where the school and church were both commandeered to house the wounded. At the crossroads, pause a moment. It will take a great deal of imagination, but

Honnechy Chateau, currently a 'Bed and Breakfast' establishment.

along here came hordes of British troops, units all jumbled up, exhausted and famished, and with a long tramp down the road to the left to Estrées before them, some eleven miles along an unrelentingly straight road (Roman

Honnechy **Maurois**

Honnechy and Maurois from the roman Road.

legionaries must have got very disheartened by the sight of such roads), before they could even begin to think of taking some rest. What a target there was for German cavalry, if only it had been properly handled and properly trained for such things.

Turn right; over the crest of the hill, on the left, will be found **Maurois Communal Cemetery (10)**. Be careful about the traffic as you cross the road to park here. There are views over the defensive line between Honnechy and Maurois and, to the north east, the line of the Roman road to Reumont and beyond, along which the battered remnants of the 5th Division retired. To the north lies Troisvilles and to the north west Bertry, site of the HQ of both II Corps and the 3rd Division.

Proceed into Reumont. About 500 yards into the village there is a turning to the church on the left; in the churchyard there are a few 1914 burials, the two identified of them both belonging to the Argylls: one a twenty one year old private, the other, forty one years old, Captain Fraser. Opposite there is a turning to the right, ignore this one, but immediately afterwards there is another: take it. At the T junction turn left, follow the road as it bends quite sharply to the right and take the next left, which starts promisingly enough but eventually deteriorates the closer it gets towards the Suffolk Hill Memorial, about three and a half kilometres as the crow flies. This is usually a passable track (for most of the distance it is metalled), but proceed with caution and be prepared to abandon the attempt, especially if there has been some nasty weather and heavy rain. After several hundred yards there is a **rough track** on the right **(11)**, where you should stop. In reaching here, a few hundred yards back, you will have passed over the position occupied in the early afternoon by the Norfolks, who straddled the road. Looking northwards, across the outer edge of Reumont, there was considerable activity. In one of the last houses of the village was where Major General Fergusson had his 5th Division headquarters. In the fields beyond the Roman road was situated 108 Heavy Battery, which fought a reasonably successful battle against German artillery

and was effective in assisting the retreat of forward units of the Division. Nearby, and alongside the road, was A Company, 2/DoW, charged with escorting the guns. Beyond them, on the east side of Bois Dix Sept, was the general location of 19 Brigade before it was split up, half heading off to form a defensive line in Montigny, west of Bertry, whilst it was from here that 1/Middx and 2/A&SH made their way to support the Suffolks and Manchesters in the vicinity of Suffolk Hill.

Suffolk Hill Memorial.

Continue along this track for about two kilometres until a **track** meets it, coming in from the left **(12)**. It was along and near (to the north) of the latter that 1/Middx and 2/A&SH advanced from their reserve positions. 1/Middx crossed the Reumont track a few yards before this junction, along with part of 2/A&SH, and joined up with half of 1/RSF and 59 Coy RE to hold a defensive line centred about five hundred yards away on the spur to the south. It was at approximately this track junction that a gun of 11 Bty RFA was overturned. Beyond this point the track tends to deteriorate – there should be no difficulty in reaching here – and the more cautious may want to take the track to the left and join the Roman road a kilometre or so away. Where the track joins the road, on the far side, was the location of the main body of 2/DofW, spread out at right angles to the Roman road.

The intrepid should now proceed along the Reumont track. Looking to the left, to the Roman road, on the far side of it was 2/RWKents, at right angles, whilst on this side of it, also at right angles, were two companies of 1/E Surrey.

After about five hundred yards (you will have to use your tachometer for this, as there are no obvious landmarks) you will be coming through the reserve positions of part of 2/A&SH and only a matter of yards beyond that, on the left hand side of the track, parts of 2/Manchesters – which moved further forward during the battle – and on the right hand side a mixed party of 2/Manchesters and

Reumont road; Suffolk Hill in the distance. Jack Sheldon looking west towards the Roman Road.

2/A&SH. It is just beyond this point that you are entering into the positions of the guns of XV Brigade Royal Field Artillery [RFA] – the 11th and 80th Batteries, intermingled with Manchesters, Suffolks and other infantry elements. About 1,200 yards after the track junction at (12) there is another **track junction** on the left **(13)**, making for quite a difficult turn into it. This track (We have always found this driveable, even in a medium sized minibus) takes you up to the Suffolk Hill memorial. However, be warned, you can only really turn around by making use of the gates that lead onto the grass surrounding the memorial. We have never found these locked, but if they are it can be a trying reverse back to the track junction.

At the area of the track junction, and extending northwards, were some of the forward elements of the units defending the right flank of the Division. The Suffolk Hill Memorial itself is impressive; not so much physically, but the list of casualties of the men who died here, the great majority of whom have no known grave, marks a spot of enormous courage and fortitude. Indeed the views from it are not particularly good north and west; the defended ground forward and to the flanks is obscured by the nature of the ground. It certainly is not ground which, given time, would have been defended in the way it was; but Le Cateau was not a battlefield where the defending general had the luxury of choosing the points on which he would make his stand. That is the nature of the problem facing an army unexpectedly forced to make a long retreat.

From here the tour takes you into Le Cateau. Retrace your way to the track junction and turn left; this eventually leads past a large school complex (and, beyond it, sports facilities). Keep to the left of the car park. When the road is reached turn left and at a T junction, left again. In a very short distance, there is a major road on the right, which you should take **(Boulevard Paturle) (14)**. After several hundred yards you will come to traffic lights: left takes you out to the N43 westbound (which is the direction of the tour) and right leads down into the main part of Le Cateau: it might be a good opportunity to stop for

The surprisingly mildly damaged Boulevard Paturle after the British took Le Cateau in October 1918.

lunch or for a reviving drink in any case.

Instead of turning off on Boulevard Paturle it is possible to continue straight ahead. However, the road does deteriorate, and although seemingly solid enough underneath, I would not attempt it in anything less than a 4 x 4, at least once the going gets tough. It has its interests, as the area would have had British troops in it on 26 August, and it will bring you out eventually to (or close to) the positions occupied by 52 and 37 Batteries and part of 1/KOYLI. If it is possible to find somewhere to put the car so that it does not block traffic, it is possible to get to the place where 37 Battery had its guns and view the place where three VCs were won. These positions are also reached by the alternative route below.

At the Roman road (D932) crossroads, turn left, heading towards Reumont. On the right of the road, within a couple of hundred yards of the turning, were the infantry of 1/KOYLI and three batteries of XXVIII Brigade RFA. Nearest the Roman road was 124 Battery, slightly beyond it to the north west was 123 and in a small hollow, just before the right hand turn to Troisvilles, was 124 Battery, amazingly enough never 'uncovered' by the Germans and which suffered very few casualties until the limbers came up as the withdrawal began. All but two guns of this Brigade were lost in the battle.

Finding somewhere to park is not all that easy. The **road to Troisvilles**, the

Area held by 2/KOYLI either side of the Troisvilles Road.

first on the right **(15)**, has a large exit area and I have felt comfortable parking tight against the bank there; whatever, special care must be taken. The tour will be continuing along this road in due course.

Cross the road and go down the track opposite the Troisvilles road. Look back across the Roman road. To the north of the Troisvilles road were the guns of XXVIII Brigade RFA and the men of 2/KOYLI. Immediately to the south of that road, facing east, was part of B Company of 2/KOYLI, the other part on your side of the road, posted parallel to the Roman road, facing in the same direction. The differing heights of the banks of the roads at the time meant that the men on the east side could fire over the heads of the men on the west side, providing a tiered effect. Proceed about two hundred yards along the track **(16)** and then look to your right, to the south. About a hundred yards away were the guns of 52 Battery, which were abandoned at the time of the withdrawal and the horse teams used to help to remove the other guns. The guns there fired for as long as they could: Captain Barber Starkey and a wounded sergeant served one gun between them, going to a neighbouring wagon for ammunition. The captain died of his wounds on 11 September (or thereabouts – there is some disagreement about the date of his death) and is buried in Le Cateau Communal Cemetery. Proceeding another hundred yards or so along this track brings you to the left of 2/Suffolk's position, with the men of C Company. As the track closes to a junction of tracks, it becomes increasingly sunken. The end in this sector of the front came at about 2.45pm, though no German seems to have come to 52's position until about 5pm.

Just beyond 52 Battery was positioned 37 (Howitzer) Battery, which straddled another track, coming out on the Roman road about six hundred yards south of the one you are on. It seems quite extraordinary to think that five guns of 80 Battery, four of 11 and four of 37 were saved when they were withdrawn sometime around 2pm – ie, five guns were lost in addition to the six of 52 Battery.

Captain D Reynolds of 37 Battery, once he got back to Reumont, sought permission to find some volunteers and try and extract the two guns of the Battery remaining on the position. Accompanied by Lieutenants EG Earle and WD Morgan (both of the Battery), Reynolds took up two teams to bring the howitzers out. Becke, in his *Royal Artillery at Le Cateau*, takes up the story.

'As they galloped down the valley [from Reumont] towards the Battery position the German infantry were commencing to swarm all over the ground on which the right batteries of the line had been in action. Nevertheless, both howitzers were limbered up, but then one team was shot down by the German infantry, who were now not more than two hundred yards away. The other howitzer, however, galloped off and, although one driver was hit, it was brought away.

'The CRA ([Divisional] Commander Royal Artillery) saw this episode himself, and personally ordered one of our batteries to stop firing in order to allow Captain Reynolds to make his attempt.' All of this happened, according to an eyewitness, an officer of 1/Norfolks, between 3 and 3.15pm. Reynolds got the VC, as did Drivers Luke and Drain. Reynolds died in 1915 from complications caused by gas poisoning and is buried at Etaples: Luke died in 1983, Drain in 1979. Earle got a DSO.

To the right of the Roman Road. Suffolk Hill in the distance – in the foreground area of advance of Middlesex and Argylls.

Proceed down the Roman road about six hundred yards and you will see a good quality **track (16) on the left**. The only sensible thing is to select a suitable off road position in the vicinity. Be warned: if you do decide to go down the track the only thing to do when coming back is to reverse onto the main road, a tricky (and probably illegal) business. Look back along the Roman road towards the track just visited. In between these two tracks were two companies of 1/E Surrey. It was along this track that Reynolds and his volunteers rescued one of the two guns and where one of the teams was shot down. Turn around, turn right and return to the Troisvilles road, the first on your left

This road to Troisvilles can be rough and one has to hope that there is nothing coming the other way, as the road is often sunken with banks on either side, leaving little room for manoeuvre. Nearly all the roads in the area of the battlefield would have been substantially more sunken than they are now, narrower and with either a dirt or pavé surface. In addition, the N43 had poplars along its sides, which provided useful aiming marks for the British.

The HQ of 13 Brigade **(17)** was situated on the north bank about five hundred yards along this road. Continue along the road and a little short of three kilometres after its commencement you will see a large, **solitary tree** (marked *Arbre on* contemporary maps) on the bank to your left **(18)**. This tree is a replacement – indeed quite possibly a replacement of a replacement. There is space to park a short distance beyond the tree. In the course of this drive, looking to the right, with outposts extending beyond the crest of the rising slope, you will see the positions occupied by 2/KOSB, the left battalion of 13 Brigade. About one and a half kilometres from the start of the Troisvilles road brings you to the right flank of 15 Brigade, whose right was held by the Bedfords. Shortly before the *Arbre* was where the Norfolks were posted, held in battalion reserve. In the fields to the right were the guns of XXVII Brigade. Two of the batteries were particularly useful in helping to cover the front of 9 Brigade as well as its own. All of these guns were extracted.

Just beyond the Norfolks was where the Brigade commander, Gleichen, had his HQ. He was able to watch the efforts to bring the tree down. The road ceases to be sunken at this point, and good views may be had of the dispositions east of Troisvilles, as well as the village itself and La Sotière. At the road junction turn left and go to **Troisvilles Communal Cemetery (19)**. There are known to be seven Le Cateau 1914 casualties here, including Captain R Stevens, the Brigade Major of 9 Brigade. It is probable that the thirteen unknowns are also from that battle. Troisvilles Communal Cemetery is typical of several villages in the battle area, where it is probable that the local communities went out and found the soldiers and buried them after the battle moved on. A number of these villages have a standardised stone with wording in French indicating the number of British soldiers buried and – occasionally – with a name or two of the casualties.

Turn around and follow the road north towards La Sotière; about five hundred yards away, opposite the (second) turning to the left, was where the

View from the Troisvilles – Roman Road.

sad remnants of 1/Cheshire were placed. At the roundabout turn right and, more or less opposite a factory, on the right there is a track where it should be safe to stop **(20)**. Some couple of hundred yards down this track there was a section of 120 Battery; on the other side of the road, in the area of the factory, was a machine gun of 1/Dorsets, instrumental in keeping the Germans at bay in this sector. Looking east, across the fields, the Bedfords were stretched out. There are good views along a good length of the Troisvilles – D932 road; but it is noticeable how the undulations in the ground obscure the view along the length of the ground to the D932. A few hundred yards further down the road there is another track to the right (which existed in 1914). You may want to drive to the junction and walk down this and get a better look at the positions of the Bedfords and of 119 Battery

The replacement 'Arbre'.

Turn around as possible and proceed straight across the roundabout and take the second turning on the right, signposted Inchy (be warned, this turning is cunningly concealed!). The road is narrow and there are not too many places to stop. There is a track going off to the left; beyond it (to the north) there was a section of 121 Battery. As the housing of the village ends **(21)**, try and find a place to stop for a while. The Dorsets' left hand boundary was on this road. There are excellent views to the north, over Inchy and Beaumont, and it is easy to see why the Germans felt disinclined to make much movement from here. To the west there are not particularly good views because of the lie of the land, but Audencourt can be made out in the distance. This was the ground held by 9 Brigade of the neighbouring 3rd Division.

This concludes the 5th Division tour. 15 Brigade suffered some 150 casualties – a striking contrast to the 1,300 or so of 14 and the 950 of 13 Brigades. From here you may drive into **Inchy** and back on to the N43. The 3rd Division tour commences in that town.

Inchy in the distance from the left of 1/Dorsets' position.

Water Tower
Area of Start, Tour 2)

Inchy Church

Tour 2: The Third Division Battlefield.

The tour commences in Inchy. The first stop is slightly off the tour map, see Map p.63.

The villages of Inchy and Beaumont blend into each other. On the night before the battle the British had outposts forward of here and both places were full of

The Germans coming out of Inchy here suffered heavy casualties from the British holding the high ground.

troops anticipating a further retreat in the early hours of the 26th. The Germans moved in and then, largely, strayed no further than the southern outskirts. Opposite them were 9 Brigade.

The road through Inchy has some tortuous turns in it. Once past the highly unusual church on your right the road takes a sharp bend to the right and then turns sharply left. At this latter bend there is a road off to the right, signposted Troisvilles. Take it. Within a hundred yards or so, as the road bends to the left, there is a narrow road on the right; take this until, within another hundred yards or so, you come to a crossroads, where you should turn left. The road soon gives out and degenerates into a track, but there is a large open space where you can stop **(1)**. If you walk up the track, past the water tower, you are coming towards the forward positions of 9 Brigade. About five hundred yards beyond the water tower is the location of the line of 1/RSF (minus two companies). To your right were the Lincolns and to the left the Northumberland Fusiliers. Situated half way along the Northumberland Fusiliers' line, to the rear, was a section of 107 Battery RFA. To your right is the village of Audencourt. If you continue to the end of the track there are

German view along the east of 9 Brigade's front.

1/Dorsets   La Sotière   1/Northumberland Fusiliers

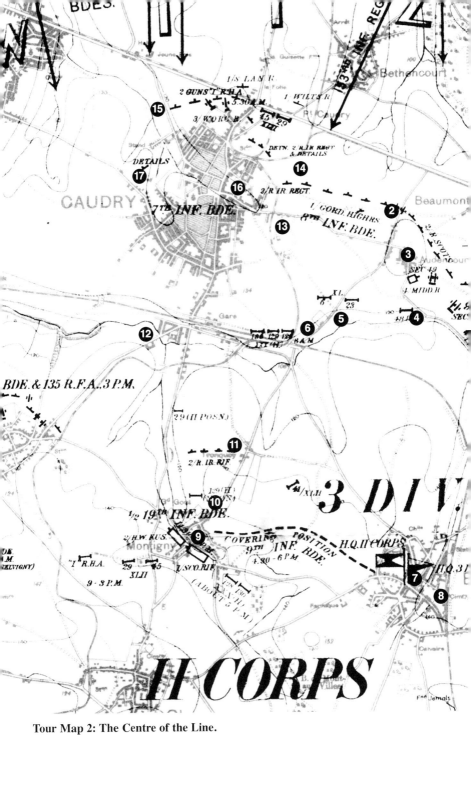

Tour Map 2: The Centre of the Line.

Audencourt   **Area of 1/Gordon Highlanders**   Caudry Church

View across the front held by 1/Gordon Highlanders.

views over to the south; at the bottom of the valley there is another track (passable only with a 4 x 4), which was used to hold the wounded and across which elements of the Brigade retired when the time came to withdraw. Again to your right, about five hundred yards away, may be seen the junction with the track which runs south from Beaumont. Behind this was a section of 108 Battery that, along with a section of 107 Battery, provided formidable support for the line. Remaining in support until the last moment, the two guns of 108 and two of 107 Batteries had to be abandoned. The Brigade suffered about 180 casualties in all for the battle; despite its exposed position it managed to withdraw with trifling loss and the Germans were not quick to follow them up.

Return to the car and drive back into Inchy. At the crossroads, go straight ahead, past the church, and then turn left onto the N43. About 500 yards after you leave Beaumont there is a turning on the right (D115a) to Audencourt, situated on high ground. Close to the junction with the N43 there was a German battery. Proceed up this busy road for several hundred yards. On your right there is a track heading off west (towards Caudry) and a rather more satisfactory road on the left heading for Beaumont. Stop (safely) at the track **(2)**. At this point the approach road was covered by a couple of machine guns (though it seems there may have been four – those of both the Gordons and the Royal Scots – see below). To the north of the track, and continuing more or less in a straight line west towards Caudry, were the Gordons, and beyond them part of the Royal Irish Regiment, continuing the line to the now disappeared railway line which skirted the east of Caudry. The track is drivable, but the last time we were there some works were in progress on it, which required a short detour on a field (once started on this track there is nowhere to turn around). The tourer should be happy to look across the lie of the land at this point, unless he wants to find a safer place to park and walk the track. A branch from it, a few hundred yards from its exit on the Audencourt - Caudry road, has now gone – the line was forward of this obliterated track. So has the small wood in front of which

218

Hay's platoon was situated during the battle.

It was somewhere near **(2)** that Hay was found on the morning of the 27th. On the opposite side of the track, bending back south east, were 2/R Scots, whose line ran diagonally across the face of Audencourt. Return to your car and, at the crossroads, take the left turn into the village. Find a convenient place near the church and stop **(3)**. Walk past the church, heading east, and down a track (which definitely nothing short of a tractor should attempt). It dips down into a deep embankment. As you emerge into the sunlight (the banks are very overgrown), on the right was a section of 49 Battery RFA. On your left was the right flank of the Royal Scots. Return to the church and the car. Continue along the road through Audencourt but go no further than the water tower on your right **(4)** as the promising road becomes, in a few hundred metres, a difficult and then a very difficult track, emerging eventually at Le Fayt, an extension of Troisvilles. Walk down the track, past another coming in from your right and south of that and to the right of the one on which you are walking was sited 48 Heavy Battery. According to Becke, it 'was busily engaged in shelling advancing infantry, who at these longer ranges gave … promising targets, as well as searching the ground from which the infantry appeared, to prevent any concentration prior to attack. It was also employed on counter battery work controlling the German batteries as far as possible.' It withdrew at about 4.30pm without loss. Nearby the 3rd Division had its advanced HQ.

Return to your car and rejoin the D115a, turning left on to it. About a kilometre or so after leaving Audencourt there is a track **(5)** that runs at right angles either side of the road. Just to the north of the track heading east was 23 Battery RFA, whilst on the other side of the D115a was 6 Battery. This latter battery was concentrating its fire in particular on Béthencourt Wood, east of that village, where German infantry seemed to be concentrating. When the time for withdrawal came (and it seemed to get the message rather later than other parts of the Brigade), three of 6's guns had to be abandoned.

Becke quotes a description of the Audencourt battlefield given by Lieutenant Armitage of 27 Battery, who had been made a prisoner and was moved from Ligny to a German hospital in Béthencourt on 1 September and walked this road.

'South of the village … in a field to the west of the road he saw some 18 pdr guns [these were of 6 Battery]. An unlimbered gun proved that the battery had been in position roughly facing north and large piles of empty cases showed where the guns had stood. One gun was halfway from the position to the gate leading to the road. Another was limbered up in the gate and stood there with the team, all black horses, lying dead in front of it.

'Further on, in the village itself, was a medley of water carts, cable carts and general service limbered wagons, each lying by the roadside with the horses or mules dead in the shafts. [The Brigade transport had not been removed to the rear.] At the northern end of the village were four machine guns, their detachments and three officers lying dead beside them. One of the guns was painted in blotches of various colours.

View from north of Audencourt towards Beaumont and Inchy, 2/Royal Scots front.

'The bank of the road at the northern end of the village, a hedgerow about four feet high, was pitted with hastily scraped hollows. Nearly every hollow held its man.

'Just to the south of the Le Cateau – Cambrai road and close to it were the remains of a German gun position. One gun, damaged by a direct hit, still stood there, the positions occupied by the others being indicated by five piles of empty cases. A little to the right was a small mound of freshly turned earth with five helmets on the top. These helmets had the artillery ball on top in

East of Audencourt looking towards Beaumont and Inchy; and across much of Brigade's Front.

II Corps' and 3 Division's HQs were situated near this unremarkable crossroads in Bertry.

place of the spike, and were obviously officers' property.'

Proceed south and go under the railway **(6)**. On the embankment here, from about 8am, were stationed the howitzers of XXX Howitzer Brigade. At the road junction on the far side of the railway turn left (D115) for Bertry, into which you drive (there is a large *calvaire* as you come into the town on your left). At a major junction, go around to the right and then turn left, direction Maurois (and still the D115), a few yards further on. It was at this junction of streets that both II Corps and the 3rd Division had their headquarters. Continue down the D115 until you see the **large church (7)** on your left. Ideally it would be best if you parked either before the church or in the parking bays situated below it. The church (which more often than not is open) was used during the battle and, perhaps more interestingly, it was also used for housing

Bertry Church.

Gordon Highlanders in Bertry Communal Cemetery.

prisoners immediately after it – for example the Gordons were brought here. Not the most beautiful of places, Bertry does have a small supermarket and a drink may be purchased here as well. Continue past the church on the small road (ie keeping the entrance on your right) and, at the junction, turn right. At the bottom of the street is the Communal cemetery **(8)**; stop near the entrance. The CWGC plot is off to the left of the cemetery. Amongst a group of Gordon Highlanders, the only one named is Lieutenant Lyon. This is one of those cemeteries where the French erected a communal marker, which is still *in situ*,

Turn right at the road junction, driving parallel to the railway, and then right at the next junction, putting you back on the D115. Drive past the church and at the junction at the top of the road turn left and then immediately right, the D98 to Clary. As you emerge from Bertry there is a turning on the right to Montigny, which you should take. Further down the road towards Clary seems to have been the place where the Gordon Highlanders were rounded up by the Germans, in the early hours of the 27th.

The road to Montigny runs parallel, more or less, to the defensive line north of it occupied by 9 Brigade until about 6pm. After about a kilometre (and up until a turning to the left), in the fields to the south, were positioned two of the batteries of XXX Heavy Brigade from about 5pm onwards.

Montigny Church, used on the day for the treatment of casualties.

Drive into Montigny, until at a crossroads you will see the church **(9)** on your right. Park by it. The church is often open and was used for casualties from the battle, particularly from 7 Brigade. There is a café nearby and a bakery, should there be need for sustenance. To the left of the road as you approached the church were the Scottish Rifles, and as you proceed, the Royal Welsh Fusiliers, both 19 Brigade and both shifted to Reumont later in the day, having already been moved once from their position near the Roman road.

Return to the main road and take

the next turning right, to Tronquoy. After a few hundred yards, on your left there is the cemetery **(10)**, but be warned, it is set well back. There is a good track alongside the cemetery that leads up to an access gate. The CWGC burials are scattered; those of 1914 are about midway up the cemetery and seem to have come from the Ligny battlefield (for example there is a gunner of 27 Battery here). Most unusually there is an ornate German headstone to a Russian who died in May 1918, most of whose inscription is in Russian and beyond our linguistic prowess. There are excellent views across the battlefield from the end of the cemetery. In the field near the cemetery was positioned 129 Howitzer Battery, until about noon, shifted from its position on the railway embankment at Caudry.

Detail of the tombstone to a Russian, erected by the Germans.

Proceed up the road to Tronquoy, a stud farm in 1914 and very attractively laid out today. The pavé road adds to the charm. In the valley to the south of the farm was a battery of RFA (41), but it did not stay long as it could find no suitable targets and was withdrawn to the west of Montigny. Immediately after the farm buildings come to an end there is a track on the left **(11)**. Stop as convenient. 2/RIF, after their exhausting trek through the 25th, that night and the early hours of the 26th, were positioned with their right flank resting more or less here, covering the withdrawal of 7 Brigade from Caudry. Again there are excellent views, particularly when you can wander across the fields after harvesting. Audencourt church is clearly visible, as is that of Caudry in the centre and Fontaine au Pire to the left.

Continue along the paved road towards Caudry. A hundred yards or so

Caudry British Cemetery. The large German plot lies alongside it.

before the junction look to your left into the fields; stretching more or less from here across to the D45 Montigny road was the final position of 3/Worcs before its withdrawal. At the junction turn left and head towards Caudry. At the roundabout continue straight on, the D16 to Ligny. After a few hundred yards the road bends to the left and a few hundred yards beyond this there are open spaces where it is easy to park on the right **(12)**. On the other side of the road, in the afternoon, was A Company of the Worcesters, whilst in the fields between here and the railway embankment were the other three companies; positions occupied prior to the withdrawal from the town. Turn around and return towards Caudry, going under the railway line (before which there is quite a reasonable restaurant) and immediately turning right, towards the station. Note the presence of a large supermarket, petrol station and so forth beyond the embankment, if not for use now, for further reference.

Beyond the station take the new(ish) eastern Caudry by-pass and follow this for a mile or so. At a set of traffic lights turn right for Audencourt and

Memorial of the German White Collar Workers, Caudry.

Caudry British Cemetery and then first right again, which almost immediately brings you to the cemetery entrance **(13)**. The British plot is in front of a large German cemetery.

Although this cemetery was not originally established until 1917, when it received burials of men killed in the Easter fighting around Arras and the Battle of Cambrai in the late autumn, between 1921 and 1924 the French military authorities concentrated here 2,000 of the German fallen from 28 communes. It is hard to avoid the conclusion that this was done in a thoroughly slipshod manner. Of the 3,193 German dead in this cemetery, no fewer than 1,562 are interred in one great mass grave. Of these only the disgracefully low figure of 90 are buried by name.

Before the Second World War trees and shrubs were planted and the wall that surrounds the mass grave was built. The memorial of the German *Handlungsgehilfeverband* [National Association of White Collar Workers], which commemorates the 30,000 of its members who were killed on all fronts during the Great War, was placed here and the Association, which around this time adopted the cemetery, paid almost all the costs of its pre-1939 development. The stone crosses replaced the earlier wooden ones in 1976.

Return to the by-pass and turn right. About 500 yards away, on the right, will be seen Hotel Fimotel **(14)**. Park there (be warned, the car park is at the southern end of the hotel site and is not necessarily very obvious when trying to come off a busy road). The hotel offers special prices for weekend stays, which may be of some interest to readers who want to be close to the battlefield. Walk further up the by-pass towards the N43. It is possible to see

Béthencourt Church, the area from which the Germans advanced against the eastern defences of Caudry.

the distinctive shape of Audencourt Church through the trees on the northern side of the hotel. In this area, guarding the awkward salient, were two weak companies of 2/RIR and extras, though only for a time – they were 'lent' by neighbouring 8 Brigade. In due course they were replaced by 1/S Lancs, who were withdrawn very early on from their exposed position north of the N43 on the northern outskirts of Caudry. Next to them were 1/Wilts, covering the north east side of the town and providing some support for 45 and 29 Batteries. These latter had been effective in dealing with the initial German artillery attack (with the aid of two guns of I Battery RHA, over on the north western side of the town), but the position was too exposed and they were withdrawn sometime before 8am (along with I Battery) and took up a position to the south west of Montigny, but leaving a section of 29 Battery a kilometre or so up the D45 to Montigny to provide close support as necessary. Note also the views towards Béthencourt on the other side of the N43. This village and the area to the rear and close to the east and west of it were the gathering ground for German assaults (such as they were) on Caudry. Turn left on to the N43. At the

Looking east down the N43 towards Beaumont and Inchy. South of the road were men from 8 Brigade.

Rambourlieux Farm

Beaumont and Inchy

153 IR

93 IR

Caudry town square.

German supply column in Caudry.

traffic lights, the ground to the right was occupied in the very early stages of the battle by 1/S Lancs. Proceeding, the guns of I Battery were off to your left, as were the positions of 3/Worcs. Unfortunately for the battlefield visitor, Caudry has expanded up to the N43 and so there is very little to see nowadays, and the views have all been destroyed. The next roundabout is adjacent to Jeune Bois (along with a helpful water tower landmark), where some German artillery engaged in shelling in the earliest stages of the battle but were driven off. At the roundabout turn left and head back in towards Caudry. There are places where you can stop after a couple of hundred yards (15). Unfortunately it is difficult to see the view to the west, towards Beauvois and Fontaine, but before the buildings become too dense on the left of the road there is the possibility of seeing the ground over which the Germans approached the main part of 3/Worcs' defences.

Proceed into the town following the D16a for a little over a kilometre. Follow the signs to the centre (to the right) and you will emerge on the eastern

The unusual Caudry Old Communal Cemetery.

View from the Fontaine road into Caudry.

View across the west front of Caudry.

side of the Grande Place. Turn left here (there is a CWGC sign in a rather poor condition) and within a couple of hundred metres, on your left, there is parking, either by an undertaker's and some shops or in an advertised parking area. Set back from the road is the entry to **Caudry Old Communal Cemetery (16)**, in which there are a number of CWGC burials. Unusually, most of the headstones are lying flat on the ground. Equally unusually – probably because so many of them are multiple burials, not all regimental cap badges are represented. It is an unusual plot, hedged off from the rest of the cemetery (about half way up) and with a memorial erected by the commune in a central position.

Caudry was a textile town with some 13,000 inhabitants in August 1914 and had a considerable number of textile factories. It was well known for its lace. During the war it became an important higher headquarters for the German army (as did Le Cateau).

Return to the square and turn left, leaving Caudry by the D45. About a kilometre from the square there is a turning on the right, the D115 to Fontaine au Pire, which you take. As you leave the town, coming up the hill, look over to the left, where parts of 3/Worcs withdrew during the day's fighting in the town. A little further on it is possible to look right, across the western side of the town, where Lieutenant Johnston and his mixed group of men formed a defensive line **(18)**. It is not easy to stop here, but an opportunity might arise and it should be taken. As you proceed towards Fontaine, recall that this space had been left undefended and therefore 11 Brigade was threatened by an open right flank; a situation made worse by the (temporary) retirement in the early afternoon.

You are now driving out of the 3rd Division's area. The Division suffered very few casualties in the battle as such – 7 and 9 Brigades about 500 between them; but 8 Brigade, with the loss of the Gordons and the other troops who had got mixed up with them, about 750 in total, had its number of losses consequently pushed up to approximately a thousand.

Tour Three: The Fourth Division's area:

The tour commences in Beauvois.

The N43 passes through the north end of Beauvois. At its west end there is a turning to the right to the village, Fontaine au Pire and Ligny, which you should take.

11 Brigade was still in a state of confusion after its arrival here in the early hours of the morning, with much of the Brigade transport still present and with efforts being made to sort out positions in the dark when the Germans came into contact. Between then the Rifle Brigade and the Somersets had to sort out the confusion here, deal with the Germans and escort the transport away to Ligny whilst the rest of the Brigade took up defensive positions. Drive through Beauvois and in to Fontaine. There is a parking area opposite the very large church **(1)** at the

Fontaine au Pire Church.

south end of the village. The church and the Mairie (in particular) were used for the wounded after the battle. Continue and take the next right, which will eventually bring you to the cemetery. Drive past the cemetery and take the small track immediately behind it; after a short distance there is a parking area at the rear of the cemetery **(2)**.

Fontaine Communal Cemetery.

Tour Map 3: The Left of the Line.

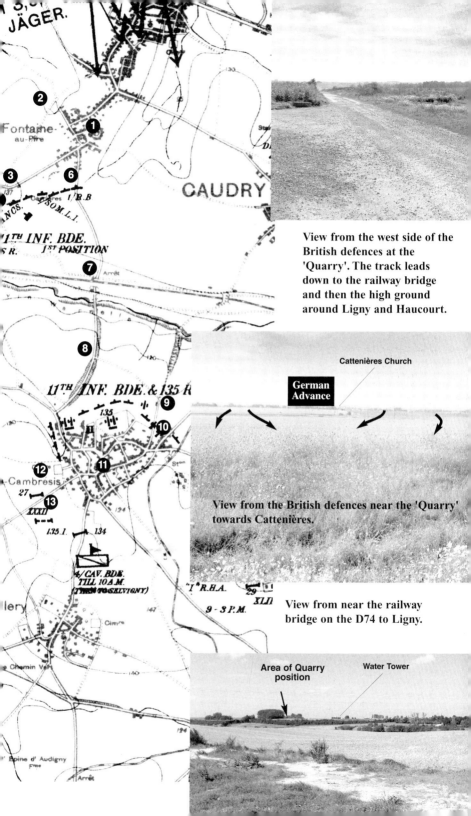

View from the west side of the British defences at the 'Quarry'. The track leads down to the railway bridge and then the high ground around Ligny and Haucourt.

Cattenières Church

German Advance

View from the British defences near the 'Quarry' towards Cattenières.

View from near the railway bridge on the D74 to Ligny.

Area of Quarry position

Water Tower

This cemetery is most interesting; besides having a large 'independent' CWGC plot there are a number of other CWGC burials scattered around it. This could be described as the 11 Brigade cemetery; a substantial number of those buried here are 'unknowns' and the great majority of them are likely to be 1914 casualties. Amongst others to be found here is Major Rickman, second in command of the Rifle Brigade, who died of wounds – his is one of the 'isolated' graves. There is also a man of the East Lancs who died in 1915: it would seem likely that he was one of a number of soldiers who were shot in early 1915 (there are others, in Ligny Communal Cemetery, for example). The Germans decreed that unless British soldiers who had taken shelter with the local population after the battle were given up by a fixed date, then all those involved in harbouring them would be executed.

Follow the track up the hill and look across to the right, over the country up which the Germans advanced towards the British positions. Very early in the day, much of the Rifle Brigade was also to be found in these fields. When you begin to approach the junction with the seemingly ubiquitous D115, find a convenient place to stop (3). Try and get as far off the track as possible, as agricultural vehicles regularly use it. From here there are good views to the north; Cattenières is really only visible because of its church spire. Walk across the road to the area of the water tower. Here you can appreciate the 'glacis' across which the Germans had to come for a frontal assault against 11 Brigade. Beyond it you may see the 'Quarry' – in fact a gravel pit. To the south there are views over the railway line and the valley of the Warnelle, with Ligny and Haucourt quite evident beyond. Turn right and head into Cattenières, driving through the village until, at the western end, you come to the church on your left (4). There are several CWGC burials in the churchyard, including the unusual sight of an unknown British and German soldier buried side by side.

Turn around and return towards Fontaine; as you are leaving the village, and before the road passes between high banks, look left: in the fields below was a covering force, including C Company of the Rifle Brigade, which came into action in the early hours of the 26th. Before the turning down to the cemetery and the water tower beyond there is a right turn, leading down towards the railway line. There is good parking near a rubbish processing area (5). Here it is best to get out and walk: boots or walking boots recommended, though the going is in fact easy.

The fighting in this area was very confused, with units getting completely jumbled. The threat came from the two flanks – an approach from the area of Cattenières and the railway embankment, or else from the gap between 11 and 7 Brigades south of Fontaine. German enfilade fire from that area was a major problem, causing frequent movements of men. The solution was to remove a substantial number to the area north of the railway embankment, in dead ground. Some were taken behind the embankment, on its south side, where Brigade HQ was also established, near the railway bridge.

Fairly early on in the proceedings the Somersets were withdrawn from the battle and moved back to Ligny – although a number were left behind because it was impossible to extract them from their position. The Rifle Brigade and some Somersets tried to form a flank guard as well, based on the road underpass between Ligny and Fontaine and making as much use of this sunken road as they could. The Hampshires guarded the left flank, straddled over the railway line, with D Company being the most exposed, facing towards Cattenières. Most of the East Lancs were held in reserve behind the railway line, at least to start with. Others helped man the Quarry position. Although there was a reasonable field of fire forward, the position was very exposed, and the line frequently had to be reinforced from the sunken road that ran behind it and from troops further down the valley. On occasion men had to be led back on to the position. Hunter Weston made himself conspicuous all over the area, encouraging and cajoling the men. This is now the time to re-read Major Collins' account of the day.

The Hampshires were able to assist the beleaguered 12 Brigade on their left; their rifle fire saw off some German artillery at about 9am. German attempts to infiltrate the position by coming along the railway were also halted, but at a cost. It was during one of these skirmishes that Lieutenant Chisholm of the East Lancs was fatally wounded, likely the first Australian fatality of the Great War.

When Caudry was temporarily vacated, Hunter Weston adjudged that the position was not tenable. The problem became one of how to get the men across the open valley up to the line at Ligny. In fact it was achieved at relatively light cost, thanks in large measure to the excellent support given by the guns, particularly of 135 Battery. It was also due to the extraordinary bravery of the men who were left in the Hampshires position and at the rear (south) edge of the quarry. A significant number of these would have become casualties as they bolted to the relative safety of the Warnelle Ravine and then came under a comforting barrage of British artillery and rifle fire as they made their way to Ligny.

The Germans attempted a follow up, but were seen off after two attempts by the defenders of the village.

It is well worth spending an hour or so here, re-reading the accounts and looking carefully at the ground, which has changed hardly at all. Crops

The view from the southern side of the railway embankment up to the Quarry position.

Area of Quarry position

allowing, you can reach the forward area of the Quarry, you can follow the (then sunken) track west towards the Fontaine - Ligny road, thereby appreciating the difficulties the defence had, threatened as it was from the right. Then you can walk down the track (Collins was wounded in the field on your left, about a hundred yards in and a hundred yards north of the railway line) to the railway and over it, viewing the area of Brigade HQ and, beyond the overgrown 'wilderness' on the left, get some idea of where the troops waited either in reserve or preparatory to making their move up the valley to Ligny. Collins' wood is no longer there, but you can see some of the issues that faced both the Germans and the British left flank defence, manned for the most part by the Hampshires.

Return to your vehicle and turn right on the D115. Whilst driving towards Fontaine note the splendid views to the south. Turn right at the junction and, as soon as possible, stop **(6)** and take a moment or two to look across to the British positions to your right (west) and then at the gap towards Caudry on your left (east). Proceed down the road to the railway bridge **(7)**; there is a space to stop just before it on the right. Elements of the Rifle Brigade, the East Lancs and the Somersets made some use of the sunken road along which you have driven; and there were men on the bank on the opposite (east) side of the road as well. It was not a particularly comfortable spot because of the increasing accuracy and strength of German machine gun fire.

Several hundred yards after the bridge there is a turning on the right **(8)**. It is a dead end and there is nowhere to turn around, but you might care to park a short distance down and, staying in sight of the car in case of agricultural traffic, walk down the road and see the view down in to the Ravine and up the slope on the north side. Collins' 'house' was possibly along here a couple of hundred yards from the junction. Return and take the track more or less opposite, in fact almost a standard road, but narrow and often with banks. At the junction swing right towards Ligny and at a convenient spot, stop **(9)**. There are excellent views over the ground across which the men of 11 Brigade retreated and up towards the defensive and gun lines in front of Ligny. In the adjacent field to the south west there was a forward machine gun guard, more or less on the north eastern flank of the defensive line before Ligny. Look about six hundred yards across the front of Ligny, roughly the middle northern edge of the village. There is a brick built, medium sized private chapel, difficult to find unless you know exactly what you are looking for (it is not even marked on the IGN maps). This is roughly where a section of 135 Battery was positioned, targeting the Germans before and behind Fontaine au Pire. Continue. Just as some buildings commence on the edge of Ligny, maybe a hundred yards or so short of the road junction **(10)**, there was another section of 135 Battery, its guns directed down the D15 towards Caudry. The Germans never located these guns, which formed such an essential element in the successful defence of Ligny and all that followed from that. The guns were successfully withdrawn in the evening, more or less under the noses of the Germans; none of the gunners were even wounded during the day's action.

Join the D16 and turn right (those in search of the elusive chapel should

View from the shrine on the southern edge of Ligny towards Fontaine and Caudry.

take the next first right: good hunting!). After five hundred yards or so you will see the large church on your right **(11)**: it is often open and there is reasonable parking in front of it. This was used for casualties in the battle (and was where Chisholm died); see Collins' description.

For someone who wants a luxury stay (and pricy menu) on this battlefield, there is the four star Chateau de Ligny Harcourt in the village.

British graves in the unusual Croix de Guerre plot in Ligny Communal Cemetery.

Ligny Church, where many British wounded from the battle were tended.

At the junction with the D15 turn right towards Haucourt. Within a hundred yards or so there is a concealed turning to the left, the approach road to Ligny Communal Cemetery. Drive down to the cemetery **(12)**.

This is a most unusual place for a variety of reasons. Immediately on your left as you enter the cemetery there is a small CWGC plot. There are a substantial number of 'unknowns', presumably 1914 Le Cateau casualties, a number almost certainly shot by the Germans in January 1915 (see above, Fontaine Communal Cemetery for the reasons for this), Lieutenant Chisholm, one of the French memorial stones and, by the pathway going up the hill and opposite the CWGC plot, the tomb of Chisholm's mother (the tomb with the large, half shrouded, ornamental vase on the top), whose ashes were buried here after her death in Sydney in 1928. Now walk to the top of the cemetery, behind the cross and through the gap in the hedge, to the French military section, the tombs set out in the form of a *Croix de Guerre*. On the far side are seven CWGC burials, which men probably have the most unusual burial arrangements of the BEF.

Return to the D15 and turn right. Just before the turning back to the church, the D16 and Caudry, there is a narrow turning on the right. This is a track, but the surface is generally quite adequate and should be driveable even in poor weather conditions. Take this and stop shortly before the junction with a track coming from the right (and along which you will proceed in due course) **(13)**. Immediately on your right was the location of 27 Battery. The achievement of this battery is well recorded by Becke and I have chosen to quote more about it than others because of the practicality of getting to its location today and seeing a very similar view to that of the gunners on 26 August.

[Between 6 and 9am.] '27 … searched for guns behind the ridge near Fontaine. Being in action in the open, it drew down on itself a heavy return fire from several batteries, which it did its best to keep employed in order to draw the fire off its own infantry. Locating one battery at 3,650 yards (the range to the German guns was checked from the fuze of a shell that landed in the battery!), 27 silenced it except one gun, direct hits being reported on two of the others. This German battery had been engaged shelling our infantry, but their switch on to 27 was very slow and 27 was able to bring Battery fire before the Germans had finished ranging. The issue of that duel was then no longer in doubt. 27 was then engaged by two or three German batteries and it became impractical to bring up any more ammunition to the guns, the detachments

236

were therefore withdrawn under cover until the German infantry advanced. Up to this moment the casualties inflicted on the Battery had been very few, for most of the HE shell burst on or beyond the sunken road [on which your car is standing].

[Between 9am and noon.] 'To the west of Ligny 27 knocked out a machine gun for 11 Brigade, but the Germans immediately opened so many batteries on it that the ammunition could not be replenished and when it was nearly exhausted the detachments were withdrawn until the storm subsided. By this time the Germans had put a direct hit on the under shield of No 5. Soon after a pause occurred and the ammunition was replenished in all the wagons, being brought up by hand [!] along the road in the rear, and the wheels of No 5 were replaced from the Wagon Body… As our infantry in front fell back, 27 opened on a German Battery in action close to the one it had knocked out earlier in the morning. But this activity drew down an intense return fire from a Heavy as well as two Field Batteries. An infantry Brigade Major now came up to the Battery Commander and said that the Battery, by drawing fire on itself, was doing just what the infantry wanted. The Battery managed to keep in action until its ammunition ran out. Then, as no more could be brought up, the men were once more withdrawn under cover.

[Between noon and 1.45pm.] 'During the afternoon the sky became overcast, the Brigade Commander went up to the guns of 27 with the Battery Commander, but any movement there at once drew down a heavy fire and all idea of getting the guns out before dark was temporarily abandoned. Later, they were again visited, when it was found that the trails were so deeply embedded that they could not be lifted until the earth around them had been loosened.'

[The Retirement: after 1.45pm.] 'Probably it was well after 5pm when, realising that Ligny must shortly be entered by the Germans, the Brigade Commander of XXXII called for volunteers from the Battery to run out the guns by hand. The Brigade Commander, Major Vallentin, and the whole Battery immediately volunteered. Men were then dribbled forward to the guns and, keeping under cover of the shields, they set to work with picks and loosened the earth around the trails. During pauses in the shelling a gun or a limber was run back to the road. Thus, by dint of steady work and seizing the opportunities offered, four guns and four limbers were withdrawn into the sunken road in rear. Then suddenly the firing increased and when the detachments were working on the next gun a heavy and accurate fire opened on the Battery. A second attempt met with the same fate and most unwillingly it was decided that the enterprise must be abandoned, for its continuance might lead to total failure. Forming up the four guns under cover they waited their time and then made a sudden dash to the south westward, pursued by the German shells – fortunately all were very short. These four guns were saved.' Major Vallentin was awarded the DSO and the DCM went to two sergeants and five gunners.'

This Battery lost two guns (according to Becke, the only ones lost in the 4th Division), one officer and seven other ranks wounded and one gunner killed:

Fontaine Church   **Ligny**

View from the west of Ligny showing the ground between the village and Fontaine.

Gunner AE Rose, who is buried in Montigny Communal Cemetery.

Looking to your left, the south west, 135 Battery was originally placed in the field nearby. Further away, on the D16 to Caullery and about 500 yards out of Ligny, was 134 Battery, whilst further along the road towards Caullery was 4 Cavalry Brigade, until it withdrew to Selvigny at about 10am.

The original, 1914, track continues beyond the junction, and it is doubtless along this that the Battery rode to safety, towards Selvigny. Take the track coming in from the right, which will lead you down to the D15, west of Ligny. There are superb views over the 4th Division battlefield; particular note might

View across to Haucourt on the left and Longsart on the right

Ruined Mill   Haucourt Cemetery   Haucourt Church   Longsart be made of the area of Haucourt and the distinctive ruined mill on the high ground south east of it. 2/Seaforth Highlanders and 1/Royal Irish Fusiliers (10 Brigade) grabbed a few moments of rest around the nearby communal cemetery in the early hours of the 26th. In addition one can see right across 11 Brigade's battlefield and get a significant view over 12 Brigade's as well. The last section of 135 Battery was positioned on the eastern side of the D15, near the junction with the D74.

At the junction with the D15 turn left. After a kilometre or so, there are some buildings on both sides of the road (le Hameau) **(14)**. These mark the eastern flank of the defensive line put up by the Warwicks; further east were the Dublins and part of the Irish Fusiliers. In the village, turn right on to the D118, Cattenières road. As the valley bottom is approached, this is where the remnants of the King's Own gathered and where the Royal Warwicks went charging up to try and assist them after the blow of early in the morning (the precipitate action of the Warwicks was not without its critics: Lt Bernard Montgomery was a junior officer with the Battalion at the time and (probably) took part in the attack). This area must have been one of great confusion and tension for a few hours from about 6am onwards – men trying to get back up to restore the line, a great number of wounded awaiting both treatment and to be got away, and the persistent sound of gunfire.

At the top of the valley, note the road to the left, but for the moment proceed towards Cattenières. About five hundred yards beyond it seek a safe place to stop for a moment **(15)**. This is the approximate area where the German machine guns were positioned which hit the King's Own at about 6am with such disastrous effect. When you have reached and gone beyond the railway line, turn around and return, observing the country over which the Germans advanced towards Longsart (sometimes spelt Long Sart) Farm and where their artillery and machine guns were deployed. Look to the left and the approach towards the Quarry position. The Germans had to be chary of the British artillery positioned on the heights above Haucourt.

Return to the right hand turn at the head of the Warnelle Ravine and go along it. There is a track going off it after about fifty yards; park on it **(16)**. What happened to the King's Own, described by Captain Nixon (presumably then a junior subaltern), was quoted in the Army's Battlefield Tour of 1933.

'We arrived at dawn by the Ligny Road at a spot where subsequently we suffered so heavily. The battalion was ordered to form close column facing the enemy's direction. Companies were dressed by the right, piled arms and placed equipment at their feet. There was a big stir because some of the arms were out of alignment and the equipment did not in all cases show a true line. A full seven to ten minutes was spent in adjusting these errors. The brigade commander (Wilson) rode up to the commanding officer and shortly afterwards we were told to remain where we were, as breakfast would shortly be up. Everyone was very tired and hungry, having had nothing to eat since dinner the day before. A remark was passed as to our safety. My company commander replied that French cavalry were out in front and the enemy could not possibly worry us for three hours. The picture at this period was as follows:

'Three companies of the battalion in close column, the fourth just about to move up to the left with the view to continuing a line with the Lanc. Fus., who had just commenced to dig in. Just about this time some cavalry (about a troop) rode within 500 yards of us, looked at us and trotted off again. I saw their uniform quite clearly and mentioned that these were not Frenchmen. I was told not to talk nonsense and reminded that I was very young. It was early in the morning and nobody felt talkative, least of all my company commander. The cavalry appeared again in the distance and brought up wheeled vehicles; this was all done very peaceably and exposed to full view. We could now hear the transport on the cobbled road and a shout went up, "Here's the cooker!" New life came to the men and mess tins were hurriedly sought. Then came the fire. The field we were in was a cornfield. The corn had been cut. Bullets were mostly about four feet high, just hitting the top of the corn stooks. Temporary panic ensued. Some tried to reach the valley behind, others chewed the cud; of those who got up, most were hit. The MGX fire only lasted about two minutes and caused about 400 casualties. The fourth company moving off to the left was caught in column of fours [on the track on which you are now parked]. Shell fire now started and did considerable damage to the transport, the cooker being the first vehicle to go.

'The CO was killed by the first burst and the second in command rallied the battalion, several of us taking up position to the right of the point where we had suffered so heavily.

'An attack was organised at once, we retook our arms and got in most of the wounded. The others were left and taken prisoner later at Haucourt church that night.'

The German 'overs' hit the 4th Division HQ in Haucourt, wounding

View of Ligny (left) and Haucourt (right) from east of Longsart.

amongst others the general's ADC; the HQ was shifted (one of numerous moves during the day) to high ground about a kilometre south of the village. Some men straggled back to Haucourt, where they were taken back into the line by the divisional staff.

Continue down the road towards Longsart Farm. Just as the road drops down and bends to the left, there is high ground on both sides of the road. On the left was C Company of the Inniskillings. On the right, where the ground evened out, about a hundred or so yards, was the right flank of the Lancashire Fusiliers. These earthworks formed part of the original (pre 1914, and no longer existing at this point even then) road between Wambaix and Selvigny.

Because this road is narrow, and the tracks are regularly used, it would be best to try and park in the farm and seek permission so to do [There is an alternative way of seeing this, though involving a slightly longer walk: see below]. Whatever, you must keep the tracks open to traffic. Beyond the farm, maybe a hundred yards or so, there is a track off to the right (**17**). It begins promisingly enough, but is not one I would really want to trust with a normal car. A Company of the Essex Regiment was positioned here. Walk up this track for a few hundred yards until you find another one coming in from the right (actually heading more or less north). To the left was B Company of the Inniskillings; to the right B Company of the Essex (though they also seem to have had a trench that was facing north south, according to the account of the Inniskilling's platoon sergeant quoted elsewhere) and beyond them the Lancashire Fusiliers. Look down the track towards the D960 Esnes – Cambrai road, and slightly to the left of the line of it. Esnes Windmill was just over a kilometre from here, on the far side of the D960.

Return to the car and continue towards Esnes to the communal cemetery (**18**). There are a large number of identified casualties from three of the battalions from the Brigade (plus a couple from the Royal Irish Rifles), but no King's Own. A substantial number (62) are also unknowns. Captain Vandaleur of 2/Essex is buried here. This cemetery, with a fine view to the south and east, as well as a view up to the D960, is a fine place to pay tribute to the men of 12 Brigade.

Continue into the town and note the picturesque Esnes Castle; one of the medieval lords was killed fighting against the English at Poitiers in 1356. The present structure dates from the late fifteenth century (the church from the twelfth). It was earmarked to be 4th Division's HQ, but this never happened.

Turn right and take the D960 out of the town. About eight hundred yards after the sharp right hand bend in the road in Esnes there is a track on the left hand side of the road, with reasonable parking space (**19**). Cross the road and follow the track on the other side: this eventually comes out near to Longsart Farm and is the alternative route to see the positions of 12 Brigade before it. The first part of the track is driveable, but you may well be pushed to find turning space – unless the ground is dry after the harvest, in which case it can be done in a field as the metalled part of the track begins to give out.

Where you are parked gives useful views to the south and the defensive line of two companies of Inniskillings. These remained, more or less, in position for

Esnes Communal Cemetery, beautifully set out – a tribute to the work of the CWGC.

Multiple burials in the cemetery; notice on the left the grave of Captain Vandeleur of the Essex.

Esnes Chateau.

most of the day, despite all the comings and goings on the ridge to the east/north east. These men would have seen the attack at about 3pm by elements of 12 Brigade to force the Germans back and to recover some of the wounded, which was at least partially successful. Esnes Mill was given up fairly early in the battle, between 9 and 10am. It was situated about 200 yards due east of the junction. There is a good track up to the site (go to the end of this track and turn right) but it deteriorates and there is no easy way to turn around. The view there is excellent – of the left of the 4th Division and of the second position of 12 Brigade before Haucourt, and is worth a walk

Elements of the Seaforth Highlanders from 10 Brigade (situated for much of the day above the village, about Point 137 – 134 on the IGN map) would have assisted with the covering of their withdrawal. 10 Brigade, the rearguard, moved off at 6pm.

Drive to Haucourt. Soon after entering the village, at a bend to the left, there is a road going off right. It is one way, but you may be able to stop nearby (alternatively, walk down to it from the church – see below). Walk up it a hundred yards or so and there is a memorial to the Parish Priest, who apparently was executed by the Germans for assisting wounded British soldiers: the church was certainly used for them. Return to the main road – 4th Division HQ was in one of the houses opposite (although none look old enough to be original) until it came under shellfire early on the 26th. At the junction with D118 turn right and, immediately after the church (which I have never found open), turn left - do not be put off by 'dead end' signs (note, you can stop near here and walk down the road on the right, which will bring you out at the memorial to the priest mentioned above). Drive out of the village a short distance, and the communal cemetery is on your left **(20)**. There are only two identified casualties here, but again it is an atmospheric place: consider the exhausted men of part of 10 Brigade who tried to snatch some rest here as night was gradually coming to day on 26 August. The ruined mill is clearly

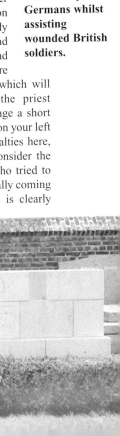

Memorial to the Curé of Haucourt, who was shot by the Germans whilst assisting wounded British soldiers.

Ruins of Haucourt mill.

Haucourt Cemetery.

Longsart Farm

View of Longsart from near the water tower and near the reserve positions of the Essex Regiment.

visible and 4th Division HQ was further south, beyond that.

Return to the village and the D15 and head back towards Esnes. You will shortly see a water tower on the right and a turning on the left (D118c), almost opposite. Take this pavé road and stop after 100 yards or so **(21)**. Look to your right, into the fields, where the reserve companies of 1/Essex were situated. Look down to the abandoned sugar refinery – a replacement, one assumes, for the one there in 1914. The track opposite leads up to Longsart Farm and also to positions where elements of 12 Brigade were under the protection of the north side of the Warnelle Ravine.

Proceed along this suspension-testing road (39 Battery was tucked away in the triangle between the roads as you come to the junction with the D118). Look across to the right as you reach the high point, to the location of the Seaforths and Irish Rifles (or parts of them), by this stage 4th Division's only reserve, situated about Point 137. Follow the D118 to Selvigny; about six hundred yards after the junction there is a road on the left. Opposite was the site of St Aubert Farm **(21)**. 88 Battery was sited to the south of the road/track; its commander, Major Raymond England, was killed and is buried in Selvigny Communal Cemetery **(22)**, which is on the outskirts of the village on the Caullery road. At the junction with the D16 turn right and after a fairly sharp right and then left bend in the road, **Selvigny German Cemetery (23)** is on your left.

This cemetery, which is located to the east of the D16 one kilometre north east of the centre of Walincourt-Selvigny, was originally established early in 1917. The village of Selvigny was a particularly important administrative base

for the German army between the end of the Battle of the Somme in 1916 and the withdrawal to the Hindenburg Line, when it housed a large field hospital complex. The majority of the soldiers found here died during the Battle of Cambrai in late 1917, but it also contains important burials from the 1914 Battle of Le Cateau. The cemetery contains the remains of 3,993 soldiers, some of whom were concentrated here after the war by the French military authorities, who removed burials from thirty one communes in a forty five kilometre radius.

In the process, the bodies of Oberst Louis von Arnim, commander of IR 93, and Hauptmann Alfred Theinert, commander of 9th Company IR 93, were transferred from the village of Clary, four kilometres to the east. Von Arnim is believed to have been the senior casualty on either side during the Battle of Le Cateau. To find the grave of so senior a German officer in a cemetery in France is an extraordinarily rare matter, so it is worth visiting this cemetery for that reason alone. It is entirely possible that some of the other 115 fatalities of IR 93 are also buried here as unknown.

Both conifers and deciduous trees were planted in the cemetery between the wars; the mass grave, which, shockingly once more, only contains fifty nine named burials out of 1,380, was enclosed by a wall and the old wooden grave markers were gradually replaced with the current ones made of Belgian granite from 1969.

Oberst **Louis von Arnim** Commander IR 93, killed by shrapnel during the failed assault on Beaumont-en-Cambrésis during the early afternoon of 26 August 1916. Block 1 G192

Hauptmann **Alfred Theinert** Officer Commanding 9th Company IR 93, killed at the head of his company in a failed attempt to push on into the village of Beaumont at around 12.00 pm 26 August 1914. Block 1 G190

From there take the D960 to Esnes, passing Point 137 on your right and along the withdrawal route of the left hand of 12 Brigade and some of 10 Brigade; and from there stay on the road to Cambrai – should that be your base.

Louis von Arnim, commander IR 93, the senior fatality from either side on 26 August 1914, killed by shrapnel fire near Beaumont

Graves of von Arnim and Theinert in Selvigny.
(see p. 88)

Tour 4: From Le Cateau to Cambrai: the German 'side of the hill'.

This tour is designed to bring you back towards Cambrai from Le Cateau by, we hope, an interesting route that negates the need to retrace your 'steps' along the N43. It starts at **Le Cateau Military Cemetery**. Because of the distance involved, there is no accompanying map as such, but we hope that the instructions will be clear enough to enable you to drive the route without too much difficulty. This route will also give you an opportunity to visit a number of British cemeteries, including three VC graves, which are well off the beaten track.

If you did not take the chance before, walk across to the west side of the road leading up to the cemetery, the D932. Here there is a good general view over much of the right flank of the British front; and yet it is possible to see how the folds in the ground provided some protection to the hastily prepared British positions.

Proceed north east along the D932, down into Montay and the valley of the Selle. Soon after you have crossed the river take the left turn (the D955) towards **Neuvilly** and Solesmes. Drive through Neuvilly and, on a right inclining bend on the further outskirts, you will find the CWGC **Neuvilly Communal Cemetery Extension**; there is plenty of space to stop outside it. This is also a good vantage point to look towards the British positions, though a ridge obstructs some views. **Rambourlieux Farm** may be seen about two kilometres to the south; 2nd Battalion Field Artillery Regiment 75 fired from here in support of the attack on Inchy. Its commander, Major Hinsch, was killed by a stray bullet and is buried in the German part of Le Cateau cemetery (Block 1, Grave 664).

Buried in this cemetery (B15) is **Private Frank Lester VC** of the Lancashire Fusiliers.

For most conspicuous bravery and self-sacrifice during the clearing of the village of Neuvilly, on 12th October, 1918, when, with a party of about seven men under an officer, he was the first to enter a house from the back door, and shot two Germans as they attempted to get out by the front door. A minute later a fall of masonry blocked the door by which the party had entered. The only exit into the street was under fire at point-blank range. The street was also swept by fire of machine guns at close range. Observing that an enemy sniper was causing heavy casualties to a party in a house across the street, Pte. Lester exclaimed, "I'll settle him," and, dashing out into the street, shot the sniper at close quarters, falling mortally wounded at the same instant. This gallant man well knew it was certain death to go into the street, and the party opposite was faced with the alternative of crossing the fire-swept street or staying where it was and being shot one by one. To save their lives he sacrificed his own.

After about two kilometres turn left on the D16 to Briastre (it is also signposted to Bellevue Cemetery, which is almost immediately on your right as you make the turn). Bellevue Cemetery is a 1918 burial ground. There are good views of Viesly, to the south west, a large village that both sides passed through in 1914. Continue towards Viesly on the D16; the road tends to jiggle about in the village, but it will be signposted Béthencourt.

At the time of writing there were major road works going on along the section to Béthencourt, but if these have finished, it is worthwhile heading into it (a little under three kilometres away). In the village the D16 comes to a T junction and goes to the right; a hundred metres or so further on is **Béthencourt Communal Cemetery**, with a number of interesting British burials there from the fighting of 26 August; judging from the dates on the headstones, some of these died of wounds in the days after the battle. The village was slightly hidden from British view by the rising ground to the N43 and the Germans concentrated men here before sending them off on the flanks (particularly the German left flank) to try the British lines.

[You can now **either** proceed along the road and turn left at the T junction (the D16 goes right) and go along the minor road to Audicourt Farm; further to the south the Germans withdrew some of their guns to La Guisette farm, to continue their attack on Caudry and Audencourt). From there go right on to the D45 to Quiévy and pick up the route in the town where the D113 comes off the D45; **or**] return to Viesly.

Soon after entering Viesly, take the D134 Solesmes road. This will bring you out at a major junction after a couple of kilometres. The mass of buildings at the junction is known as **Ferme de Fontaine au Tertre**; it was one of the places that the British guarded on the retreat back to Le Cateau. As you turn to the left, note the formidable bunker in the field on your right. Proceed into **Quiévy**; there is a sharp bend to the left and, after a hundred metres or so, a

Bunker at Ferme de Fontaine au Tetre.

turning on the right, the D113 to Bévillers. [Should you be so inclined, almost opposite this turning there is a minor road that leads, after about five hundred metres, to Quiévy Military Cemetery. This is unusual in that there are far more Germans buried here than British. The British casualties are all from the 1918 fighting.] Note that there is a one way system in the town, and so you will be sent on a circuit around the parish church.

From **Bévillers** continue on the D113 towards **Boussières en Cambrésis**. The road between these two villages offers occasional views south, towards Beauvois and Fontaine au Pire. Just as you enter **Carnières** there is a minor road going off on the right; you will know that you have gone too far if you pass the D113a, almost opposite the turning, which heads sharply south east off the D113. The road goes into the town, bending slightly right at a meeting of roads and then take the left fork: there are CWGC signs, but you do need to keep your eyes peeled. After a couple of hundred metres you will come to **Carnières Military Cemetery**, a 1918 burial ground and where **Guardsman William Holmes VC** (I B3) is buried.

Guardsman W Holmes VC.

For most conspicuous bravery and devotion to duty at Cattenieres on the 9th Oct., 1918. Pte. Holmes carried in two men under the most intense fire, and, while he was attending to a third case, he was severely wounded. In spite of this, he continued to carry wounded, and was shortly afterwards again wounded, with fatal results. By his self-sacrifice and disregard of danger he was the means of saving the lives of several of his comrades. Very few people appear to visit this cemetery.

Return to the D113; there is turning on the left to the N43 and then, a few metres later, the D118 on the right, heading north towards Rieux en Cambrésis. Go along this for about three kilometres until you come to a junction with the D942. Turn left on to this road, which eventually goes into Cambrai. At this point you are roughly in line with western extremity of the Le Cateau battlefield, some kilometres now to the south of you. Again, after three kilometres or so, there is a turning on your right, the D157 to Cagnocles. Drive through this village until you come to the (fast) D114: Naves is off on your right, but you should turn left. In a couple of hundred metres you will come to Naves Communal Cemetery Extension on your left; there is parking along the road by the cemetery and, immediately before it, very extensive parking in a set aside area. The entrance to the CWGC cemetery is on the far (western) side of the communal cemetery and has its own approach path.

For some reason, many of the fatalities of the

Many of the casualties at Longsart were finally laid to rest here at Naves Communal Cemetery Extension, miles from their place of death

fighting to the north of Longsart Farm were brought for burial here, particularly King's Own and Lancashire Fusiliers. Only a couple are identified, though there are a number of cap badges on the graves of a number of the unknown. Also buried here is **Corporal James McPhie VC** (II E4).

For most conspicuous bravery on the 14th October, 1918, when with a party of sappers maintaining a cork float bridge across the Canal de la Sensee near Aubencheul-au-Bac. The further end of the bridge was under close machine gun fire and within reach of hand grenades. When Infantry just before dawn were crossing it, closing up resulted and the bridge began to sink and break. Accompanied by a sapper, he jumped into the water and endeavoured to hold the cork and timbers together, but this they failed to do. Corporal McPhie then swam back, and, having reported the broken bridge, immediately started to collect material for repair. It was now daylight. Fully aware that the bridge was under close fire and that the far bank was almost entirely in the hands of the enemy, with the inspiring words, "It is death or glory work which must be done for the sake of our patrol on the other side". He led the way, axe in hand, on to the bridge and was at once severely wounded, falling partly into the water, and died after receiving several further wounds. It was due to the magnificent example set by Corporal McPhie that touch was maintained with the patrol on the enemy bank at a most critical period.

Corporal J McPhie VC.

Continue along the D114 for two and a half kilometres. About five hundred metres before a minor turning on your right there are a number of buildings; ahead, near the turning but beyond it, there is a speed limit sign and immediately beyond the turning there is a building. Take this minor (and rather unpromising) road, which is surprisingly busy until it emerges by a large factory on to a junction with the D942. Turn right, towards Cambrai. After about two kilometres, on the left hand side of the road, is Cambrai East Military Cemetery, a joint German/CWGC plot. The British burials do not include any from Le Cateau 1914, but the German plot is most interesting.

It is one of the most impressive of all the German cemeteries on the Western Front and, thanks to the fact that it was laid out in permanent form in

Cambrai German Cemetery.

1917, it is far less stark than some of the great concentration cemeteries. Throughout the war, Cambrai was an important town in the German rear areas, housing headquarters, logistic units and several field hospitals. These hospitals treated Allied soldiers as well as German ones so, from the start, Cambrai cemetery was designed also to house the fallen of the British and French armies in plots specially set aside for them. Its central memorial, a massive stone cross, was designed in 1917 by Dr. Wilhelm Kreis, one of the founders in 1919 of the *Volksbund*. All the original burials date from 1917 and 1918, as does the statuary placed within it, some of which honours the French and British fallen. It was expanded between 1921 and 1924 by the French military authorities, who moved a great many graves of the 1914 – 1916 period from temporary cemeteries in the surrounding area. The great majority of these soldiers were placed in a mass grave. 442 of 2,746 burials are known by name. The trees, shrubs and hedges were planted during the 1930s and the original wooden crosses were replaced by the current ones in stone in 1977.

There are comparatively few named 1914 burials in the cemetery, but it does contain the grave of **Kürassier Friedrich Schlue** (Block 11, Grave 279). Schlue was a trooper with 4th Squadron, Kürassier Regiment 7, who was killed, along with Unteroffizier Arthur Loese, whilst carrying out a reconnaissance on foot near the railway line south of Cattenières during the early afternoon of 26 August 1914. Schlue's squadron commander, Rittmeister Detlef von Kotze, who ordered the patrol, was also killed during the day. Of the three, Schlue is the only one to have a known grave in France.

From the cemetery it is only a short distance to Cambrai.

Kurassier Schlue. One of the few German casualties with a known grave.

INDEX

(Italics = Illustration)